Foreign Flowers

East-West Center Studies

Books bearing the imprint "East-West Center
Studies" are works developed with substantial
support from the East-West Center, an internationally recognized education and research
organization established by the U.S. Congress
in 1960 to strengthen understanding between
the United States and the countries of Asia
and the Pacific. The Center is located in
Honolulu, Hawai'i.

Foreign Flowers

Institutional Transfer and Good Governance in the Pacific Islands

Peter Larmour

University of Hawai'i Press
Honolulu

Library of Congress Cataloging-in-Publication Data
Larmour, Peter.
    Foreign flowers : institutional transfer and good governance in the
Pacific Islands / Peter Larmour.
        p. cm.
    Includes bibliographical references and index.
    ISBN 0-8248-2901-8 (hardcover : alk. paper) — ISBN 0-8248-2933-6
(pbk. : alk. paper)
    1. Oceania—Politics and government. 2. Public institutions—Oceania.
I. Title.
    JQ5995.L37 2005
    306.2'0995—dc22

                                        2004027593

Portions of this book originally appeared in *Pacific Studies* 17(1): 45–76;
Public Administration and Development 22(2): 151–161; *Asian Journal of
Political Science* 10(1): 41–54; *Public Administration and Development* 22(3):
249–260; and *Pacific Economic Bulletin* 18(1): 115–120. The author is grateful to the editors of these journals for permission to reproduce them here.

Designed by University of Hawai'i Press Production Staff
Printed by The Maple-Vail Book Manufacturing Group

Contents

Acknowledgments

This book began as a project on states and societies in the Pacific Islands. Then I stepped back and realized that the state was just one of many examples of transfer that I had been interested in or had worked on. Many of the ideas presented here come from work and discussions with Yash Ghai, and I am very appreciative of his insight and encouragement. Adrian Leftwich strongly encouraged my writing. David Marsh's work on policy transfer, and his visits to the Australian National University (ANU), helped me frame the material. Ben Reilly pointed me to work on electoral systems, and Diane Stone to work on knowledge transfer. I am particularly grateful to Christine Sylvester, Raymond Apthorpe, Clay Wescott, Nand Hart-Nibbrig, Hal Colebatch, Ron Crocombe, Donald Denoon, Barrie Macdonald, Yash Ghai, and Ted Wolfers for reading and commenting on lengthy drafts. Maree Tait, Publications Director at my part of the ANU, was supportive throughout. Ann Nevile relieved me of my administrative duties during 2001 so that I could work on this project, and Francis Hutchinson sorted out tangled referencing. I also want to thank Eddie Hollingsworth for his personal support.

Some of the ideas in this book arose from a consultancy for the Asian Development Bank, and I am grateful to Steve Pollard, Cedric Saldhana, Clay Wescott, and Bob Beschel for that experience. The material on Transparency International in Papua New Guinea is part of a larger project with Barry Hindess and Luis de Sousa—Transparency International and the Problem of Corruption—funded by an Australia Research Council Discovery grant. I am very grateful to the late Sir Anthony Siaguru and Mike Manning for their cooperation in that research.

The final draft was written during a visiting fellowship at the East-West Center in Hawai'i in early 2003. I would like to thank Nancy Lewis,

Director of Research, and her colleagues for that opportunity to concentrate on writing and, later, for the generous grant toward publication. I am especially indebted to Geoff White for his consistent support and sensible advice, to Bob Kiste for his comments and suggestions, and to Elisa Johnston at the East-West Center, Masako Ikeda at the University of Hawai'i Press, and Rosemary Wetherold for their thoughtful editorial advice. I of course am solely responsible for the content of the final product. I would also like to thank Nicola Davis, who was already painting flowers and weeds as symbols of invasion, for her elegant and apposite artwork on the cover.

Abbreviations

ADB	Asian Development Bank
ANU	Australian National University
AusAID	Australian Agency for International Development
AV	Alternative voting
CCF	Citizens' Constitutional Forum
COFA	Compact of free association
CPC	Constitutional Planning Committee
CRC	Constitution Review Commission
ERP	Electoral Reform Project
FATF	Financial Action Task Force
FAO	Food and Agriculture Organization
FPP	First-past-the-post (electoral system)
FSM	Federated States of Micronesia
GDP	Gross domestic product
GNP	Gross national product
G7	Group of Seven
IASER	Institute of Applied Social and Economic Research
ICAC	Independent commission against corruption
IDEA	Institute for Democracy and Electoral Assistance
IFI	International financial institution
IMF	International Monetary Fund
INA	Institute of National Affairs
IPS	Institute of Pacific Studies
LCC	Leadership Code Commission
MCC	Micronesian Constitutional Convention
MIRAB	Migration, remittances, aid, and bureaucracy
MP	Member of Parliament

NGO	Nongovernmental organization
NPM	New public management
OECD	Organisation for Economic Co-operation and Development
OFC	Offshore financial center
PNG	Papua New Guinea
PR	Proportional representation
RAMSI	Regional Assistance Mission to the Solomon Islands
RSS	Rueschemeyer, Stephens, and Stephens (1992)
SI	Solomon Islands
TI	Transparency International
UN	United Nations
UNESCAP	UN Economic and Social Commission on Asia and the Pacific
USAID	U.S. Agency for International Development
USP	University of the South Pacific

Introduction

Aid donors have been promoting "good governance" in the Pacific Islands since the 1990s. They have funded projects to promote democracy or reduce corruption, and international financial institutions like the World Bank made good governance a condition of some of their loans. However, they have met some active resistance. In Papua New Guinea (PNG), for example, students rioted and soldiers mutinied over recommendations for land registration and public sector reform.

Governments often choose to learn from abroad. Sometimes they are forced to, through loan conditions, colonization, or military defeat. U.S. attempts at "nation building" in Afghanistan and Iraq are extreme examples. In June 2003, Australia led a force of troops, police officers, and other officials to restore order and rebuild institutions in Solomon Islands, labeling the country a failed state.

Institutions from one country may not suit another, but the Pacific Islands have also suffered from the partial application of idealized and standardized models with no particular national origins. Colonization, decolonization, fiscal crises, and membership in international organizations have made the islands open to prevailing ideas of "best practice." Missionaries and consultants have been active and creative participants in this process. So have members of professions with well-organized bodies of doctrine, like economists, accountants, and surveyors. Local elites have been active partners as well. Traditionalist appeals to a version of the past have been countered by transformative appeals to the future.

The region provides the opportunity to see how similar institutions were adapted to different local contexts. A number of relatively isolated islands provide the conditions of a natural experiment. All but one, Tonga, were subject to direct colonial rule. Similar constitutions were overlaid on both the highly centralized chiefdoms in the eastern parts of the region and the small-scale, more egalitarian systems in the western areas. Systematic attempts were also made to incorporate local circumstances into so-called homegrown constitutions. These constitutions are now being questioned, particularly by intellectuals in Samoa, which was the pioneer. Resentment toward foreign institutions in the South Pacific still continues, along with attempts to devise or restore indigenous alternatives. After Fiji's first coup d'état, in 1987, a local newspaper wondered if democracy might not be a "foreign flower," unable to survive in the hostile local soil (Larmour 1994).

The promotion of good governance in the South Pacific is nothing new. In the mid-nineteenth century the *Sydney Morning Herald* criticized the regime in Tonga as being "totally inefficient except for the wants of the merest savages" (Latukefu 1975). The king of Tonga took a study tour of New South Wales in 1853. He was shocked by the signs of poverty he saw but was impressed by the leasehold system of land tenure, which he then introduced to Tonga. He went on to adopt a constitution modeled on Hawai'i's, which in turn borrowed elements from Britain's. In making these changes, the king was advised by missionaries. Now consultants and nongovernmental organizations (NGOs) play a similar role in promoting "international best practice."

Transfer

"Transfer" means "conveyance or removal from one place, person, etc., to another" (*Shorter Oxford English Dictionary*, fifth edition). The phrase "institutional transfer" was used by David Apter, in his study of politics in what was then called the Gold Coast, now Ghana, in the 1950s (Apter 1955). He asked if the institutions of parliamentary democracy modeled on Britain were suitable for African circumstances. Similar questions were asked before independence in Solomon Islands, where a government report wondered if "political progress, following the Westminster model, is suitable or desirable" (British Solomon Islands Protectorate 1968, 3).

The argument against transfer was made most influentially by German legal theorist Von Savigny (1814). He saw the law, like language, as embedded in a distinctive Volksgeist, or spirit of the people. His argument was part of a more general Romantic reaction against the universal claims of the Enlightenment. Yet countries are not different in every respect. They often copy from each other and look for examples of best practice abroad. Nineteenth-century Japan modeled its police force on France's and its postal system on Britain's (Westney 1987, 13). In turn, the Japanese system of *koban*—police boxes in urban areas—has been copied by American cities. Ombudsmen have proliferated from their origins in Scandinavia, as has Hong Kong's Independent Commission Against Corruption. Privatization was promoted by the British accounting, advertising, and stockbroking firms that had done well out of its application to Britain in the 1980s. In the 1990s, borrowers looked to New Zealand for examples of "new public management," based on market principles.

Law has always been particularly mobile. Most private law in the West, apart from Scandinavia, derives from Roman civil law or English common law (Watson 1974, 22). Even family law has been open to change as a result of foreign influence. Thus Alan Watson, the author of *Legal Transplants*, concludes that "the creation of law for that precise society in which it is operating is neither always common nor very important" (ibid., 100).

"To transfer" means to take from place to place, but there are a variety of possible sources and destinations. Policy makers typically look to the past, or precedent, as a source. Generals are accused of fighting the last war. Ideas may be invented, and every borrowing is, in a sense, a reinvention as an idea is taken up and adapted to circumstances. Some ideas may be derived from first principles, like the assumptions of economics, and to that extent are borrowed from nowhere. The involvement of international organizations such as the Asian Development Bank, the World Bank, the Commonwealth, or Transparency International contributes to a sense of placelessness. "Best practice" might be found anywhere. And revolutionaries typically look forward, in a sense "borrowing from the future." Six possible combinations of place and time are summarized in table 1.

In the first column for place, the borrowing is from somewhere: specifically named places or regions, like Africa. In the second column for place are more abstract sources, such as the first principles of economics and accounting, myths, or utopian fantasies. I have called these sources

TABLE 1. Sources of Borrowing

	Somewhere	Nowhere
The present	Other countries or regions	First principles
The past	National history	Myth and religion
The future	The West, China, or the former USSR	Utopia

"nowhere," after William Morris' "utopian romance," *News from Nowhere*, first published in 1908 (Morris 1970). Morris' protagonist wakes up in the future, thus facilitating a critique of the present. The rows in table 1 point to borrowing from the present, the past (though this is often forgotten or selectively remembered), and the future. The typology also points to the sources that cut across the categories: "the West," for example, is partly a region, but it is also something more placeless, abstract, and futuristic. "Westminster" is similarly abstracted but draws its prestige from the past. The Bible—which became a source of inspiration for nineteenth-century constitution makers—sits between the columns for place. It refers to real Middle Eastern places, but they are far away and almost mythic.

In his pioneering study of lesson drawing in public policy, Richard Rose (1993) distinguished "great examples" from "siren calls." The former were highly desirable foreign models that were also highly practical for implementation. The latter were equally desirable but impractical. An Independent Commission Against Corruption might, for example, be highly desirable, but impractical in terms of its costs or demands on scarce legal or forensic talent. Rose opened up two other possibilities: undesirable but potentially practical, and undesirable and impractical, amounting from the recipient's point of view to a lucky escape.

Engineering or Gardening

Giovanni Sartori (1997) talks of "constitutional engineering," though the results may be unpredictable—a small change in a constitutional rule may have quite unexpected effects. Donors tend to use a metaphor of construction. As part of its "cooperative intervention" into Solomon Islands, for example, Australian officials would be "inserted" into the Department of Finance and the central bank, while "jurists are also likely to be sent to rebuild the justice system" (*Sydney Morning Herald*, 26 June 2003). Johan Olsen (2003) contrasts "gardening" and "engineering" as approaches to reform. The former recognizes the organism and autonomy of institutions. Reformers can plant, implant, or transplant, but their "foreign flowers" grow at their own pace, and in accordance with their own internal logic. Reformers can only hope to prune here or fertilize there. The engineering metaphor grasps the intentional and deliberate quality of institutions: they are products of human design. The gardening metaphor grasps their autonomy and independence: they have lives of their own.

The results of transfer are not necessarily the replacement of one institution by another. Often the new and the old coexist. One may dominate the other, which is forced into the shadows, like magic in the West. In settler societies like Australia or the United States, the institutions of native or aboriginal people tended to be downgraded, marginalized, or co-opted. Some of those institutions are now being revived. In New Zealand, for example, the Treaty of Waitangi, signed between Maori and British leaders, provides the framework for an emerging dual political order, drawing on Maori and European institutions. Institutions also mix and blend. Esin Orucu (1995), looking at the reception of laws in the European Union, used a culinary metaphor: systems might be pureed, in which case the origins of the mixture were invisible; they might be blended, in which case lumps of one or another of the original systems were still visible; or each system might rest separately, like salad on a plate. Tonga, for example, has a blended system of government—parts of its Tongan and imported origins are still visible but are well mixed together all the way through. Fiji, by contrast, is more like Orucu's salad, with parallel administrative systems for Fijians and non-Fijians still largely distinct and with little interaction between them.

Why Does Transfer Matter?

Introduced institutions are often blamed for political problems in the South Pacific. Barak Sope, once prime minister of Vanuatu, believes that the Westminster system is unable to cope with ethnic conflicts in Melanesia (interview on Radio Vanuatu, 19 December 2000). These views are endorsed by journalists and academics writing from outside the region. An Australian newspaper comments that the introduced system of government "didn't work" in Papua New Guinea because "it was irresponsibly grafted on to an already sophisticated society that worked in a completely different way to our own" (*Canberra Times*, 14 March 2000).

Historian Judy Bennett argues that the "failure of the transplanted political system based on the Westminster model" resulted because "few Solomon Islanders own the national system as theirs": "Introduced by the colonial ruler it is still seen as a foreign superstructure, not a product of their efforts, so they lack both a commitment to it and a critique of it" (2002, 14).

A transfer of political institutions came with colonization and decolonization. A third wave of transfer has taken place in the Pacific Islands after decolonization, as fiscal crises have forced governments to borrow from financial institutions like the World Bank and the Asian Development Bank. Independence was accompanied by aid agreements that have expired or been renegotiated. The international financial institutions now promote "good governance"—including democracy, the rule of law, and anticorruption—and can insist upon it as a condition for a loan. Many of these institutional reforms run up hard against "homegrown" beliefs in chieftaincy, custom, and duty to support one's family and kin. From a study of Kiribati, historian Barrie Macdonald asserted that the approach taken by the World Bank and other donors was "ideologically driven" and that "standard checklists of good governance characteristics make insufficient allowance for cultural diversity, historical context, local economic circumstances or the dynamics of political process" (1996, iii).

A fourth wave of transfer may be breaking over the region, as Australia leads the Regional Assistance Mission to the Solomon Islands (RAMSI). It followed on Australia's intervention in East Timor and its contribution of troops to the United States' "coalition of the willing" in Iraq

The experience of the South Pacific is of wider relevance. International organizations like the World Bank and private consulting firms promote models of good governance in formerly socialist and developing countries. The collapse of socialist societies provided the opportunity—and the demand—for new political and economic institutions such as stock markets and private property. Some were restored from a precommunist past. Others were borrowed. Some were insisted upon as a condition for entry into the European Union. Political theorist Claus Offe wondered at the relevance of the constitutions being adopted in Eastern Europe: "No Western political or economic or social institution has been invented for the purpose of extricating an entire group of societies from the conditions of state socialism and its ruins" (Offe et al. 1998, 216). Western political institutions, Offe says, arose in response to Western problems, which in turn have shaped the cultures on which these institutions depend to perform their functions. Nor were they invented for such purposes as the economic development and management of an ethnically diverse society —typically tasks for government in postcolonial states like, say, Malaysia or Fiji.

Yet opposite lessons were drawn from the Asian financial crisis of 1997. One was that there was no alternative, "Asian" route to development. An Australian newspaper headline put it bluntly: "We tell Asia: Westernise to end the crisis" (*Canberra Times*, 24 October 1998). Malaysian prime minister Mahathir drew the contrary lesson, that there was no single prescription: "The real issue is whether we will willingly allow our economies to be governed by a 'doctor with only one pill for every illness'" (*Australian Financial Review*, 25 June 1999). Mahathir was doing more than objecting to foreign ideas—though he might have been doing that as well. He was criticizing the standardization of the advice and hinting at the exercise of power in the doctor-patient relationship.

Transfer is now promoted by management gurus, academic economists, policy analysts, and their students. These days, as sociologists Strang and Meyer pointed out, "theorists do the travelling" (1993, 492). Yet, as they noted, there is a loose link between theory and rationality. Global theorization tends to ignore important local differences. Behavior based on it, Strang and Meyer suggested, will produce more standardized and ritualized action than behavior based on personal information will. Borrowing environmentalist imagery, other writers have worried about the spread of "institutional monocultures" (Crouch and Streeck 1997).

Déjà Vu

My own interest in "institutional transfer" began with trying to reverse it. My first job in the Pacific, as a lands officer in Solomon Islands, involved returning freehold land to the descendants of its original customary owners. My first consultancy, in Vanuatu in 1980, involved recommending that Vanuatu not borrow from the example of its Melanesian neighbor in land policy. Given that the Vanuatu government lacked the bureaucratic capacity of Solomon Islands, I thought it should get out of the way of direct negotiations between expatriate freeholders and traditional owners.

I had been brought up at university on varieties of Marxism, which tended to see political institutions as determined by more fundamental economic conditions. However, in the 1980s I got excited by what the property rights school of institutional economics had to say about the customary land tenure I had been working on in Solomon Islands. Vincent Ostrom (1987) also showed how a right-wing "political economy," or what became known as public choice theory, could recast the study of public administration. When I started teaching at an Australian university, a colleague and I devised a textbook that tried to combine simple economic and sociological ideas about institutions (Colebatch and Larmour 1993). Occasional consultancy work since—particularly an assignment for a multilateral bank—kept me thinking about the relevance of standard or introduced ideas, the role of brokers of ideas, and why some reforms stick and others do not.

The idea of good governance brought institutional thinking back into development policy in the 1990s. However, like others working on comparative politics and development administration, I was uneasy about the standard package of privatization and public sector reform that was being promoted after the collapse of communism in 1989 or during the fiscal crises of the late 1990s. My concerns were sharpened by a 1999 article in the American journal *Public Administration Review*. Watching the flow of consultants engaged in "building institutions in the image of the West" in Bosnia in the mid-1990s, Huddleston saw "a return to a foreign assistance tradition that had largely been abandoned in the 1960s superseded by the more culturally sensitive insights of development administration" (1999, 147). The editors' introduction used the phrase "here we go again." Huddleston wondered at the "disconnect between what public administration specialists are now being sent abroad to do, and what we as a profession ostensibly learned decades ago" (ibid., 148). Yet he concluded reassuringly that the space for national differences was closing as international norms emerged. I was less reassured about the loss of space. I also wondered who was closing it and why and how it was being closed.

What exactly had been learned from the 1960s and 1970s? Then the major actors included the United Nations Public Administration Division; the technical assistance missions of the governments of the United States, Britain, and France; and the Ford Foundation. Together they all promoted a program of "administrative reform," involving "the replacement of expatriate administrators, the establishment of training in administration and management, long range institution building, the application of sound managerial concepts, and attitudinal change" (Caiden 1991, 54). They produced a network of consultants and contractors "mostly located in North America, many of whom had known each other from service in World War II and met together formally at briefings and academic gatherings" (ibid., 57).

In the 1960s, the Ford Foundation funded conferences that found, for example, that those promoting rational legal models of bureaucracy were underestimating the "survival power and capacity of traditional administrative systems" (ibid.). National governments were resisting ideas for their own reasons. They realized that "ostensibly neutral matters of means carried with them Western ideas at odds with national objectives." So the governments reacted opportunistically. They picked the "technical operations (management) readily assimilable without fundamental changes (administrative reform)" (ibid., 58). A later international conference on development administration went on to conclude that "reforms have to be country specific" (United Nations 1985, 1). "Country specificity" defers to the sovereignty of national governments represented in international organizations like the United Nations and is now a cliché of development assistance.

These early conferences also anticipated the 1990s concern with democratic institutions. They concluded that Western countries should be less concerned with marginal technical adjustments and more concerned with ideology and social changes—particularly the encouragement of "democratic, private and local government institutions and progress towards the rule of law, freedom of expression, and individual freedom, initiative and private enterprise" (Caiden 1991). In 1966 the U.S. Foreign Assistance Act was amended to include "the utilization of democratic institutions in development."

My sense of déjà vu was increased in two other ways. First I reread Sione Latukefu's history (1975) of the Tongan constitution. The nineteenth-century arguments about the role of missionary advisers seemed very similar to those about the role of NGOs and consultants in the region today. Second, newspaper stories in March 2003 described how Afghan factions and their advisers were jostling over the content of a new constitution, particularly the role to be played by traditional leaders and by Islamic and customary law. They were doing so after a violent invasion by the United States and its allies. Similar issues of "nation building" arose during the decolonization of the Pacific Islands and in the Australian interventions in Timor and Solomon Islands.

Approach

In a recent survey, De Jong, Lalenis, and Mamadouh (2002) identify two perspectives on what they call "institutional transplantation." The first perspective looks at what makes actors seek answers abroad—what they call "actors pulling in." The second looks at the relationship between introduced and indigenous institutions, or "goodness of fit." In the Pacific Islands there has been more pushing from outside than pulling in, and the imposition of introduced institutions is often blamed for their poor fit.

This book focuses particularly on the process of transfer and on the role of power in that process. It uses a framework devised by Dolowitz and Marsh (2000) to guide studies of policy transfer. The word "policy" emphasizes deliberate choice and actors pulling in. The word "institution," by contrast, emphasizes what is fixed or given and issues of fit. Dolowitz and Marsh also recognized that transfer might be coercive, along a scale that ranged from the pressures to keep up with competitors, through

conditions attached to loans, to outright imposition of institutions following military defeat. And without a choice, countries were particularly vulnerable to standardized solutions peddled, for example, by consultancy
firms.

This book tries to answer several questions:

- Where did the institutions come from? Were they invented or borrowed or some combination of the two? Did they come from metropolitan models, other colonies, or first principles?
- Why did so many local institutions end up looking like those in the
  West? Was it because the institutions were forced on their recipients? And what was the role of the consultants and advisers who
  played such a visible part in the process?
- Why did some transfers take hold, and others not? What was the
  fate of alternatives?
- What were the effects of transfer? In what ways did transferred or
  hybrid institutions perform better or worse than indigenous ones?
- What has been the fate of a particular institution, the state? (Many
  of the current diagnoses of Melanesia's economic problems hinge
  on ideas about the state, its weakness, or even its failure. The state
  was imported into the region, and countries became independent
  states at about the time that official opinion in Western countries
  was turning against statism, in favor of privatization and NGOs.)
- What role does culture play in the transfer of institutions and in
  resistance to the transfer? (Critics of imported institutions often
  bring up ideas about culture.)

The book answers these questions in several linked ways. Chapters 1 and
2 identify institutional transfer as a persistent theme in the study of the
Pacific Islands, reflected in ideas like homegrown constitutions, invented
traditions, and weak states. Chapter 3 examines the "institutional" in the
phrase "institutional transfer." The so-called new institutional economics
has become influential in the study of development, and ideas about institutions appear in several disciplines. The argument for good governance
is partly an argument that institutions matter and have a causal impact on
rates of growth or on economic development more generally.

Chapters 4 through 6 are more empirical, analyzing about forty cases
of institutional transfer, beginning with Tonga's borrowing of foreign
institutions in the nineteenth century and ending with current attempts
to induce island-states to give up money laundering. The cases are of insti-

tutions associated with good governance: property, constitutions, democracy, public sector reform, and the prevention of corruption. Aid donors believe that these institutions are important for development, yet transfers of them often fail or are resisted.

The final chapters are more reflective. There is a presumption that institutional transfer is difficult or prone to failure. The image of the foreign flower is a rather pathetic one, of a plant beleaguered or starved of nourishment. Yet some transfers—for example, of Christian churches—seem to have taken place quite successfully. Chapter 7 identifies some common themes in the earlier chapters, such as the role of timing and crisis, and the techniques and sources of transfer. It goes on to identify factors that determine whether or not transfer took place, including social conditions, sympathy with local values, and misunderstanding.

Chapter 8 turns to the question of power. Many of the political institutions in the Pacific Islands were introduced during the colonial period. The World Bank and the Asian Development Bank have often insisted on institutional changes as a condition for loans. Governments, students, and soldiers have sometimes resisted. The chapter draws on recent political theory to identify the types of power involved in transfer. Chapter 9 considers how the transfers have been evaluated by those involved, including the consultants who advised on them and the donors and financial institutions that hoped that institutional transfer might lead to improved economic performance. The final chapter summarizes the results of the analysis of the Pacific Island cases and uses those results to answer questions about institutional transfer.

1 Institutional Transfer in Pacific Studies

About a thousand years ago, the Polynesians fanned out from a central location in the Southeast Pacific, settling on islands as far west as New Zealand and as far north as Hawai'i. Along with animals and seedlings, they brought their chiefdom-based institutions with them. These introduced institutions developed differently—from highly stratified systems of government, sometimes called protostates, in Hawai'i and the Marquesas Islands to much more egalitarian ones in the outlying islands of the Melanesian archipelago.

Thus the South Pacific region provided the arena for a vast natural experiment in the evolution of institutions. The large number of isolated cases has allowed scholars to search for links between demographic and environmental determinants of the evolution of institutions. Archaeologist Patrick Vinton Kirch (1989) looked at the development of institutions of chieftaincy. He wanted to understand how that type of institution became highly stratified and divided religious and secular functions on some islands yet was quite egalitarian in others. In Hawai'i, for example, a sharp distinction was made between commoners and chiefs, and fine distinctions were made among chiefly lineages. In Tonga the religious and secular functions of senior chiefs had become distinct. Elsewhere, chiefs lived more closely with commoners and combined religious and secular roles.

Yet in spite of the methodological potential of the "natural experiment," Kirch concluded that innovation and invention were as important as environmental determination in explaining the variety of institutions that developed from common Polynesian roots. Population pressure and environmental constraints were insufficient explanations of political differentiation. Agency mattered as much as structure. "The power of overarching symbolic systems, themselves the products of human creativity"—in short, institutions—could not be overlooked (ibid., 283).

In the south and west of the region, Polynesian settlers came across people with more decentralized traditions of government. Political units in Melanesia typically included a few hundred people or fewer. Continual face-to-face contact made it possible to maintain order by a combination of factors. An individual's right to retaliate, if attacked, was recognized. There were traditions of reciprocity: if I helped you now, you would help me in the future. Gossip, shaming, and supernatural sanctions enforced shared values (Taylor 1982). If power was given up to leaders, it could be taken back from them. Within such political systems, the responsibility for maintaining order was distributed widely, rather than concentrated in one person (Southall 1968). Political systems—within which people accept an obligation to settle disputes without fighting—were embedded in larger, more extensive networks of competition and exchange.

Colonial rule was preceded by a long period of contact with explorers and traders. Nineteenth-century experiments in combining introduced and indigenous institutions were overturned by colonial rule everywhere except in Tonga. Hawai'i's constitution, one of the models for Tonga's, was overthrown in a settler coup that provided a pretext for U.S. intervention (Kuykendall 1940). A "federal government" that reconciled chiefly and settler interests in the Cook Islands was set aside by New Zealand (Gilson 1980). Each island came under a system of government from London, Paris, Canberra, Wellington, or Washington, D.C.

In some cases, colonial institutions were modeled on the institutions of the colonizing country: Britain, France, Australia, or the United States. In others, they were devised for specifically colonial purposes or imported from other colonies. Indigenous institutions were sidelined or co-opted. Colonial officials ruled directly by carrying out patrols and holding court and indirectly through chiefs and headmen they selected. Samoa's Mau rebellion was in part an attempt to reassert chiefly authority that had been undermined by direct colonial rule.

In the 1960s and 1970s, New Zealand, Australia, and Britain withdrew from direct colonial rule, and the United States restructured its relationships with its Micronesian colonies. Decolonization offered the prospect of revival of traditional institutions but also brought international expectations about democracy, the rule of law, and human rights to bear more closely on the new states. Ten countries became independent, starting in 1962 with Western Samoa (now simply called Samoa). Another five adopted their own constitutions, while entering into relationships of "free association" with New Zealand or the United States. Others—Hawai'i and the Northern Mariana Islands—moved closer into the U.S. orbit.

The authors of the first independence constitution, Samoa's, were mainly expatriate but put great effort into making it "homegrown": devised by Samoans, in Samoa, and reflecting indigenous political traditions. They were also mindful of the coups and conflicts that they had seen following decolonization in Africa. They hoped that homegrown constitutions might be more robust and resilient than those based on foreign models.

Institutional Issues in Pacific Studies

The most influential way of thinking about Pacific Island politics has been anthropologist Marshall Sahlins' contrast between Melanesian "big men" and Polynesian "chiefs" (1963). Sahlins distinguished these different types of political leadership according to the degree to which the roles were achieved or ascribed. The authority of the Melanesian big man was achieved by his own efforts, whereas the authority of the Polynesian chief was ascribed by inheritance.

Sahlins' argument provoked all sorts of rejoinders, qualifications, and extensions. Like any ideal typification, it was overdrawn. On the one hand, some big men got a head start from their parents (Standish 1978). On the other hand, weak and ineffective inheritors of chiefly status might be bypassed or sidelined by higher-achieving siblings. In any case genealogies could be constructed and reconstructed to incorporate insurgents.

The geographical side of Sahlins' argument was also criticized, on empirical grounds and in principle. Well-established systems of inherited chieftaincy existed in parts of Melanesia—among the Mekeo in the central province of PNG and southern Vanuatu. Outlying Polynesian islands were also included in Melanesian states—Tikopia, Anuta, Rennell, Bellona, Sikaiana, and Ontong Java in Solomon Islands, for example. A more general criticism was that Melanesians used the word "chief" to describe all sorts of local leaders (White and Lindstrom 1997).

The division between Melanesia and Polynesia (and additionally Micronesia) was made by European explorers and colonial rulers. The reference to "black"—the "Mela" in the word "Melanesia"—was frankly racist. Linguistic and archaeological research was showing similarities across the region, as well as new distinctions within it. Political sympathies and common causes against colonialism served to underplay the distinctions on which Sahlins' typology depended.

Nevertheless, the distinction between Melanesia and Polynesia is important for arguments about institutional transfer. A single set of Polynesian chiefly institutions was relatively quickly and recently disseminated across the region. They then developed more or less in isolation from each other, some becoming more centralized, others more decentralized. Some became protostates—one of the few examples in world history of states emerging endogenously and independently of other state systems. They were transformed rapidly with contact, and as we have seen, only the Tongan monarchy survives.

Melanesia, on the other hand, provides prototypes and evidence for the conditions of statelessness. Political theorist Michael Taylor (1982) used Melanesian anthropology in his study of the conditions for anarchy. Melanesian examples also featured in institutional economists' discussions of conditions for self-management of open-access common property resources (Ostrom 1990).

The decolonization of the South Pacific—and the subsequent fate of the independent states—has also reinforced a distinction between Melanesia and Polynesia. Of the ten fully independent states, the vast majority of the population live in Melanesia, particularly in PNG. Their land areas, highlands, and dependence on natural resource exploitation distinguish Melanesian states from their smaller neighbors. Polynesians tend to have more access to metropolitan countries, larger overseas diasporas, and more limited political independence. And two of the three current candidates for state failure—Solomon Islands and PNG—are Melanesian (the third, Nauru, is Micronesian).

Homegrown Constitutions

The first Pacific Island country to become constitutionally independent was Samoa, which did so in 1962 on the basis of a constitution whose authors deliberately tried to combine introduced and indigenous forms of government. High chiefs were to take turns at being head of state, and colonial legislation that restricted suffrage to *matai*, chiefly heads of households, was retained. "Homegrownness" referred both to the content of the constitution and to the participatory process by which it was adopted. Samoa's pioneering approach influenced other countries in the region. Touring committees canvassed popular opinion in the highlands and outer islands of PNG and Solomon Islands. A constitutional convention brought local leaders to the capital in Kiribati. Referendums accompanied each stage of the process of adoption of constitutions in the U.S. territories. National constitution-making processes were mirrored in the process of adopting state, and even municipal, constitutions in Palau. Many countries' constitutions provided a special place for traditional leaders, in councils of *ariki*, *iroij*, or simply "chiefs." Most of the constitutions protected indigenous systems of land rights. Many provided for decentralization to more traditional levels of self-government.

Fiji's 1970 constitution stands out against this trend. It was decided upon behind closed doors by the leaders of Fiji's political parties in London and enacted by the British parliament. It was overthrown by the Fijian army in 1987. Both its successors—the 1990 constitution, which was leaned toward indigenous interests, and the 1998 constitution, which was acceptable internationally—followed the process of touring the country and holding village-level discussions.

The doctrine of the homegrown constitution, and the story of constitution making in Samoa, was set out by one of the advisers, Jim Davidson (Munro 2000). He was a founder of a tradition of Pacific history that emphasizes the active agency of islanders—rather than explorers, traders, and colonial officials—and stands against the idea that contact was necessarily a "fatal impact" (Moorehead 1966). Homegrownness can be called a doctrine because its practitioners wrote up what they did in ways that allowed their ideas to spread. Jim Davidson was followed by Norm Meller (1982), Yash Ghai (1983, 2000), and then Brij Lal (2002), and each of them wrote explanations and justifications of his role as constitutional adviser or commissioner.

Homegrownness was an issue in PNG, in the strictly legal sense that PNG's Constitutional Planning Committee (CPC) believed not only that the constitution should be adopted by a convention of Papua New Guineans, rather than granted by the Australian parliament, but also in the broader political and cultural sense that it should reflect PNG ways, values, and institutions. In the end, as Peter Fitzpatrick (1980) remarked, the result was rather "ordinary," for two reasons important to the transfer of institutions. First, politicians were more comfortable with borrowed institutions that carried with them the legitimacy of their origins (the honors system, which CPC had recommended be abolished, and the role of governor-general, which the CPC had recommended be divided up among other officeholders). Second, the constitution was drafted and later interpreted by lawyers with their own international networks of standards and precedents.

Consulting the people, of course, did not necessarily mean adopting their views. The planning committees were explaining and advocating as well as listening. Opinions had to be given a written legal form. Governments took positions different from those of committees, which only advised, and there were other pressures—particularly international expectations. The result was a negotiation among political parties and the former colonial power: a kind of political settlement rather than an expression of popular opinion or political culture. On a more conceptual level, Yash Ghai, reflecting on the process of constitution making in Solomon Islands, in which he had played an active part, wrote: "Despite consultation with the people and active involvement of their leaders, the constitution cannot be said to be rooted in indigenous concepts of power, authority and decisionmaking" (1983, 50).

Constitution making did not stop with decolonization. Several constitutions made provision for their own review. Fiji's 1970 constitution, for example, provided for the review of the communal voting system in what came to be called the Street Commission, but the government decided not to enact its recommendations. PNG has amended its constitution to reduce the autonomy of provincial governments and, more recently, to strengthen political parties.

After a coup in 2000, the Solomon Islands parliament appointed a committee to come up with a more homegrown system of state (i.e., federal) government. In Fiji, Sitiveni Halapua, the director of the Pacific Islands Development Program at the East-West Center in Hawai'i, has been acting as mediator between the government and the opposition in a structured dialogue called the *talanoa* process. In Bougainville, after ten years of secessionist conflict, Australian adviser Anthony Regan is helping with the drafting of a homegrown constitution.

Invented Traditions

The doctrine of the homegrown constitution accepted that the conflict between indigenous and introduced traditions was a real one that might be difficult to reconcile. The doctrine was vulnerable to the charge of supporting oppressive or outmoded traditions. More surprising was the charge that the apparently indigenous traditions were themselves introductions. The phrase "invented traditions" came from an influential book by historians Hobsbawm and Ranger (1983), who pointed out that institutions of tribe and chieftaincy in Africa had often been constructions of colonial rule. The argument was not new to Pacific studies. Peter France (1969) and Ron Crocombe (1964) had already made similar arguments about institutions of land tenure in Fiji and Cook Islands. France argued that communal ownership was a construction of colonial land policy, drawing on a resident commissioner's romantic ideas about Scottish clans. Crocombe showed how Cook Islands land tenure had been selectively reinterpreted by colonial policy.

Politically, the theory of the invention of tradition implicated chiefs. In Polynesia, colonial governments had worked with and through chiefs. Tonga had reinvented its government as a constitutional monarchy. The French government recognized (and paid) chiefs in Wallis and Futuna as *rois* (kings). In Samoa the *matai*, whose suffrage was conserved in the homegrown constitution, were themselves partly creations of colonial rule. In Solomon Islands the contrast was often made between "real" chiefs and those who had attached their signatures to fraudulent land sales or acted as intermediaries with the colonial government.

White and Lindstrom (1997) discovered a more complex set of positions for chiefs today, whom they found throughout the region. Chiefs might act as symbolic representatives of unity (like Fiji's former prime minister and then president, Ratu Mara) or minor functionaries, as well as being arrayed against the state, as representatives of marginalized interests. Jeffrey Sissons (1999) saw the Cook Islands government manipulating the traditional system according to the needs of electoral politics and the national economy. At one time it emphasized the monarchical and unifying aspects of chieftaincy; at another, the decentralized, ethnic, and touristic character of chieftaincy.

The homegrown constitutions often created special places for chiefs. Such institutions honored chiefs by recognition but often at the same time isolated and marginalized them. However, Fiji's Great Council of Chiefs suddenly acquired political weight after the 1987 coup. It had been established by colonial legislation, but it later sought to set itself outside, above, and historically prior to any constitution. The thing being transferred here was sovereignty. The Deed of Cession, the council argued, had transferred sovereignty from Fiji's chiefs to the British Crown and that sovereignty should be handed back to the chiefs (rather than to elected politicians) as Fiji became a republic.

The argument about invented traditions made colonialism doubly

overweening. Two transfers needed to be explained: of the colonial institutions that now appeared so solidly traditional, and of the later introductions that now seemed arrayed against them.

Nation Making

During the period of decolonization there was often concern about the
absence of nationalism. Nationalism was seen as something unfortunately
limited to the bureaucratic elite and university students or relegated to
local, separatist forms. Political scientist Ron May (1982) included cargo
cults in a broader category of "micronationalist movements," and university students, particularly in PNG in the 1970s, were often active in them.

New Zealand, Britain, and Australia—as well as the United Nations
—were seen as pushing countries into independence rather than as sur-
rendering to nationalist pressure to withdraw. PNG, Solomon Islands,
and Vanuatu each became independent during a secessionist crisis, which
pitted a new national government against popular pressure for a separate
independence (for Bougainville separately from PNG, for the Western
Province separately from Solomon Islands, and for Espíritu Santo and
Tanna separately from PNG). PNG, once independent, was able to give
"nation-building" military support to the Vanuatu government in suppressing its separatist rebellion in 1980–1981.

Nationalism was not completely absent. Jeffrey Sissons (1999) pointed
out the early nationalism of Sir Albert Henry's Cook Islands Party and its
unifying monarchical picture of chieftaincy. Sissons contrasted it with later
emphasis on interisland differences and local chieftaincies. Anthropologist
Robert Foster (2002) found nationalism in unexpected but everyday places
in PNG: in advertising, the mass media, and campaigns against chewing
betel nut. For him, transfer was a much more decentralized and discur-
sive process, involving the private sector as much as the government and
driven by globalization as much as by national actors. Foster drew particularly on Benedict Anderson's influential work (1983) on nation-states as
imagined communities—imagined because members could never hope to
meet everyone face-to-face. Anderson had pointed to the "mimetic" and
"modular" character of nationalism. It was something easily transferred,
as a package that slotted comfortably into place beside other nationalisms
(subnationalisms might also nest within supranationalisms). The downside of borrowing was, as Margaret Jolly (1992) put it, the "spectre of inauthenticity" that also haunted invented traditions.

The State in Pacific Studies

European explorers, missionaries, and traders brought their own ideas about government, particularly the virtues of a centralized bureaucratic state. These ideas were unfamiliar in Melanesia but meshed relatively more with the protostates already emerging in parts of Polynesia. Historian Richard Gilson summarized why Europeans might want to deal with a centralized monarchy in Samoa: "centralized because the unification of the group was considered essential to the conduct of external relations as well as the maintenance of internal order, and a kingdom because monarchy, apart from being 'naturally' suited to Polynesians, and traditional with many settlers, represented a form of entrenched and concentrated authority through which Europeans might hope to exert influence generally upon the Samoan people" (1970, 188).

Hybrid forms emerged in the period between contact with European traders and missionaries and the formal imposition of colonial rule. The Cakobau government in Fiji (1871–1874) (Routledge 1985) and the federal government in Cook Islands (1891–1900) were precarious combinations of chiefly and bureaucratic rule. The Hawaiian monarchy was eventually overturned by a settler coup. The hybrid Tongan monarchy survives from well before the time it adopted a written constitution in 1875.

By the late nineteenth century the whole region was divided up and parceled out among colonial empires. The region became governed by bureaucracies whose senior officials were responsible to distant governments. Penetration of the new and arbitrary political spaces created by the partition of the South Pacific was slow and uneven. As late as the 1920s, the Australian government was publishing maps of Papua and New Guinea that showed degrees of official control around the coasts, as measured by population censuses (Wolfers 1975). The Highlands were simply left blank. The first government patrols and contacts there did not take place until the 1930s.

Colonial states in the South Pacific were strongly differentiated from the societies they governed and were relatively autonomous. Their senior levels were staffed from abroad. Racial segregation increased the differentiation between rulers and ruled. Particularly after the Second World War the budgets of colonial states were supplemented by grants from Canberra, London, Wellington, Washington, the Hague, or Paris. These states were centralized around capitals—Port Moresby, Honiara, Port Vila Suva, and so on—and were coordinated by governors and high commissioners at the center and by district officers in the field. In many ways they corresponded to sociologist Max Weber's idea of the state: separate from society, governed by its own official ethos, and gathering to itself the monopoly of the legitimate use of violence.

Colonial governments and their successors—the aid donors and international financial institutions—typically think of the state in terms of the job it is supposed to be doing. This job is often traced back to Adam Smith's "three duties of the sovereign": defense, police, and construction of public works that would be unprofitable for the private sector but of benefit to society—a potentially big category. Reports by PNG's Institute of National Affairs and by the Australian Agency for International Development (AusAID), for example, tend to take this functional road, seeing the state in terms of its ability to correct market failures and to secure economic development. Marxist accounts of the state in PNG also tend to see the capitalist state in functional terms, as a vehicle or an arena for class interests.

Yet there is also a moral or ethical dimension to "stateness." Weber's famous definition of the state as a "human community that successfully claims the monopoly of the legitimate use of violence" is partly functional but also ethical. The claim is recognized as legitimate. Killing done in the name of the state may be regarded as admirable, but done privately, as immoral. Rule by states also introduces a distinction between public and private that may have sometimes disadvantaged women, who became relegated to a new private sphere while men took on new opportunities in the public world of politics and government. Bureaucracies in Melanesia have norms of impersonality that may be regarded as ethically suspect in the wider society, where people are expected to help their friends and kin.

The Postcolonial State

Marxist arguments about the state were influential in the 1960s and 1970s. Marxist theories tended to see the state as an effect of broader and more fundamental social conflicts. However, some theories of the postcolonial state saw it as more autonomous from society than counterparts in developed countries. Its support was transferred from abroad, and its officials might have class interests of their own as a bureaucratic bourgeoisie. Marxist writers associated with the University of the South Pacific, such William Sutherland (1992) tended to see the state in this way. Later, Ian Frazer (1997) indicted the whole Solomon Islands bureaucracy as complicit beneficiaries of the timber boom in the 1990s. Their bureaucratic salaries depended on taxation of resource exploitation. In Scott Mac-

William's work (1986), institutions like commodity boards, provincial governments, and holding companies provided the terrain—and sometimes the prizes—in struggles between different branches of the bourgeoisie. Marxist theories tended to be skeptical about the possibility of transferring institutions between countries at different stages of development and skeptical about the importance of institutional forms, such as representative democracy, as opposed to the class purposes to which they were put.

Weak, Quasi, and Failed States

Theda Skocpol (1985) "brought the state back in" to political science, and Joel Migdal has developed the most sustained theory of state weakness that influenced studies of Melanesia in the 1990s. Migdal (1988) first defined state strength in terms of the ability of the elite to impose its preferences on the rest of society. That strength could be measured by compliance with legislation, popular participation, and the legitimacy accorded to institutions. Later Migdal (1994) emphasized the interaction between state and society, rather than the opposition between them. More recently he has tried to explain why ostensibly weak states nevertheless continue to survive. Migdal (1998) explained this surprising survival in terms of international support, successful interactions with citizens, and the ability to create meaning in law, ritual, and public space (each of the latter involving institutions). In the South Pacific, for example, international recognition brings aid, loans, and technical assistance to weak states. Cash is handed out to citizens during election campaigns or through special parliamentary slush funds. States also draw on traditional forms of government, such as councils of chiefs, and on nationalist feelings to create support for themselves. They may also, when necessary, draw on images of modernity and development, as Sissons (1999) described in Cook Islands. These factors may allow the states to persist, without substantially changing the societies in which they find themselves.

The idea of the weak state became influential with regard to governments that seemed increasingly incapable of performing basic tasks like maintaining law and order. The authority and the capacity of the weak state were challenged by all manner of social forces and local leaders, including chiefs. The theory was applied particularly to Melanesia (Dauvergne 1998; Dinnen 2001). Jane Turnbull (2002) argued that while the Solomon Islands state had the appearance of a Western liberal democratic state, the power relationships that were institutionalized within it were more traditional, fluid, and personalized. The state was reluctant to impose law and order and failed to engage with the lives of the population, most of whom were still illiterate. There was an absence of everyday bureaucratic disciplines, such as coming to work on time, maintaining records, and planning. As a result the state had little capacity to encourage rural development.

The idea of the weak state in PNG was sometimes driven by a nostalgia for the supposedly strong state of late colonial rule, which stood apart from society but capably delivered services like health and education. Faced with the "weakness" of Melanesian states, aid donors like Australia increasingly turned to the missions and civil society to deliver social services. Development-oriented NGOs often had religious backers.

Robert Jackson's related idea (1990) of the quasi state, sustained by international recognition and aid rather than its own domestic legitimacy and taxes, echoed an earlier idea in Pacific studies: that of the type of economy known as MIRAB (migration, remittances, aid, and bureaucracy), in which international migration, remittances, and aid fund a local bureaucracy (Bertram and Watters 1986). These international dimensions of stateness made it particularly open to transfer and vulnerable to conditions set by donors, but its limited capacity to affect local society implied that transfer might go no further than the planning office, the central government, or the capital.

By the end of the 1990s, policy makers and journalists were talking of Solomon Islands and Nauru as failed states (Dobell 2003). Justifying Australia's proposed military and police intervention in Solomon Islands, Australia's prime minister argued that it was "not in Australia's interest to have a number of failed states in the Pacific" (*Sydney Morning Herald*, 26 June 2003). Writing for a think tank in Australia, Susan Windybank and Mike Manning warned that PNG was following Solomon Islands into "economic paralysis, government collapse, and social despair" and was on the brink of becoming a failed state (2003, 10). Political scientist Stephanie Lawson looked back at Fiji's coups of 1987 and 2000 and concluded that although the state had been weakened, it was not yet "prone to significant failure," as least in comparison with places like Somalia, the Congo, and parts of the former Yugoslavia (2003, 283).

Governance

The word "governance" originally derives from "steering," and it has gained currency as ideas about the state, its value, and its capacity have been questioned. In political science, governance refers to "order without hierarchy"—the idea that order need not depend on top-down regulation by chiefs, kings, or parliaments. This idea is realized in stateless societies, like those in Melanesia, and in international relations, where there is no "world government" to police law and order.

The word has also been applied to the new public management and to the management of public-private networks in the delivery of health, education, and other social services—a necessary consequence of privatization or downsizing that left provision to the private sector or NGOs (Rhodes 1997). The word also appears in the phrase "corporate governance," referring to the role of boards of directors. When the World Bank and the Asian Development Bank (ADB) sought to introduce greater accountability and transparency in the financial sector in East and Southeast Asia, they tried to transfer models of corporate governance from the United States and Australia or ideas of best practice in the accounting profession. Some of the language of "good governance," such as "transparency" and "accountability," derives as much from accountancy as from economics or political science. Accountants have been as influential as economists in institutional transfer, particularly through established networks of international consulting firms such as KPMG.

The World Bank also adopted and promoted the word, which it first used in 1989 as a kind of code, for the bank's charter prevented it from talking about the domestic politics of its members. The meaning of the word was thus intended to be vague. Later, the bank adopted a bland definition—"the manner in which power is exercised in the management of a country's economic and social resources in development"—and linked the term to its own long-standing concerns with public sector management, accountability, the rule of law, transparency, and information (World Bank 1994). More recently, the bank's Web site has linked the term "governance" to anticorruption. These ideas gained particular influence through the ability of the bank to disseminate them through its publications (like the *World Development Report*), the data it collected, its consultants, and the advice it gave governments. The bank could also insist on them as a condition for loans. The Asian Development Bank followed the World Bank in adopting a "governance policy," and ideas about public sector reform, privatization, accountability, and transparency were written into the conditions of a series of ADB loans in the late 1990s.

The World Bank's interest in governance is embedded in a wider intellectual and professional framework. The bank's concerns with efficiency, transparency, and oversight come from the worlds of accounting and auditing. In a general way, it is market friendly, with a preference for letting markets solve problems (like the exchange rate or industrial development), but recognizes the need for state action to provide the conditions within which markets can operate. It is not suspicious of all state activity—after all, the bank itself is a highly bureaucratic intergovernmental organization. During the 1990s the bank and the bilateral donors like Australia that followed its intellectual lead came to believe that institutions matter in achieving development. Institutions like parliaments, courts, and the media had an independent effect that was not simply reflective of social conditions. And institutions mattered, rather than other political factors such as leadership and ideology.

The World Bank's usage of the word "governance" overlaps with that of another phrase, "good government." An organization called the Good Government League was founded in Louisiana in 1912, part of the politics of corruption and reform that produced the populist governor Huey Long. Formed by "a collection of patrician and business leaders devoted to honest government" (Williams 1970, 133), it sounds rather like an early version of Transparency International (TI), an anticorruption NGO. "Good government" was also part of colonial theory in Britain after the Second World War. It "became a slogan in colonial affairs because it implied that 'self government' meant incompetent administration" (Lee 1967, 5). "Incompetent administration" remains a concern for the promoters of "good governance." Being nagged about good governance reminds recipients of the colonial origins of many bilateral aid agencies.

Governance and good government enter the argument of this book in several ways. The book is particularly concerned with international transfers from country to country and from international organizations to particular countries. These transfers take place in an international system without a central authority that can enforce agreements or insist that sovereign states reform themselves. Donors demand reform as a condition for aid, and international banks can make it a condition for a loan. But there is not a lot they can do if the recipient reneges on the agreement or fails to comply with the condition. There is no international court that can enforce such conditions. The political pressures that drew donors to give aid in the first place continue to apply. And the raison d'être of international financial institutions is to keep lending—including lending to cover earlier defaults. They rarely, if ever, foreclose on a loan. Instead, good governance has been promoted indirectly, by statistical comparison, the creation of rankings, visiting missions, international conferences, and the emulation of best practice. It may be insisted upon by donors, but it may also be self-imposed for fear of being left behind or outside the club. Good governance, in the particular sense the World Bank defines it, has been promoted by processes of governance in the wider sense of self-management and peer pressure.

Conclusions

The political ideas in Pacific studies discussed above are not distinct: they overlap, feed into each other, and react against each other. They have also influenced events as intellectuals and professionals advise governments. The University of Papua New Guinea's Law Faculty, including recruits from East Africa in the 1970s, taught Marxist approaches to law in its social context and also advised on homegrown constitutions. Those constitutions entrenched and standardized invented traditions of chieftaincy or custom. The apparent weakness of Melanesian states contributed to the absence of good governance, though it was far from clear that the World Bank's battery of remedies—downsizing, privatization, accountability, and transparency—had much purchase on the problems they were called upon to address.

New ideas have entered the discourse, but they have not simply displaced or replaced older ones. For example, to analyze the current peace process on Bougainville, we would need to take into account cargo-cultish political movements, the economic interests of regional and national elites, invented traditions of Bougainvillean nationalism, and the weak but surprisingly resilient PNG state, unwilling to let Bougainville go but unable to subdue it. Anthony Regan, a constitutional lawyer, is following in the footsteps of Yash Ghai and Jim Davidson by drawing up a homegrown constitution, including local government by chiefs. Donors worry about good governance, while Robert Foster's type of nationalism would be expressed in the T-shirts or cassette tapes of the young men who fought the war and are now hanging around looking for work.

Why then do we need another concept, "institutional transfer"? The "institutional" part points to the relationship between structure and agency that is important for reformers as well as analysts. One of the contributions to the anthropological perspective to understanding South Pacific politics (e.g., in cargo cults, invented traditions, or nation making) is the agency it recognizes in ordinary people affirming or withdrawing their recognition of larger-scale institutions. From another direction, much of the work on homegrown constitutions and good governance has been done by individual consultants and local politicians, concerned with the limits of what can be achieved by individuals. Chapter 3 will show how institutional theories encompass individual purposive action and the constraints on it—though different theories give different relative weight to each. The "transfer" part of the phrase is useful as a neutral alternative to a progressive language of evolution or a nationalist language of resistance. It refers to a process that may be promoted, accepted, resisted, or reversed.

2 Cargo, Culture, and Context

The study of the Pacific Islands has created and then exported two powerful images of institutional transfer. The first is the image of the cargo cult, in which islanders construct models of aircraft, airfields, and wharves in order to attract material wealth. It is a poignant image of failure. Sham institutions are constructed, and the cargo never comes. The second is the image of Trobriand cricket, in which islanders reconstruct the rules of an introduced game, folding them into long-established patterns of local politics and ritual. It is a cheerful image of revival and reconciliation. Both images are now widely disseminated beyond the region. Anthropologist Lamont Lindstrom (1993) has charted the diffusion of the idea of cargo cult, from its first mention in a settler newspaper to its appearance in the scholarly literature and then its escape into global popular culture. Trobriand cricket has similarly escaped its origins, mainly through an influential ethnographic film, produced by the Papua New Guinea government's Office of Information at the time of PNG's political independence. Political scientist Christopher Hood (1998), for example, uses it as an image of the unintended effects of reform in an article on the use of contracts in the public service. Here I have used these images to introduce some ideas about institutions and institutional transfer.

Cargo Cults

"Cargo" in the term "cargo cults" refers to expectations of material wealth and the use of supernatural means to achieve it. The first recorded use of the phrase was in 1945, in a reference to the prewar "Vailala madness" in Papua: "livestock has been destroyed, and gardens neglected in the expectation of cargo arriving" (Bird 1945). Settlers and administrators often saw cargo cults as political threats. Worsley (1970) saw the "Vailala madness" as one of many millenarian movements in Melanesia that grew up in reaction to colonial rule and missionary influence. They were millenarian in the sense that they expected and prepared for "the coming of a period of supernatural bliss" (ibid., 22). While gardens were abandoned, airfields and jetties were built to receive the coming cargo.

Here resistance to colonial rule seemed to be borrowing its forms and playing them back in a sketchy, attenuated way. On postwar Malaita in Solomon Islands, for example, the leaders of Marching Rule, or Maasina Ruru, borrowed the institutional forms of the American soldiers whom they had admired, constructing new villages like barracks along the coast (Cochrane 1970, 87). The movement also modeled itself on colonial institutions: "The 'custom chief' was the D.O. [district officer]; the 'head chief' a Government headman; 'leader chiefs' and 'line' chiefs were the same as the Government's village officials" (ibid., 91). Its military drill drew on colonial, American, and traditional forms of fighting. Marching Rule courts made plans to codify customary law (Worsley 1968, 177).

The Maasina Ruru movement was successfully co-opted into a form of local government, the Malaita Council, which became a prototype for homegrown, "provincial" government at independence. Worsley called movements like Marching Rule "protonationalist"—they anticipated more secular political movements. Some members of the movement certainly did engage in local and national elections. But others resisted normalizing.

Cargo cults did not bother just administrators and planters. Their millenarianism challenged religious orthodoxy. Christianity expects a coming bliss, but the Melanesian movements expected it to happen quite soon. They also challenged the authority and organization of missions and of the churches the missions sought to implant. In Solomon Islands, for example, Silas Eto led a breakaway Christian Fellowship Church. "Etoism" was another cargo cult, combining indigenous beliefs with introduced ones. Its followers were frustrated with the paternalism of white men and later became involved in secular politics after independence. The Methodist Church commissioned a study by Alan Tippett (1967), a missionary turned anthropologist, to recommend how it should respond.

The missionary is in many ways the paradigmatic agent of transfer, facing strategic choices about how to achieve conversion and how to balance local autonomy and enthusiasm with conformity to doctrine. The missionary is, above all, a believer in the transformative power of ideas and beliefs. Should a missionary be sent to establish a local church, or should one be sent only after such a church exists and calls for an expatriate pastor or priest? How far should indigenous beliefs be incorporated into church doctrine and practice? Should conversion proceed from the top down, by converting chiefs, or from the margins, by converting young people, women, or marginalized people? And how should the metropolitan church respond to local initiatives in doctrine and organization and to combinations of local and introduced forms of worship? In the 1960s a conference convened by the World Council of Churches concluded: "Much of what is being undertaken by missions, with foreign resources, would be immeasurably more effective as a witness to the Gospel if spontaneously undertaken, according to their own means, by members of the local church" (World Council of Churches 1963).

Tippett's sympathetic study is concerned with ideas and beliefs and makes comparisons with agricultural extension work and public health programs that depend on popular acceptance (Tippett 1967, 86–87). Tippett distinguishes three kinds of church growth that correspond to more general types of institutional transfer. The first is conversion growth, in which individuals break with past beliefs and join the church. The second is organic growth, in which a local church grows out of a mission: "A biological analogy could be used of a cell separating from its parent cell and becoming an independent organism" (ibid., 31). The third is "quality growth," in which adherents engage more intensively with the church, as indicated by baptisms and confessions.

Tippett's kinds of growth can be traced in other institutional transfers: the conversion, the splitting off, and the intensified commitment. Churches are now often talked of as being NGOs. The relationships between international NGOs like Transparency International and Greenpeace and their national counterparts are in some ways like those between a church, its missions, and spontaneous local movements drawing on indigenous traditions.

Trobriand Cricket

Methodist missionaries introduced cricket to the Trobriand Islands in 1903. Among the missionaries were Fijians, transferring what had earlier been transferred to them. Cricket is a powerful symbol of British colonialism. Until the 1950s it was played in Trobriand according to the rules introduced by the missionaries and colonial officials, its sponsors: eleven players on each side, two batsmen, runs, wickets, and so on. Sometime after that, it began to be adapted to local political purposes and to tap into local traditions of dance, chants, and magic. A documentary film, *Trobriand Cricket* (Leach and Kildea 1974), shows how the game had changed by 1974. There were still two batsmen, but the number of fielders had grown to include all the young men in the community (fifty-nine in the case filmed). Bats had become smaller, more curved, and highly decorated. The teams entered and left the field in highly choreographed displays of dancing, which were also triggered whenever a batsman was caught or run out. The dancing and chanting were inflected by the islanders' experience of the American occupation during World War II. One team, whose village land had been used for a runway, called itself Aeroplane. The players' arm movements imitated wings and propellers, and they chanted "oil here, petrol there, fueled up" to taunt their opponents with their preparedness.

Whereas the scorekeeper was chosen for his impartiality, the umpire became a more partisan figure, chosen from the batting team and deploying magic and commentary on its behalf. Games were convened by ambitious chiefs and were followed by ostentatious distributions of ritually important food. The home team was always allowed to win, but never by an excessive margin. Thus Trobriand cricket was adapted and incorporated into longer-established patterns of competition among villages and their leaders.

Trobriand cricket was a self-conscious and playful amalgam of traditional and introduced institutions. Its development involved invention as much as revival, and its appearance had been a kind of delayed reaction. Trobriand cricket did not emerge at first contact, when Trobriand Islanders were struggling to make sense of alien institutions. The islanders had picked up cricket fast and started modifying the rules only late in the colonial day.

Institutions and Organizations

Trobriand cricket is a good place to begin a discussion of institutional transfer, because institutions are often compared to the "rules of the game" (North 1990, 4). As with Trobriand cricket, parliamentary and electoral rules provide opportunities and constraints for ambitious politicians. Economic historian Douglass North distinguishes organizations from institutions (ibid., 4–5). If institutions are the rules, then organizations are the teams, like those competing in Trobriand cricket. Institutions and organizations may get transferred out of step with one another, perhaps because organizations are easier to transfer than the rules within which they operate. The idea of an ombudsman commission, for example, has spread widely beyond its Scandinavian origins. Such an institution depends on a flow of complaints from the public. It also relies on a normative framework that does not stigmatize or punish complaints made against officials. And if it is to work without sanctions, it must depend upon a public service ethos that is responsive to its reports, and it must be ready to act on complaints reported to it. It is not difficult to imagine a context in which people are reluctant to complain, one with a normative framework in which public complaints are treated as treasonous or partisan and a public service ethos that is intolerant of outside advice. An organization may be successfully transferred but fail to fit into such a context, which lacks the shared values and assumptions necessary to make the organization's operations possible.

The reverse is also possible: the organization stays the same, but the rules change around it. The Trobriand cricket team finds that it is now expected to play soccer. Or a department set up to protect local industry is now expected to promote competition. This form of transfer—in which the rules change but the team stays the same—may be becoming more common as countries sign international treaties, like those establishing the European Union or the World Trade Organization.

Rationality and Instrumentality

Convening Trobriand cricket matches may suit the calculations of ambitious chiefs, but playing it involves everyday magic. The world of foreign aid and multilateral banking is rational and instrumental in style. It sounds rational to talk about the aims of transferring systems of land registration (with the aim of improving productivity or reducing disputes), adopting constitutions, reforming the public service, and limiting corruption. Yet one of the defining characteristics of institutions may be that they do not require practical justification. They are simply there, to be respected but not questioned. In nineteenth-century constitutional language, their "institutional" quality depends on their being "dignified" (like the monarchy) rather than "efficient" (like parliament). In the language of 1950s sociology: "To institutionalize is to infuse with value beyond the technical requirements of the task at hand" (Selznick 1957, 16–17).

Individuals—including those teamed up as "organizations"—play games with great intensity and rationality. Yet the games themselves are harder to make sense of. Typical means of institutionalization include imitation of the form of other, already established institutions or validation by the state (Zucker 1977). Institutionalization is often associated with increasing similarity, and so new constitutions cleave to the form of older ones. Thus (to return to the analogy of a game), players seeking to institutionalize a new sport may adopt the organizational forms of other, established sports and seek recognition from the state. Other institutions—perhaps chieftaincy, a church, or an NGO—may provide the model and confer recognition where states are absent, weak, or failed.

Formality

Trobriand cricket combined formal elements (like the exchanges of food and other gifts) and informal ones (like the sotto voce grumbling about the way that the host village is always allowed to win). The distinction between formal and informal introduced institutions is important to Joseph Stiglitz' criticism of transfer as "downloading the best practice." Stiglitz was a controversial chief economist at the World Bank. He distinguished between codified knowledge and tacit knowledge; the latter was "the rest of the iceberg" and could be transmitted only by face-to-face methods such as "apprenticeship, secondment, imitation, study tours, cross training, twinning relations and guided learning by doing" (Stiglitz 2000, 34). Adaptation had to be by local "doers of development." In practice, informal, or tacit, understandings may be harder to transfer or must be transferred in different ways—perhaps by personal contact with visiting consultants or by overseas study tours.

Culture

The film *Trobriand Cricket* relishes the dancing, chanting, and body painting—that is, culture in the sense of artistic achievement and creativity. The narration also points out that the game is embedded in a broader context of local food production and politics, in, for example, the postmatch exchange of gifts—that is, culture in the sense of way of life. Culture is a tricky concept but is central to many arguments about the transfer of institutions in the Pacific Islands and Africa. Culture can mean quite different things, with different implications for transfer. It may refer to common beliefs and attitudes (particularly when they are resistant to change); to self-evident differences, rather like "race"; and to politicized personal identities (Appadurai 1996). The still influential doctrine of cultural relativism provides an ethical critique of transfer, claiming that it is unfair to judge one culture by the standards of another.

Time magazine quotes veteran opposition politician Tuiatua Tupua Tamasese Efi of Samoa as having said, "For us the Westminster system is part of an alien culture" (*Time* 24 April 2000). Political scientist Daniel Etounga-Manguelle argues, half ironically, for a "cultural adjustment program" in Africa (2000). Reflecting on his experience as an education planner, Geoffrey Coyne (1992) considers how Solomon Islands culture affects the way the public service works. By "culture" Coyne means the relationships and expectations that people bring with them from village life. Status within a village, for example, may depend on marriage, age, and one's ability to distribute wealth. A great premium is put on diffusing conflict through long meetings and achieving broad consensus. People who may depend on each other during a lifetime of village living are reluctant to say no to each other and are reluctant to tell others what they should do. In a bureaucracy, however, status depends on one's office, official housing and transport are not supposed to be shared with others, vigorous debate may be valued as a means of reaching decisions, and senior officers are expected to tell their juniors what to do. More personal values also affect the way the bureaucracy works in Solomon Islands. A desire to avoid shaming discourages people from correcting mistakes that have been made. Individual initiative is frowned upon. Personal, family, and official matters are not kept distinct. People treat knowledge and information as a personal resource and are reluctant to share it. The result is a civil service, which tends to react to events and where wide consultation often leads to delays.

Political scientist Samuel Huntington argues that culture matters but that defining culture too broadly as "way of life" ends up explaining nothing. By contrast he advocates a narrower, subjective definition of culture as "values, attitudes, beliefs, orientations and underlying assumptions prevalent among people in a society" (Huntington 2000, xv). A subjective definition keeps open the possibility that some people may be more attached to a particular culture than others are. The practice of transfer assumes that some people hold on to attitudes more strongly than others. Missionaries who aim to convert marginal groups may also trade on their looser attachment to supposedly shared attitudes.

Culture is also often cited as a source of inertia or resistance to change, as in Coyne's account of Solomon Islands. Where anthropologists have become involved in development, it has typically been to explain to engineers or economists why the changes they propose may be resisted. Anthropologists have been less involved in promoting cultural change, except perhaps in issues concerning women or in public health campaigns, like those against HIV.

Yet research on the reception of laws in Ethiopia found culture providing less resistance than the researchers expected. Academic lawyer John Beckstrom (1973) followed the introduction of a new legal code in Ethiopia in the 1960s. The research was particularly interested in the role of the legal profession as interpreters of the code. It identified different groups of users and potential victims. Judges were poorly educated, but the research found "no evidence of hostility, on the part of judges, to the new codes being 'foreign law' imposed upon the country" (ibid., 566).

Indeed, local traditions of deference to authority made the judges' job easier. Judges were acting flexibly, ignoring some of the nuances of divorce law and punishing youths for "troublesomeness" even if they had broken no law. Beckstrom found examples of neutralization, the process of judicial modification or abandonment of the rule where it caused conflict with tradition (e.g., when widows turned to the courts for compensation that custom had assigned to families). It was hard to tell if elders were now using courts more than traditional forms of arbitration. Nor was it clear if preference for traditional methods related to brevity, simplicity, or access rather than to substantive content. However, there was evidence of a preference for traditional methods and of more recourse to them, but introduced courts were better able to enforce outcomes.

Rather than culture, pragmatic calculation of costs and benefits (including transaction costs and the likelihood of enforcement) seemed to be determining choices between introduced and indigenous institutions in Ethiopia. Family and other "personal" kinds of law and institutions—where culture might be thought to have a stronger hold—were no less transferable than others.

Talk about culture now sometimes draws on older ideas about race. Anthropologist Marilyn Strathern notes that statements about cultural differences sometimes draw conclusions in the same way that ideas about race used to in the West (1995, 156–157). If people are essentially and self-evidently different—in race or, more politely, culture—then the institutions devised by one race or culture for its own purposes might not be appropriate for others. Ideas about essential and self-evident differences between groups of people and their institutions are still widespread, in spite of official and academic revulsion against racist thinking since the defeat of the Nazis and the end of colonial rule.

Culture is now often thought of as a source of personal identity and of authenticity. It points to how people see themselves and hence to the kinds of institutions they may be comfortable or uncomfortable with. Anthropologist Arjun Appadurai (1996, 11–16) links new understandings of "culture" to processes of globalization, indicating the way in which differences are used to mobilize group identity—like ethnicity. He is particularly interested in migration and media images. Both of these have been important in transferring ideas among Pacific Islanders, particularly Pacific Islands diasporas in Auckland, Sydney, and Los Angeles.

So it may be that identities have to be transferred along with institutions. People may have to come to see themselves as members of a team before they can play cricket properly, and as individuals before democracies or markets can work as expected. Particular people, of course, may move between identities as they play in different games: a cricketer one week, a soccer player the next. They may also be criticized as "mimic men," for failing to completely transfer from one identity to another.

Cultural Relativism

Cultural relativism is the idea that different cultures needed to be understood in their own terms and should not be judged by the standards of others. The film *Trobriand Cricket* adopts a neutral, nonjudgmental tone and explains Trobriand cricket mostly in its own local terms. The idea of cultural relativism is associated particularly with anthropologist Franz Boas, and debates about it led the American Anthropological Association to criticize the 1948 United Nations (UN) Universal Declaration of Human Rights as ethnocentric. Now it is under criticism, particularly from feminists over issues such as genital mutilation and, more generally, the subordination of women or gays and lesbians.

Cultural relativism was, until recently, dominant in discussions about corruption in developing countries. What looks like corruption to Westerners, it was argued, can be acceptable as familial obligations in other cultures. This kind of relativism is now less prevalent in international institutions. Transparency International, for example, takes a robust attitude toward the "myth" of culture, quoting one of its founding fathers, now the president of Nigeria: "In the African conception of appreciation and hospitality, the gift is usually a token. It is not demanded. The value is usually in the spirit rather than in the material worth. It is usually done in the open, and never in secret. Where it is excessive it becomes an embarrassment and it is returned" (Olusegun Obasanjo, cited in Pope 1996, 5).

Yet the gift giving in *Trobriand Cricket*, for example, seemed to amount to something more substantial than token. Its value was material as well as culturally significant (though more highly valued and spiritual items, like betel nuts, were exchanged among leaders). The gifts were also part of deliberate processes of political self-aggrandizement. Milton Esman, a pioneer of development administration, took a strongly relativist approach to institution building (IB) in developing countries. He was writing about the time of the Vietnam War, which was giving foreign advisers a bad name: "The IB perspective explicitly rejects the notion that meaningful change can be a straightforward transfer of technology or the installation of pre-packaged know-how or organizational forms from one culture to another whether managed entirely by indigenous innovators or assisted by foreign advisors" (Esman 1972, 37). Nevertheless, Esman recognized that most people working in institution building had a background in international technical assistance and that sponsoring governments hoped their work would be effective. Now the language of institution building persists in U.S. discussions of postconflict Afghanistan and Iraq and in Australian discussions of intervention in the South Pacific Islands.

Context

Historian Barrie Macdonald's study (1996) of governance in Kiribati explicitly takes on the task of specifying the local context of aid, in an unfolding account of the ways that the culture, society, history, and politics of Kiribati affect its government's capacity and style of dealing with donors. Macdonald sets his study up against the template approach taken by the World Bank. He cites "cultural norms and values" that are unsympathetic to "individual displays of wealth, personal aggrandisement, or leadership by direction" (ibid., 5). He also finds that public service pay and promotion practices undermine individual ambition "already rendered tentative by cultural mores." So aspects of introduced institutions seem to be reinforcing indigenous predispositions. Similarly, both traditional and modern Kiribati society are highly elitist. Where Coyne (1992) presented a simplified contrast between village and public service life in Solomon Islands, Macdonald points to ways in which each might reinforce the other. Macdonald's idea of context encompasses much more than culture and includes the country's history, economic circumstances, political structure, and processes.

The film about Trobriand cricket is as interested in the context as the game itself. It goes behind the scenes and to the day after, placing the match in a rich context of local life. The terms "context" and "culture" are sometimes used interchangeably—indeed, anthropologist Clifford Geertz (1963) argued that culture *was* context. For Geertz, culture was the frame within which social life can be described and understood. In this broad sense, culture is an institution itself.

It is now commonplace that proponents of institutional transfer must take into account the context in which institutions are meant to operate. Political scientist Shamsul Haque has criticized introduced institutions for being "contextless" (1996, 323). But what "context" amounts to is less clear. Philosopher Ben-Ami Scharfstein (1989) links the belief that context matters to broader arguments for relativism. He also draws on non-Western intellectual traditions to consider how it matters and identifies typical ways in which problems of context have been presented. The first is that context is linked to misunderstanding, and the idea that misunderstanding might have been avoided if context had been better taken into account. This points to the cognitive issues involved in transfer—the role of research, local knowledge, evidence, and testing for validity.

Second, there is a frequent argument that abstraction is not enough and that experience from the inside is necessary to get a full picture. Thus, as we saw above Stiglitz (2000, 34–35) emphasizes tacit knowledge and horizontal learning, picked up through study tours, cross training, twinning, and secondments. Texts and manuals can document the technique and facilitate learning, but they cannot completely substitute for hands-on experience. Training and consultancy both deal in experience as well as abstract knowledge.

Third, there are often complaints about overgeneralization. Terms like "Indian" or "Melanesian" need to be unpacked and disaggregated. To do so points away from generalizations like "Africa," "the Pacific," "developing countries," and "the West" toward knowledge about particular countries, places, and subgroups.

Fourth, Scharfstein points out that claims to uniqueness are often the same as those made by other groups. People often assert that their attitudes toward child rearing, hospitality, or the virtues of family are what distinguish them from their neighbors or enemies. But Scharfstein writes, "The claims to peculiarity were sometimes so like others that they seemed to refute themselves" (1989, 48). There is a strange universality to some of the values that groups believe distinguish themselves from others. That universality points toward a skepticism about claims of cultural distinctiveness.

Scharfstein is suggesting a set of moderating principles—inviting more research, more hands-on knowledge, the unpacking of generalizations, and skepticism about claims of uniqueness. They would moderate the urge to transfer without thought to context (and they would also moderate the urge to desist in the face of untested claims to distinctiveness). As Scharfstein notes, whatever one's predisposition to universal or particular explanations, there are practical limits to the degree to which context can be discovered and identified. Technical assistance grapples with these practical issues, and its techniques of the visiting mission and the short-term consultancy are famously prone to ignorance or misunderstanding of context.

Sociologist Bruno Latour (1986) calls "context" a "weasel" word that is always available to explain events away and forestall further research. He adds: "The context is not the spirit of the times which would penetrate all things equally. Every context is composed of individuals who do or do not decide to connect the fate of the project with the fate of the small or large ambitions they represent" (ibid., 137).

Projects like the mass transit system that Latour studied have to create and sustain their own context, by keeping key players interested. Projects create their own contexts, as well as swim within them. Research needs to be done to discover why individual actors behave as they do—giving or withdrawing support. As well as enjoining research, Latour is also directing attention to the political dimensions of context and to the task of creating and sustaining interest among the networks of actors that might facilitate or block it. He likens the task to attaching pots and pans to the tail of the project to ensure that it "makes enough commotion to wake up a minister" (ibid., 143).

3 Institutional and Policy Transfer

To produce a theory about the diffusion of innovations, sociologist Everett Rogers compared studies of how farmers adopt new crops and how doctors prescribe new drugs. His categories of early adopters and late adopters have since become commonplace in, for example, the marketing of consumer electronics. He found an S curve of adoption—slow at first, gaining momentum, then slowing down again as holdouts proved hard to convince. A number of characteristics of innovations helped explain their different rate of adoption. Innovations should offer a perceived advantage over existing ideas. They should be compatible with the adopter's existing values and experience—and simple. They should be able to be tried experimentally first, and the results should be plain to see. Rogers described technical assistance as a form of diffusion and offered as his first example a story of public health officials' efforts to persuade Peruvian women to boil their drinking water, a concept that ran against well-established indigenous beliefs (1995, 267–289).

In Rogers' story the users of drinking water resisted attempts by a public health official to get them to boil it. The reason was that local people had an indigenous system of categorizing foods into hot and cold. By custom, only people who were already ill used boiled, or hot, water, and people learned from childhood to dislike boiled water. Rogers develops the story by distinguishing three types of people. First is the person who will drink boiled water because she feels sickly. She is following her indigenous beliefs rather than concerns about bacteriological contamination. From the point of view of public health officials, she is doing the right thing for the wrong reasons. Second is the marginal outsider, who acts as a change agent and accepts the need to boil water to avoid illness. She is an innovator, but her marginal status may mean that few others follow. Third is the rejecter, who does not believe the story of biological contamination and believes strongly in her own theory of hot and cold water.

In Rogers' often-repeated story, people take different positions toward their indigenous beliefs and the alternatives proposed by health workers. They may also do the same thing—such as drinking boiled water —for quite different reasons. Yet, to understand the variety of responses, we need to understand indigenous beliefs, as well as differences between personalities.

Rogers' research influenced one of the earliest systematic accounts of the transfer of an institution between countries, political scientist Donald Rowat's study (1973) of the spread of the ombudsman idea. The first ombudsman was established in Sweden in 1809, and the next in Finland in 1919. The spread of the institution came after the Second World War. Denmark created one in 1955, followed by Norway and New Zealand in 1962. The diffusion of independent commissions against corruption (ICACs) follows a similar pattern: initiated in Hong Kong, borrowed by New South Wales, then adapted to jurisdictions in Queensland and Western Australia, and proposed in PNG. In a separate borrowing, Korea set up an ICAC in 2002.

Rowat (1973) considered the factors that determined what we might call the transferability of the institution. He formalized his argument as a hypothesis about the balance between agency and structure: "New ideas spread and new institutions are adopted partly because intellectuals promote them, but mainly because social conditions are ripe for their spread and adoption" (ibid., 70).

On the structural side, Rowat linked the spread of the institution to the postwar expansion of state activity, and the shift from the laissez-faire to the "positive state." An ombudsman, addressing individual complaints and grievances, was a necessary and perhaps inevitable response. (Rowat was writing in 1973, just at the time Western governments began to turn against the idea—if not the practice—of big government.)

On the agency side, the first Danish ombudsman was a tireless promoter of the concept. He was also willing to speak and publish in English, and the idea was spread through academic journals, international professional organizations like the International Commission of Jurists, and conferences and seminars run by international organizations, such as the UN and the Council of Europe. However, public opinion and pressure do not seem to have played a large part in the diffusion of the institution.

Rowat showed that transfer needs promoters, both local and from the outside, but that the conditions also have to be right. The balance between structure and agency is important for reformers, both domestic and international. Domestic reformers wonder if the time is ripe for change (structure), while aid donors and international financial institutions promoting good governance wonder if individuals (agency) can make a difference. Sometimes the agency is seen to lie with collective actors, like the government or the state, whose choices of economic policy, for example, may be restrained by larger, more structural conditions as well as by the agency of other states.

Institutional Theory

A revival of interest in institutions has been gathering across the social sciences. It has blurred and crossed boundaries between law, economics, political science, and sociology. It has also become influential in thinking about development: the World Bank now tells us that institutions matter.

Generally, institutional theories today are concerned with the relationship between rational purposive action and the social and political constraints on it. A common metaphor is that institutions are the rules of the game, in which players compete for advantage. Theories differ about what is regarded as fixed and given in this relationship and about what needs explaining. Actors' goals and preferences can be treated as given ("exogenous" in economists' language) or as needing to be explained. Actors' strategies can be seen as the product of calculation, availability, or social acceptability. The rules can be seen as something fixed and given or as products of human action and therefore subject to reaffirmation, revision, or revolution. So institutional approaches are not alternative to rational, individualistic ones but include them. A sociological dictionary, for example, defines an institution as "an enduring set of ideas about how to accomplish goals generally recognised as important in a society" (*Blackwell Dictionary of Sociology*, 2nd ed., 2000). The reference to goals points to rationality. The phrase "generally recognised" points to the ways these goals are socially constructed and valued. It includes as examples the family and the state.

Institutions such as constitutions, parties, and legislatures are a long-standing concern of political science. Detailed, historically informed accounts of constitutions and particular institutions have been a staple of the study of public administration. They are often criticized for being atheoretical and merely descriptive, and the so-called new public management has attempted to recast the discipline on more individualistic grounds. Nevertheless, the story is not one of steady progress toward rational choice. At least since the late 1940s, the study of public policy has steadily chipped away at the idea of policy making as a rational choice among alternatives. The consideration of alternatives was constrained by time, computational capacity, and the cost of acquiring information. Decisions were (and should be) incremental. In any case, the point at which decisions were made was often not clear or was clear only in retrospect. March and Olsen (1989, 11–14) found policy making to be a matter of timing and availability, rather than of choice and relevance. Solutions went looking for problems—a typical mode of transfer.

There have been "rational choice" revolutions at different points in the development of several disciplines—in economics in the late nineteenth century, in political science in, say, the 1950s, and in public administration in the 1980s. The revolutions are partial—there are always holdouts. And, in a kind of dialectical way, there is backlash and rediscovery. Thus in the 1980s Theda Skocpol (1985) wrote about "bringing the state back in" to political science, and March and Olsen (1989) wrote about "rediscovering institutions." Similarly, economists talk of the *new* institutional economics, reevaluating work done before neoclassical economics dominated the field.

Several issues in the revived theory of institutions seem particularly relevant to understanding transfer:

- *Functions of institutions.* Institutions provide instrumental constraints and opportunities. They also define what is more broadly right or wrong and help make sense of events and give them meaning (W. R. Scott 1995). Thus, for example, "the market" refers not only to a particular group of people buying and selling but also to an ideal by which their activities can be understood and evaluated. Watching the buying and selling, we can say cognitively that "a market is emerging," and we can evaluate government policy, as the World Bank does, according to how "market friendly" it is. Different functions may transfer in different ways or out of step with one another. The meaning may transfer ahead of or behind the transfer of the activity it was formerly connected with.
- *Role of individuals, agents of transfer, middlemen, and brokers such as consultants.* Are "new people" required to act within "new institu-

tions," or can the same motives be assumed everywhere? Can agency also lie with groups of individuals, as in North's idea (1990) of the teams that compete in a soccer match? Some writers distinguish purposive, self-conscious organizations from impersonal, mysterious institutions.

- *Similarities among institutions.* Why do some institutional forms proliferate at the expense of others? For example, there are strong similarities in the organization of schools and hospitals, whatever the political and economic system or the level of economic development.
- *Role of the state.* Why and how has the state become the dominant political form throughout the world, and is its time coming to an end due to policies of privatization, welfare reform, and the rise of private corporations and NGOs? In the West the state has for some time seemed like an effective and admirable institution. States can authorize and regulate other institutions. States have been able to transform their environments to make themselves fit. Westney's study of organizational emulation in Japan found that "the fit between new institutions and their social environment was not the result of the perspicacity of the organization-builders nor of some uncanny compatibility between the new and the existing social structures, but of the capacity of the new institutions for transforming the environment" (1987, 24).

Questioning the need for states still seems faintly impertinent or irresponsible. Public choice theory, which became influential on policy in some Western countries in the 1980s, started to formulate impertinent questions. Arguments from first principles showed that states might "fail," just as markets did. States were vulnerable to capture by well-connected interest groups. They might embody no higher purpose than the self-interest of the bureaucrats and politicians who staffed them. By the 1990s there was a widespread lack of conviction in the state as an agent for development. Development economics used to have a strongly historical and statist flavor. Much of the academic work in this area was funded and driven by the World Bank, the UN, and the ADB—which are bureaucratic creatures of the international state system—and by government aid donors. In the South Pacific a reaction against statism was led by Helen Hughes, embodied in some of the work of the National Centre for Development Studies at the Australian National University. The neoliberal discrediting of the state in the 1980s justified programs of privatization and the public sector reforms of new public management, whose transfer is analyzed in the following chapters.

States, as we saw in chapter 1, are also moral, or ethical, orders. The moral character of states is partly a matter of legitimacy. In the Weberian picture of the state, it is also a matter of the ethos of officials. In colonial administrative theory this ethos was embodied in ideas about trusteeship. Colonial states were certainly set apart from society, but they often seemed biased in favor of the interests of settlers. Their independent successors might close the gap with society—bringing government "closer to the people"—but at the cost of autonomy and impartiality and a pervasive sense of corruption, as a derogation from an ideal of impartial administration.

The idea or ideology of stateness, and the resources needed to support it, might be transferred out of step. So there might be implanted a strong desire for autonomous, impersonal political institutions, but no capacity to sustain them. In this case, supporters of the idea of the state might turn to NGOs like Transparency International, resourced from outside and promoting statelike values. Or the resources might be transferred, in the absence of the idea of autonomy and impartiality. In this case, foreign aid would support corrupt, tribalist, or personalistic regimes.

Coercive Transfer

One result of successful transfer is increasing similarity. Sociologists Paul DiMaggio and Walter Powell (1991) suggest three ways in which organizations become more alike (isomorphic). The first they called coercive transfer, when organizations respond to pressures from other organizations or from their legal environment. The authors assert that as states come to dominate social life, organizations increasingly adapt to the state's rules. Nonstate organizations that depend on state funding, for example, must adopt state-sanctioned accounting practices. They must create their own hierarchies in order to interact successfully with other, hierarchical organizations. Chiefly political systems, for example, may have to adopt some of the forms of European states in order to deal with those states.

Colonial rule is often seen as the extreme case of forced transfer. It introduced new institutions and transformed others. When Papua New Guinea became independent, there was debate about the transfer of Australian institutions and their appropriateness. Comparing PNG with West

Africa, political scientist John Ballard wrote that during decolonization "the models chosen were almost inevitably those of metropolitan governments, altered to fit the needs of colonial administrative structures and the political constituencies they shaped" (1981, 4).

Ballard and human geographer Gerard Ward traced the construction of institutions in PNG by Australian officials "in their own image." Yet oddly the construction began quite late in the colonial period, after a postwar period of local experiment in which "imaginative department heads in Papua New Guinea attempted with minimal resources to devise health, education and agricultural programmes adapted to local needs and resources" (R. G. Ward and Ballard 1976, 441). From the 1950s to the 1970s, however, Australian policy became more assimilationist. A system of generalist district administration was replaced by a system of direct administration through functionally specialized departments that took directions from Canberra and were organized like their counterparts there.

Mimetic Transfer

DiMaggio and Powell's term for the second way in which organizations become more alike is through mimetic transfer. Not all change comes as a result of external or intentional pressure. Faced with uncertainty, organizations will model themselves on prestigious others, according to DiMaggio and Powell (1991). Here the authors cite the Japanese emulation of Western organizational systems in the nineteenth century, and the reverse process of American imitation of Japanese management practices in the twentieth century. These were deliberate attempts to emulate the other's successes. But there was also a ritual element: U.S. companies adopted Japanese practices to enhance the legitimacy of the companies and to show that they were trying to improve working conditions (ibid., 69). The extreme case might be the cargo cult (discussed in chapter 2). The authors also find that "despite considerable search for diversity there is relatively little variation to be selected from" (ibid., 70). Organizations adopt the limited number of forms of other organizations that are regarded as successful and legitimate. Nationalists paradoxically assert their own difference to claim the right to institutions that are much like everyone else's. Hence Meyer (1981) has argued: "Peripheral nations are far more isomorphic—in administrative form and economic pattern—than any theory of the world system of economic division of labour would lead one to expect" (Meyer 1981).

Decolonization involved mimesis as much as coercion. Independence brought colonial territories into membership of a system of nation-states and international organizations such as the British Commonwealth and the United Nations. Ten countries in the Pacific Islands became independent in the 1960s and 1970s. Others adopted new constitutions and less colonial relationships of "free association" with the United States or New Zealand that were approved by the UN but fell short of full sovereignty. Several of these new constitutions deferred to traditional forms of political organization—in setting up national councils of chiefs, in returning land to its traditional owners, and in reasserting the value of customary law. Yet decolonization did not lead to a reversal of transfer or a wholesale restoration of precolonial systems of government. In many ways, it accelerated transfer. Acceding to membership of international organizations and joining the international community produced pressures for common standards and forms of government, particularly liberal, representative democracy. Sociologist Bernard Badie concludes: "The years following decolonisation clearly revealed the failure of all mimicry in the constitutional area. Everything indicates, however, that it has not ceased and that it has even intensified" (2000, 2).

The states that emerged from colonial rule in the Pacific Islands were very small, and to that extent they were weak and vulnerable. Emerging international norms and the politics of the cold war had protected the sovereignty of what Jackson (1990) rather sourly labeled "quasi states," dependent on aid and international recognition rather than on their own domestic resources. This protection is now lifting, as aid donors, the World Bank, and the ADB become more intrusive in promoting good governance among their clients.

Now most countries' suites of institutions look quite similar, in spite of huge differences in population, scale, and wealth. In any capital city, there will be a police headquarters, a legislature, and an office of the prime minister or president. Departments dealing with foreign affairs, health, and education are likely to be found. In this way, very large countries like China and India are similar to very small countries like Solomon Islands or Tuvalu. Strang and Meyer (1993) called it the "surprising isomorphism" of modern states. This similarity makes them particularly conducive to transfer. As Strang and Meyer explain, "States subscribe to remarkably similar purposes—economic growth, social equality, the political and human rights of the individual. States are also understood as possessing identical standing as sovereign, despite extreme disparities in military and economic capacity. And while these cultural definitions can be and are violated, they provide fertile ground for the rapid diffusion of public policies and institutional structures" (ibid., 491).

These similarities may be only apparent or skin-deep. Similar-looking institutions could be carrying out quite different functions. In one country the army may be involved in choosing the government and running businesses. In another the army simply prepares to fight foreigners. In socialist countries the ruling party plays a much wider role than it does in capitalist ones. In very poor countries the institutions may look more like empty shells—inside the "department of X" there is no money to pay the phone bills, while officials are running their own businesses to stay alive. Other similarities run quite deep: the internal organization of schools, hospitals, and prisons is remarkably similar, however they are funded, under socialism or capitalism.

Normative Transfer

The third way in which organizations become more alike, as suggested by DiMaggio and Powell (1991), is through normative transfer, which the authors relate to the increasing professionalization of work. This kind of transfer took place through colonial bureaucracies and grew rapidly after the Second World War. The bureaucracies provided links sideways, with other colonies, as well as back to functional departments like those for health and agriculture in Canberra, Wellington, or London.

The formal training required to enter professions produces standardized ideas and values, which are transmitted and reinforced by professional associations. International consulting firms, for example, transmit the professional values of accountants, such as transparency, and their language of corporate governance. International financial institutions transmit the professional values of bankers ("soundness," for example) and the professional biases of economists, in favor of market solutions. Tippett's research (1967) on conversion to Christianity was itself part of the process of professionalization of missionary work.

The three types of transfer presented by DiMaggio and Powell (1991) are ideal types. In any case of transfer there is likely to be a mix of coercion, mimesis, and professionalization. However, the authors' point is that each of these processes can proceed "in the absence of evidence that they increase internal organizational efficiency" (ibid., 73). The process of transfer is fundamentally irrational. With luck, organizations will be coerced by regulation into being more efficient, will copy more efficient organizations, or will be advised by the right professionals, but there is no necessity they will.

Institutions and Institutionality

The premise of proposals for good governance is that institutions matter. Architects of homegrown constitutions sought to root laws in local beliefs and affections. In Marxist arguments about the postcolonial state, the institutions that mattered—classes—lay behind and below the surface, whose solidity might be deceptive. Weak states were supposed to lack the solidity of their strong counterparts in the West, and there were degrees of weakness and failure short of collapse. Invented traditions sounded whimsical and lightweight, while the institutions adopted by cargo cults—the barracks and airfields—seemed particularly ghostly and ephemeral.

To talk about transferring institutions may beg the question. The institution—"stable, valued and recurring" (Goodin 1996)—is usually the intended result of transfer. The thing transferred might be something more lightweight (like an idea, a policy, or a law), material (like a grant or a loan), or personal (like a consultant or trainer). The result, as Esman (1972) suggested of Apter's argument (1955), might be called institutionality, and there could be degrees of it.

This book is more concerned with the process of transfer than the results. So we shall analyze the thing transferred as a "policy" and reserve the word "institution" for the anticipated results. In current English usage, "policy" tends to mean a rationale or manifestation of considered judgment (Parsons 1995, 14). Politicians in Western countries are expected to have policies and to compete with each other in offering them to voters at elections. In this sense, "policy" conveys something deliberate and prospective. The influence of economics and economists has reinforced this idea of policy as plan and of policy making as choice between alternatives. Rationality in this context involves a process of calculation and comparison of means to achieve a given end.

The study of how policy makers actually behave has tended to undermine this picture of policy making as a rational choice between alternatives. There are practical and intellectual limits to the number of alternatives that can be identified and considered. Their outcomes in any case are unpredictable. Faced with the costs of gathering information and with uncertainty about the future, policy makers tend to react to problems, rather than anticipate them, and tend to opt for familiar solutions. Charles

Lindblom (1992) describes this process as one of "disjointed incremental-ism." He also commends it as "the science of muddling through," appro-priate to a democracy that was suspicious of central planning. Political scientists March and Olsen (1976, 26) see an even more radical disjunc-tion between problems and solutions. They find policy making to consist of a messy mix of issues, problems, and solutions, ordered not by linkage of means to ends but by coincidence and timing. Decision makers deal with problems one by one, as they come up, rather than comprehensively and simultaneously. Within the shifting muddle of actual organizations, problems and solutions are picked up and dumped in temporal, rather than logical, order. March and Olsen argue "Suppose we view choice activity as a garbage can into which various problems and solutions are dumped by participants. The mix of garbage in a single can depends partly on the labels attached to the alternative cans; but it also depends on what garbage is being produced at the moment, on the mix of cans available, and the speed at which garbage is collected and removed from the scene" (March and Olsen 1976, 26).

March and Olsen's garbage-can model points to issues of timing, coincidence, and availability that become particularly important in trans-fer. As we shall see, local crises lead policy makers to look abroad for models, yet the models available at the time—or being pressed on them—may not necessarily suit.

The rational view of policy making has spawned a series of studies of the gap it opens up between policy and implementation. The pioneers in this area were Pressman and Wildavsky (1973), who studied a job creation program in Oakland, California, and examined the number of links that had to be made between various actors. More recent studies have shown policy making to be less like the unfolding of a blueprint and more like a reiterative process of negotiation between those who are proposing the policy and those who are charged with implementing it or have the power to block it.

Policy Transfer

Transfer has been a long-standing concern of the study of public policy, beginning with transfers between component states in federal systems. Richard Rose (1993) deals with transfers within countries that belong to the Organisation for Economic Co-operation and Development (OECD), though his conclusions about transferability might apply more generally.

Rose sought to identify the conditions under which "lesson drawing" in public policy was successful. Many of these conditions were familiar. Transfer was easier if programs contained few unique elements, had a simple cause-effect structure, sought small changes, and were consistent with the values of the recipients. Transfer was also easier if similar resources were available in both the donor and the recipient nations, suggesting that North-South transfers, from rich to poor, might be less successful than South-South transfers. So far these points are fairly commonsense. But Rose identified two additional interesting conditions. The first was that the program should be able to be carried out by more than one agency. It should not be hostage to one department, which might be ineffective or opposed. He also found that agencies that already dealt with the outside world were more receptive to transfer. Reformers might best look to departments like customs or civil aviation (ibid., 118–142).

The next three chapters will analyze a number of cases of transfer, using a framework developed by political scientists Dolowitz and Marsh (2000). The authors define "policy transfer" as "the process by which knowledge about policies, administrative arrangements, institutions and ideas in one political system (past or present) is used in the development of policies, administrative arrangements, institutions and ideas in another political system" (ibid., 5). For Dolowitz and Marsh, the distinctive character of developing countries is their vulnerability to coercive policy transfer. They note the role of the World Bank and the International Monetary Fund in imposing conditions on loans, as well as the rise of international consultancy firms that provide standard or "best practice" answers to complex local problems. The authors asserted that the freedom to pick and choose policies and the direct imposition from outside are endpoints on a continuum. In between are "bounded rationality," which recognizes the cognitive and practical limits on the search for models from abroad—the choice that is driven by necessity or by fear of being left behind—and conditionality, which the developing country may reject, with dire consequences (ibid., 13).

The approach taken by Dolowitz and Marsh has several advantages. First, the authors directly address questions of power, which seem to be particularly important in relation to developing countries and which we examine more closely in chapter 8. Second, their neutral term "transfer" is without the teleological or progressive overtones of "development" or "evolution." Transfer cannot necessarily be assumed to involve improvement or even rationality. Third, their approach asks where the policies came from, and we have already noticed that policies are increasingly "borrowed from nowhere," derived from first principles, and transmitted through international organizations.

This framework was used in the most systematic study of policy transfer to developing countries to date, Richard Common's analysis (2001) of the spread of new public management (NPM) in Hong Kong, Malaysia, and Singapore. NPM encompassed structural changes, mainly involving decentralization, such as the creation of single-purposes agencies, and privatization. NPM also included changes to the processes of government, borrowing techniques from the private sector (ibid., 49–51).

Common considers the history and the context of administration in each country with great care. The countries inherited colonial styles of government that, at upper levels, fused politics with administration. Local cultural traditions, loosely labeled "Confucianism," were generally respectful of hierarchy, collectivism, and bureaucratic leadership: "Paradoxically, the resilience of colonial administrative models has allowed indigenous politicians and bureaucrats to serve their own interests by emphasising bureaucratic features such as lifelong tenure, inflexibility and hierarchy" (ibid., 102). Local elites picked and chose among elements of NPM and its rhetoric to suit their political purposes. Singapore's PS21 (Public Service for the Twenty-first Century) reform program, for example, emphasizes strategic management and better-quality services. But it does not embrace NPM's more structural reforms, such as decentralization and privatization (ibid., 212–213). Common concludes: "The notion that policy transfer results in an increasing number of 'inappropriate' policy adoptions that are unsuited to local political, cultural, social, economic and administrative contexts now appears false" (ibid., 236).

Common's conclusions are consistent with lessons drawn about administrative reform by the Ford Foundation in the 1960s: Common also found that national elites were picking and choosing among the techniques offered, choosing those that consolidated their authority and ignoring the others.

Episodes of Transfer

In the following chapters, five policies are analyzed:

- *Customary land registration*. Involving the extension of land law out from colonial capitals and settler plantations onto land owned according to custom and tradition, customary land registration demonstrates a drive to universalize, standardize, and bring life under bureaucratic control that political scientist James Scott (1998) characterized as "seeing like a state."

- *Constitutionalism.* The policy of constitutionalism expresses the universal but self-limiting character of state power. The constitution applies to everyone, the government included, throughout the territory of the state. In the liberal tradition transferred to the South Pacific, the constitution also claims to set limits to the exercise of state power—limits set out, for example, in human rights provisions or in the prohibition of compulsory acquisition of land.
- *Representative democracy.* The idea of representative democracy— and the mechanism of elections, by which modern states claim legitimacy—is often said to contradict indigenous forms of political organization, by chiefs or big men.
- *Public sector reform.* During the 1990s, public sector reform came to mean downsizing and the privatization of state-owned enterprises. It might have been driven by the urgent necessity to restore public finances by cutting wage bills and realizing assets. But it was packaged in a liberal ideology that was suspicious of state action, and it preferred market solutions.
- *Anticorruption.* During the 1990s, criticism of politicians and bureaucrats in developing countries grew, on the grounds that they were corrupt: favoring their own private or political interests above the interests of the country, the people, or the nation as a whole. Some of this revulsion drew on liberal suspicions of rent seeking. Some of it was a reaffirmation of the idea of a coherent, impartial state. Some drew on religious or other moral traditions, against the visible display of wealth or other misbehavior. It had an ambiguous relationship to arguments for indigenous institutions, which did not recognize any liberal line between the public and the private.

The protection of private property rights, the rule of law, and the suspicion of state action embodied in NPM and anticorruption efforts are all part of a more general package of liberal forms of government. They stand against arguments, on the one hand, for development through public ownership and, on the other, for government by custom and chiefs.

Interactions among the five policies have reinforced their treatment as different aspects of good governance but have made it more difficult to disentangle their separate results. The constitutions generally protected customary and private land rights. Customary land registration and public sector reform were combined in a controversial land mobilization program in PNG. The public sector reforms in Cook Islands were followed by the establishment of a political review commission. The constitutions in Melanesia contained anticorruption Leadership Code provisions. Concern about corruption in the National Provident Fund precipitated riots and a state of emergency in Vanuatu, and rebuilding the fund became part of the Comprehensive Reform Program in an agreement with the ADB. Transparency International has recently become involved in promoting a change to alternative voting in PNG.

Each of these five policies represents a different aspect or dimension of stateness, which is an international as well as a domestic phenomenon. Each policy has also involved international organizations, as well as transfers from country to country. The World Bank is involved in promoting land titling, public sector reform, and anticorruption measures. The Commonwealth provides a network of support for officials and politicians using Westminster constitutions. The Group of Seven (G7) rich countries set up the Financial Action Task Force and housed it in the offices of the OECD.

Chapters 4–6 analyze about forty episodes of transfer. They do not consider every transfer to each country. Nor do they pretend to be a sample of all such episodes in the region. Rather they are examples that are well documented or that I am familiar with. The purpose of analyzing them is to uncover and demonstrate some general principles about transfer that are discussed in later chapters. An episode here means a deliberate attempt, which may or may not have succeeded. Some countries have experienced several episodes.

Each chapter considers a different subgroup of Pacific Island states. That subgroup is defined by the policy or the intended institution. Chapter 4 deals with attempts to transfer a standard system of customary land registration to three Melanesian countries. It provides an opportunity to see how a similar system was adopted or rejected in different places. The scope of Chapter 5 is wider. It mainly deals with the transfer of Westminster constitutions to eleven Pacific Island countries. Chapter 6 focuses on the World Bank's attempts to get PNG to adopt public sector reforms and on the ADB's efforts to promote similar reforms in six other countries. This chapter also looks Transparency International's promotion of ideas about preventing corruption and at the OECD's attempts to regulate Pacific Island tax havens, particularly in Nauru and Cook Islands.

Thus the next three chapters do not provide a comprehensive account of policy transfer in the Pacific Islands, nor an assessment of its effects. However, the number and variety of episodes will allow us to identify some common determinants of the process (in chapter 7), to test some explanations (in chapter 8), and to consider some evaluations (in chapter 9). Finally, these are all episodes of transfer into, or within, the region. I also looked for transfers outwards, but without success.

4 Customary Land Registration

In his book *The Mystery of Capital*, Hernando de Soto (2000) describes the disappointment felt by leaders of developing countries who reformed their economies after the collapse of communism. With varying degrees of enthusiasm they balanced budgets, cut subsidies, and reduced tariffs. The result was "glaring inequality, underground economies, pervasive mafias, political instability, capital flight, [and] flagrant disregard for the law" (ibid., 9). What had gone wrong, de Soto asked? Why did capitalism seem to work so well in the West but fail in many parts of the world? His answer was property. Legal systems in developing countries failed to convert assets held by the poor into capital, which they could use to invest. A good example was their traditional, customary, and informal rights to land.

Customary land tenure is the institution regularly blamed for lack of development in Melanesia, and land registration is regularly recommended as the solution. Registration would create titles that could be bought, sold, or mortgaged. In PNG, Solomon Islands, and Vanuatu a system of registration had been put in place for so-called alienated land— land that had been bought by foreigners or taken by the government. Sometimes dubious titles were investigated and adjudicated and the land surveyed. The issue became whether and how the system of registration should be extended to so-called customary land, land still in the hands of Melanesians. The promise was of clear titles that would reduce disputes and could be used as security for loans. De Soto had borrowed Braudel's image of capitalism confined to particular places and sectors, as if in a bell jar (ibid., 66–67). In Melanesia, capitalism had been confined to towns, plantations, and other enclaves. Registration of customary land would allow it to break out and include the whole of the society. The fear was that registration would be a prelude to further alienation, because registered land was easier to sell—to other Melanesians or to foreigners.

That fear was exploited by leaders of demonstrations against the World Bank in PNG in the mid-1990s. The government was negotiating with the bank for a loan. One of the conditions being discussed was that the government would "complete framework legislation for customary land registration" and "complete registration in East New Britain and East Sepik." Alerted by local NGOs, university students set up barricades and roadblocks and burnt government vehicles (Filer 2000, 32–37). The government quickly backed down, and the loan condition was dropped. Similar demonstrations in June 2001, over public sector reform conditions, led to three students being shot dead by police.

When

The five periods of transfer of policies for customary land registration in Papua New Guinea, Solomon Islands, and Vanuatu are summarized in table 2. The first, which could be characterized as modernizing, occurred in the 1950s and 1960s, when a Kenyan model of land registration was tried in Solomon Islands and proposed in PNG. The second period, in which PNG was influential on Solomon Islands, amounted to a nationalist reaction to the first. The third period applies only to Vanuatu, where radical right-wing proposals for a free enterprise system based on freehold title and the gold standard were defeated by force. American property developers who had bought plantation land to divide for residential subdivisions became alarmed at losing it to traditional claimants at independence, which came in 1980. Some of the developers had links to the Phoenix Corporation, a Far Right organization that was promoting "new countries," which would be free of government regulation and would protect liberty through freehold land tenure and the gold standard (Oliver 1968). Similar ideas became more respectable and mainstream in the 1980s, the fourth period particularly in PNG. At that time, land policy was influenced by liberal ideas promoted by the private sector–funded Institute of National Affairs, founded in 1976. The fifth and current period has been defined by the influence of the World Bank, which has supported land titling schemes in many countries throughout the world. The periods overlap, and the countries were influenced differently and at different rates. The nationalist reaction that began in the second period persisted in Solomon Islands until the 1990s, when new legislation to create customary land records was passed in 1994.

TABLE 2. Transfer of Customary Land Registration Policies to PNG, Solomon Islands, and Vanuatu

When	How	Who	What	From where / to where	Degrees of transfer	Factors involved
1950s and 1960s	Official networks and study tours	Consultants: Rowton Simpson, Jerry Lawrance, Jim Fleming	Systematic adjudication Text: *Land Law and Registration*	Sudan/Kenya Kenya/SI Kenya/PNG Kenya/Vanuatu	SI: legislation enacted and 13 schemes completed PNG: legislation withdrawn from Parliament Vanuatu: legislation drafted	Centralisation of advice in London Hostility from legislatures Local rebellions
1970–1980s	Land commissions Consultancies Research and training	Consultants: Ron Crocombe, Alan Ward, Jim Fingleton, Peter Larmour IPS Suva IASER Port Moresby	Systematic adjudication with group titles Text: *Agricultural Revolution: Handle with Care*	South Pacific/PNG New Zealand/PNG PNG/SI PNG and SI/Vanuatu	PNG: provincial experiments in 1980s	Regional University of South Pacific Australian and New Zealand aid
1970s	Advice and financial support for secession in Vanuatu	Phoenix Corporation Michael Oliver	Individual freehold title Text: *A New Constitution for a New Country*	Libertarian theory/Vanuatu	Nil	PNG and Australian support to defeat rebellion
1980s	Think tank Consultancies Conferences Publications	Institute of National Affairs Consultants: Michael Trebilcock, Robert Cooter	Sporadic adjudication Development of common law	USA and Canada/PNG Public Choice theory/PNG Native American tenure/PNG	Public/private task force Land Mobilisation Program	Private sector financial support
1990s	Consultancies Loan conditions	World Bank Henao Lawyers	Sporadic adjudication	Washington/PNG	Legislation drafted in 2001	Government need for World Bank loans NGO resistance

In Solomon Islands in the 1950s, a land commission had diagnosed a breakdown in customary tenure and had recommended land registration as a remedy. But none of the three countries had an obvious crisis on customary land to galvanize action. The crisis took place over alienated and government-owned land, where there were violent disputes and occupations. The breakdown of customary tenure was, if anything, slow and progressive rather than catastrophic. It was difficult to find the point at which governments might feel that something should be done. Local politicians who came to power in the late 1960s and early 1970s did not necessarily see that a problem existed. Some believed that customary tenure was working quite well. They favored simpler records that would recognize and entrench it (Solomon Islands 1976).

How

The methods of transfer of customary land registration included study tours, commissions of inquiry, foreign consultants, a think tank, and loan conditions. A group of officials from what was to become PNG visited Kenya. In the 1970s, PNG's Commission of Enquiry into Land Matters brought expatriate academics and consultants into the process. So, to a lesser extent, did Solomon Islands' Select Committee on Lands and Mining, which was influenced by PNG's model. The final decisions on their reports, however, rested with governments, and legislation depended on parliaments within which governments were unstable coalitions. The Institute of National Affairs (INA) held seminars and invited North American academics to report on issues such as land of interest to the private sector in PNG. The institute's influence on government was institutionalized in a National Development Forum, which brought businessmen and senior ministers together. Whereas the INA relied on lobbying, seminars, and publications, the World Bank had a more powerful instrument for transferring its ideas through loan conditions.

Who

Several distinct networks of advisers influenced governments in Melanesia and facilitated the flow of ideas between them. The first included Rowton Simpson, Jerry Lawrance, and Jim Fleming, colonial officials whose careers had intersected in Kenya. The origins of a second network, which grew out of PNG's Commission of Enquiry into Land Matters and spread its influence to other parts of Melanesia, were more accidental. Alan

Ward was a visiting historian at the University of Papua New Guinea. His research had been on the conversion of Maori land tenure. He was asked by Percy Chatterton, a member of Parliament, for comments on land legislation then in front of the PNG parliament. They circulated a paper among members called "Agricultural Revolution: Handle with Care" (A. Ward 1972). In it, Ward sharply criticized the assumptions behind the bills and predicted dire consequences if they were enacted. He argued that the colonial government was going too far and too fast in converting customary rights into fully negotiable titles that could be freely mortgaged and sold. He doubted that the control boards proposed in the legislation and borrowed from Kenya would be able to prevent lands being lost to banks and other outsiders. He favored a "more evolutionary adaptation of traditional institutions" (ibid., 32) and drew on New Zealand policies toward Maori land, rather than British policies toward African land, for examples and warnings.

The land bills were already running into opposition from the legal profession, which objected to the administrative provisions, and from newly elected Papua New Guinean politicians, who objected to lack of consultation (Bredmeyer 1975). The uproar forced the colonial government to withdraw the bills, and the PNG government—led by its prime minister, Michael Somare (now Sir Michael)—set up a Commission of Enquiry into Land Matters instead.

A new network then ramified throughout Melanesia. Ward (1983) became a full-time consultant to PNG's Commission of Enquiry into Land Matters. The commission recommended a system of registering group titles, from which the group could grant use rights to individuals. Controls were to be written into the titles rather than vested in boards (Papua New Guinea 1973, ii–vi). Ward advised the PNG Lands Department during the 1970s and became the director of lands in Vanuatu in the early 1980s. Jim Fingleton, who had been a public solicitor's lawyer advising Papua New Guineans on land claims, became the research officer for the Commission of Enquiry into Land Matters in PNG. He then moved over to the Lands Department, advised Solomon Islands on the drafting of its 1977 legislation that ended foreign ownership, and advised the Vanuatu government on its 1980 Land Reform Act and subsequent implementation. He was back in Papua New Guinea again in 1986, advising the East Sepik provincial government on its land registration proposals. I was the secretary to Solomon Islands' Parliamentary Committee on Land and Mining Policy, the counterpart to PNG's Commission of Enquiry into Land Matters, and had visited PNG to report on the policy changes there.

I went on to be an adviser to the newly formed Ministry of Lands in Vanuatu in 1980. There I recommended a system of direct dealing between customary owners and foreign investors, minimizing government intermediation, and Fingleton and Ward came in as additional advisers.

Ron Crocombe's role overlapped with this network but was more institutionalized. His work involved training, research, and publications as much as direct policy advice. From 1962 to 1969—as the director of a research program on land tenure and then the head of the New Guinea Research Unit at the Australian National University (ANU), which became the Institute of Applied Social and Economic Research (IASER) at independence—he had been a vocal critic of the economic development plans of the colonial administration upon which the new land legislation was based. Under his direction, the research unit carried out a series of studies of tenure issues. Crocombe was a visiting consultant to PNG's Commission of Enquiry into Land Matters, and he taught and published authors such as Barak Sope, an organizer for the political party Vanua'aku Pati and the prime minister of PNG in the 1990s (Sope, n.d). Crocombe's position as the director of the Institute of Pacific Studies (IPS) of the regional University of the South Pacific (USP) later gave him a base and a network through which to promote research by indigenous scholars and training through extension services, including a course on land tenure (in which I was enrolled). Crocombe's approach inspired the research Ian Heath and I set up on the performance of systematic adjudication in Solomon Islands.

Michael Oliver and the Phoenix Corporation tried to influence what became Vanuatu with far-right ideas about property in the 1970s. From the mid-1970s, consultants to PNG's Institute of National Affairs drew on the lively tradition of public choice and the new institutional economics, introducing a fresh set of ideas into what had become a rather tired debate between modernists and nationalists on land matters. This third network came from Canada and North America, rather than New Zealand, Australia, and the United Kingdom. Knetsch and Trebilcock's report (1981) on land policy for the Institute of National Affairs influenced government thinking. Their economistic language and preference for a reduced role of the state were in contrast to the paternalism of colonial policy and to the nationalism of the parliamentary committees and academics who reviewed land policy at independence. Melanesian landowners were assumed to be self-interested maximizers, like everyone else. Their report led to the establishment of a joint public/private-sector task force, which pressed the PNG Lands Department to draft new legislation for the sporadic rather than systematic registration of customary land. That legislation was in turn criticized by a consultant for the World Bank, bringing a new, more global network of advice into play, armed with the tool of loan conditions.

What

The arguments were about legislation, and the substantive differences in the advice offered concerned systematic versus sporadic adjudication and individual versus group title. The arguments reflected ideological differences between the consultant groups and the ministers and civil servants they advised. In systematic adjudication, the government took the initiative, moving through the country and registering large areas at once that included many parcels with different owners. Sporadic adjudication, by contrast, took place in response to individual applications. The Kenyan model was systematic, and each of the schemes implemented in Solomon Islands (SI) was systematic within a small community. Solomon Islands' Select Committee on Lands and Mining, the 1990s SI legislation for customary land records, and PNG's public/private task force favored sporadic registration. The differences can be overstated, though, for limited resources would force governments to focus their activity on areas where there was interest in registration, and in practice governments could not proceed unless particular owners were interested. There were much stronger and more ideological differences over whether the underlying title should be registered in the name of groups or individuals and whether group ownership should be recognized through nominated representatives or trustees.

Key texts summarized and crystallized the ideas being promoted at the time. Rowton Simpson's *Land Law and Registration* (1976) was a scholarly and practical handbook, published as part of the UK aid program. Alan Ward's *Agricultural Revolution* (1972) was a timely polemic that rationalized opposition, already gathering for other reasons, to the Australian administration's legislation in PNG. Michael Oliver's *New Constitution for a New Country* (1968) was a libertarian text, which later found its opportunity in the rebellion against the Lini government in Vanuatu in 1980–1981.

From Where

The Kenyan model itself drew on precedents in colonial Sudan and elsewhere. The academic advisers in the 1970s, such as Ron Crocombe and

Alan Ward, drew on examples of Maori land tenure in New Zealand and in other South Pacific countries. The North American advisers to the INA in PNG drew on Native American land tenure, as well as the first principles of public choice theory. The World Bank, based in Washington, drew on its own experience of supporting land titling throughout the world.

Results

The Kenyan customary land registration legislation was not completely transferred to Melanesia. Solomon Islands' 1968 act and Fleming's 1976 draft for Vanuatu provided only for systematic adjudication, as in Kenya, and so was a throwback to the 1960s. Under the transferred legislation the Solomon Islands Lands Department initiated thirteen land registration schemes, registering a total of 6,990 hectares and yielding 576 titles between 1965 and 1978. The pace slackened in the mid-1970s as political attention turned, as in PNG and Vanuatu, to alienated land, and no new schemes were started.

In PNG the Commission of Enquiry into Land Matters found a need for the registration of "some" customary land. Its main difference with the Kenyan model was its preference for the registration of group rather than individual titles. Legislation to incorporate such groups was passed. So was legislation for the mediation and arbitration of disputes over customary land. But the main preoccupation of the government was with foreign-owned land, where it faced determined opposition. The government's enthusiasm for reform began to dissipate after 1975, according to Fingleton, who was then in the PNG Lands Department trying to promote reform. Legislation proposed by the department in 1978 to register customary land was not brought to Parliament (Fingleton 1981b, 234).

Nevertheless a strong demand for registration of customary land continued. It was met by the legal expedient of "lease-leaseback." Because customary land was automatically registered if the government acquired it, the government started taking leases of customary land—only to lease it back to the new owners. This expedient created more than 200 titles in coffee development schemes in the Highlands and generated more than 6,000 applications (McKillop 1991, 79).

In the 1980s the Institute of National Affairs, a private-sector think tank, kept the pressure on for reform in PNG. Customary land registration became linked to a wider project to reform the structure, procedure, and performance of the Lands Department. Donors became involved, and a Land Mobilisation Programme was funded by AusAID and the World Bank from 1989 to 1996.

The initiative for reform then moved down to the provincial level. The East Sepik provincial government, impatient with the delays in the central government Lands Department, moved to take on powers and functions over land matters. Its government adopted its own Land Mobilisation Programme and passed legislation for the registration of customary land (also drafted by Jim Fingleton) in 1987. It too would register group ownership but allowed other additional interests—perhaps of individuals or lessees—to be registered. Two areas were declared for registration, but no titles were ever registered. East New Britain also showed an interest in adopting its own legislation.

The PNG government did not give up on national legislation for the registration of customary land. In spite of the unrest in 1995, a local law firm, Henao Lawyers, was commissioned to draw up new legislation in 2001. According to the minister of lands, Charlie Benjamin, the government had learned lessons from the opposition to the Land Mobilisation Programme: its "successes are outweighed by its failures" (quoted in Choi 2001, 3). The legislation he outlined would make registration voluntary and would prevent registered customary land from being sold or transferred to banks through mortgages. It would allow leases, but it would also protect lessees against disturbance by landowners. The existing Land Titles Commission would arbitrate ownership and "must be absolutely free of political interference"—a growing problem among statutory authorities in PNG (Choi 2001, 3). Older concerns that registration would lead to a loss of land through sales and foreclosure on mortgages were supplemented by newer concerns that corruption and political interference would follow state intervention.

Generally, the transfer of land registration from Kenya to Melanesia has been a failure. Table 2 shows how meager the results have been. Thirteen schemes were implemented in Solomon Islands but have since been largely abandoned. Two provincial schemes got as far as legislation in PNG but lacked a national framework and implementation. The final column in table 2 suggests some of the reasons for the failure.

Transfers were facilitated by networks, such as one centered in the Colonial Office in London, or by the University of the South Pacific, centered in Fiji. Parliamentary resistance was important in blocking the Kenyan model in PNG. Fingleton (1981, 232–236) blamed the loss of momentum for reform in PNG on an overloaded reform agenda and on specific resistance from officials, many of whom were expatriates in the

1970s. Fears of popular rebellion, spreading from universities to provincial centers, caused the government to back away from the land conditions in the proposed World Bank loan, but governments have not completely given up on sporadic registration.

Outside the thirteen schemes implemented in Solomon Islands, all the debates have been about doctrine and legislation. Implementation will require the active participation and consent of landowners themselves—which may be easily withdrawn.

The Fate of Alternatives

Alternatives to introduced institutions were sometimes proposed or experimented with. The proposal made by Robert Cooter (1991), as consultant to the PNG's Institute of National Affairs, was the most subtle. He rejected the centralization of Kenyan and other models of adjudication, proposing instead a common law process that based decisions on custom in particular cases. Instead of trying to register all the land under a central statute carried out by bureaucrats, local courts would be encouraged to record and share their decisions, made as and when conflicts occurred. Over time, Cooter argued, a practice-based, nationwide common law would be built up out of ad hoc decisions, generalized, adapted, and shared through legal conferences and training. In this case, an external adviser recommended an endogenous process, not borrowing from Africa or looking to neighbors. Cooter was also realistic about the costs of a centralized approach.

Jim Fingleton, the lawyer who was a research officer for PNG's Commission of Enquiry into Land Matters, developed legal ideas about registering groups rather than land, which were embodied in a Land Groups Incorporation Act. The legislation recognized the corporate nature of customary ownership, and it specified rules about how members could make collective decisions about it. As such, it stood firmly against the individualizing tendencies of the Kenyan model. It was intended to facilitate the return of foreign-owned plantations to their traditional owners, but it was rarely used. It reappeared in Fingleton's drafts of land registration legislation for East Sepik, but again the legislation was unused. Instead it found new and unintended uses in dealings between local people and mining and forestry companies. The legislation provided a way for Chevron to deal with payments to traditional owners around the Kutubu oil fields. And PNG's 1991 Forestry Act required traditional landowners to become legally incorporated as land groups before negotiating agreements to harvest their timber (Fingleton 2002). Similar legal devices were transferred by Fingleton and his colleague Kathy Whimp to forestry legislation in Solomon Islands, under the auspices of the UN Food and Agriculture Organization, for whom Fingleton was a regular consultant.

The Solomon Islands equivalent to PNG's Commission of Enquiry into Land Matters—a parliamentary select committee—was critical of the Kenyan model's urge to individualize and instead recommended "another simpler and cheaper way of recording customary rights and boundaries that people can do for themselves" (Solomon Islands 1976, 18).

Similar ideas had been endorsed by an earlier 1971 committee of inquiry into land registration (the Nazareth Committee) and by the students commissioned by the late colonial Lands Department to inquire into the success or failure of systematic adjudication. These ideas were eventually enacted in 1994 legislation for the creation of customary land records. The legislation was drafted by an expatriate former government surveyor, George Scott, who was then charged with implementing the system. It was presented as an alternative to government-driven, individualistic forms of registration meant to achieve "development." It was linked more to local and cultural projects to "write down custom," influenced by anthropologists, and to cultural revivals associated with political movements like Maasina Ruru.

5 Constitutions and Representative Democracy

Most of the constitutions in the Pacific Islands date from the period of decolonization, which was inaugurated in 1962 by Samoa. That period ended with the independence of Vanuatu in 1980, though U.S. negotiations with Palau dragged on until 1994. The constitutional relationships between France and its Pacific territories, and between the U.S. and its territories, are likely to keep changing, but independence is not necessarily the terminus. The steady international pressure that led New Zealand, Australia, and Britain to decolonize has abated. There is now international discussion about resurrecting ideas of trusteeship over "failed states" (Bain 2003; Jackson 2000). Australia is leading a program called the Regional Assistance Mission to the Solomon Islands (RAMSI). It has an "Enhanced Cooperation Programme" that puts Australian officials and police officers back in operational, rather than advisory, roles in PNG (Sugden 2004). Australia has also agreed with Nauru to provide Australian officials as Nauru's financial secretary and commissioner of police.

If decolonization begins to look like a distant historical period, now closed, it also becomes easier to compare it with earlier periods of constitution making in the nineteenth century. In the introduction to this book, we saw the king of Tonga being nagged by the *Sydney Morning Herald* about what we would now call governance. The king went on a study tour, appointed a consultant, and borrowed laws from New South Wales. Rather than stages of development, there is a kind of rough constitutional symmetry between the fifty years before colonial rule (say, from 1840, the date of the first Hawaiian constitution) and the fifty years since (say, from 1962). Colonialism interrupted a process of transforming indigenous political systems that had begun in Hawai'i and continues in Tonga. The independence constitutions purported to start with a clean slate, but they contained features of what James Tully (1995) calls treaty constitutions, which preceded colonial rule and included recognition of traditional authorities at the center and in local government. The international system continues to demand, and sometimes to enforce, standards of good governance on local politics. Tables 3 and 4 summarize the processes of transfer in the nineteenth and late twentieth centuries.

Constitutionalism and representative democracy tended to march in step, although, as David Held (1987) points out, they are quite different ideas, emerging at different periods in the West and occasionally being antagonistic to each other. The word "democracy" means "rule by the people," and it can take many different forms. "The people" may rule directly, through village meetings and mass demonstrations or through referenda on particular issues. Or they may simply vote for representatives to act on their behalf. There are forms of participation that fall short of "rule," and there are questions of who counts as members of "the people." Leaders may consult the people but retain the right to decide. Women, young people, and those without property or citizenship may be excluded. Representative government is an invention of the eighteenth and nineteenth centuries. Its proponents argued that it made democracy feasible in large political systems, while protecting citizens from the excesses of mob rule. It has been consolidated only since the Second World War (Held 1987). It has triumphed since the collapse of socialist systems, in which rule by the people was supposed to be exercised through the Communist Party. A similar principle was expressed by proponents of one-party states in Africa.

The spread of representative democracy has been caused by a combination of domestic and international factors. It has often been resisted by landowners, who have feared that popular rule would dispossess them. Middle classes have not always been in favor (Rueschemeyer et al. 1992). Requirements that voters own property or pay taxes have been designed to reassure them. The spread has not been all one-way; political scientist Samuel Huntington (1993) shows that democracy has spread in several waves, with periods of reversal in the 1930s and 1970s.

Democracy has also been actively and sometimes coercively transferred. The Allies imposed representative democracy on Germany and Japan after the Second World War. The United States, other donors, and the international financial institutions began to promote democracy in formerly socialist countries and developing countries after the end of the cold war. The U.S.-led invasion of Iraq has also been presented as a campaign to create the conditions for democracy.

TABLE 3. Transfer of Constitutions in the Nineteenth Century

Where	When	How	Who	What	From where / to where	Degrees of transfer	Factors involved
Hawai'i	1840, 1852, 1865, 1887, 1894	Proclamations by king Negotiations between king and legislature	King Missionary and legal advisers Convention 1864	Constitutions with adult male suffrage	Feudal, U.S, UK, and biblical influences/ Hawai'i	1864, property qualification for voting 1887, excluded "Asiatics" from voting 1893, monarchy deposed 1894, republic 1898, annexation by USA	Relative power of settlers Immigration Relations with United States
Tonga	1875	Proclamations by king	King and missionary advisers Shirley Baker	Constitution with adult male suffrage	Hawai'i, the Bible, UK/Tonga	Pro-democracy movement since 1989	End of civil war in Tonga Great power competition International support for pro-democracy movement after 1989
Fiji (Bau and Lau)	1867 (Bau), 1869 (Lau)	Proclamations by chiefs	Chief Cakobau and European settlers (Bau) Chief Ma'afu and European settlers (Lau)	Kingdom (Bau) Chiefdom (Lau)	Hawai'i, UK/Fiji	Reforms in Bau in 1873 introduced residence requirement for voting 1874, Cakobau resigned and chiefs ceded Fiji to UK	Struggles between chiefdoms in Fiji Relations between settlers and chiefs
Samoa	1873, 1875	Promulgation by chiefs	Chiefs and American consul Steinberger	Rotating monarchy	Hawai'i/Samoa	Steinberger deported; civil wars resumed 1899, Samoa partitioned between Germany and the USA	End and then resumption of civil war Great power competition
Cook Islands	1891–1899	Proclamation by British resident commissioner	Resident commissioner, Ariki (chief) Makea	Bicameral federal government	UK/Cook Islands	Reformed in 1894 to include adult male and female suffrage Removed with annexation by New Zealand in 1900	New Zealand more willing to intervene Ariki acquiescence

Sources: Gilson 1980; Kuykendall 1940; Latukefu 1982; Meleisea 1987; Routledge 1985.

TABLE 4. Transfer of Constitutions in the Late Twentieth Century

When	How	Who	What	From where/ to where	Degrees of transfer	Factors involved
1962–1980	Decolonization negotiations	Constitutional planning committees, conventions Commonwealth Secretariat Influential consultants: Jim Davidson, Colin Aickman, Yash Ghai	Westminster constitutions with some provision for traditional or local authority	India, Pakistan, East Africa/PNG Liberation theology/ PNG	Samoa independent in 1962 Cook Islands, 1965 Niue, 1974 PNG, 1975 Solomon Islands, 1978 (but coup in 2000) Kiribati, 1979 Vanuatu, 1980	Colonial interests in withdrawal or staying Geopolitical location Aid agreements
1965–1994	Negotiations and referenda about self-government and terms of Compact of Free Association	Congress of Micronesia Influential consultant: Norm Meller	Constitutions and a compact of free association (COFA)	USA/Trust Territory of Pacific Islands, which divided into 4 entities	Northern Marianas became U.S. Commonwealth in 1978 FSM entered COFA in 1986 Marshall Islands entered COFA in 1986 Palau entered COFA in 1994	U.S. military interests
Late 1970s	Advice and financial support for secession	Phoenix Corporation	Constitution for separatist rebels in Vanuatu	USA/Vanuatu	Rebellion defeated	External assistance from PNG
1990s	Sanctions Donor funding of constitutional review	Constitution Review Commission Influential consultant: Donald Horowitz	Fiji 1998 constitution	Nigeria, Malawi, Northern Ireland, Sri Lanka, Mauritius, South Africa/Fiji	Adopted in 1998 Abandoned in 2000 coup Reaffirmed by appeals court in 2000	Australian, European Union and Commonwealth pressure Rabuka's support

Since the 1990s there has been a growth in the supply of external advice about constitutions and in donor willingness to fund it. The collapse of the Soviet Union and then Yugoslavia created a demand for new constitutions. Organizations like the United Nations Development Programme, the Institute for Democracy and Electoral Assistance (IDEA), and the United States Institute of Peace hired consultants and developed expertise in constitutional design (Carothers 1999; Ottaway and Carothers 2000). Donors like the European Union and the U.S. Agency for International Development (USAID) were ready to fund it. The spread of the Internet allowed the instantaneous transmission of constitutional models and precedents (and the curricula vitae of the consultants ready to advise on them).

When

Tables 3 and 4 distinguish several broad periods of transfer and some interesting smaller waves. The nineteenth century saw a flurry of constitution making as local leaders tried to stave off foreign intervention by demonstrating they could govern themselves in ways acceptable to foreign traders, missionaries, and governments. Hawai'i's experiment was cut short by a coup d'état (for which the United States apologized in 1993). Tonga's constitution survives and has been under pressure from an indigenous pro-democracy movement to make it more representative.

A wave of democratization occurred in the French territories of New Caledonia and French Polynesia in the early 1950s. The next big wave was the period of decolonization and nationalism, running from the 1960s to about 1980, when Vanuatu became independent. Extreme libertarian constitutional advice emerged for a brief period, affecting only Vanuatu. It is more than a historical curiosity, however, for the ideas promoted then—hostile to public enterprise, defensive of individual freedom—went on to become more respectable and mainstream in the 1980s and were promoted by the public choice advocates hired as consultants by the Institute of National Affairs in PNG.

The crises that drove decolonization, which involved the transfer of constitutions, existed as much in the metropolitan countries as in the colonies. In PNG the decision for independence in 1975, rather than later, was a product of domestic circumstances in Australia. Britain's decision to divest itself of its Pacific colonies was the product of a global review of its overseas commitments, in the context of what was then perceived as a long-term decline in British economic fortunes. In Vanuatu, however, the process was accelerated by a local crisis, as the Vanua'aku Pati steadily took control of the countryside.

The first major reverse came in Fiji in 1987, and a fourth period can be characterized as one of good governance—in which donors pressed for reform of the racially biased, pro-indigenous constitution that Fiji had adopted after its first military coup, and Australia later became more interventionist in Solomon Islands and PNG. But as we have seen, international pressure for good governance and constitutional "best practice" is a persistent theme in Pacific Island constitution making, and many of the issues and methods of the late twentieth century were anticipated in international pressure on Tonga in the mid-nineteenth century.

Pressures for democracy also came from within. In 1991, Samoa—which had become independent with suffrage limited to *matai*, or chiefly heads of household, adopted universal adult suffrage. But candidates still required a title to stand for election. Samoa's reforms did not come in response to much international pressure. They are more the results of internal shifts, like those that led to the creation of a pro-democracy movement in Tonga, when 'Akilisi Pohiva led a walkout of commoner members of Parliament (MPs) in 1989. In 2002 the movement proposed a program for a "democratic monarchy," with a popularly elected House of Representatives and a House of Nobles, to be elected by nobles. The king would appoint a prime minister from either house and would hold a power of veto over legislation, which could be overridden by a joint meeting of both houses (*Pacific Islands Monthly*, June 2002).

How

The methods of transfer of Westminster constitutions were similar to those for land registration: study tours, commissions of inquiry, and networks of consultants. Western Samoa set precedents for other countries. It was the first to become independent, it tried to adapt many features of the Westminster model, and the constitutional advisers—Jim Davidson and Colin Aikman—went on to become advisers in Cook Islands (Ghai 1986, 597).

Jim Davidson (1967) argued that there were two opposing approaches to the transfer of Westminster constitutions. In the first, a local constituent assembly draws up and enacts a constitution that breaks with colonial law. This approach harks back to the process by which the United States, followed by India and Pakistan, broke with Britain. In some ways, it is a process of reversal and rejection, rather than of transfer. Yet India and Pakistan both adopted quite conventional constitutions, in Westminster terms. In the second approach, the constitution is the result of negotiations between the colonial government and local politicians. Enactment by the metropolitan legislature formalizes a transfer of power and institutions. This approach was followed by Britain in relation to many of its African colonies. The final negotiations took place in London, free from local politics.

Different combinations of each approach were followed during the decolonization of New Zealand, Australian, and British territories in the South Pacific. In Samoa the Working Committee of the Legislative Assembly came up with proposals. Its draft was debated point by point by a constitutional convention consisting of the assembly members and other leaders drawn from outside the assembly, but none of its proposals were defeated (Davidson 1967, 401). The process was overseen by the UN's Special Committee on Decolonization, as New Zealand's "trusteeship" of Western Samoa would have to be formally terminated. Although the New Zealand and Samoan leaders would have preferred otherwise, the committee insisted that the constitution—and independence based on it—should be put to a plebiscite.

The last colonial governor of what became Kiribati, John Smith, tried to adapt the Westminster model to what he perceived to be local cultural characteristics. He believed that many former British colonies had found themselves with constitutions "which have not worked well . . . and which have had to be changed, often by an unhappy and bloody process" (Smith 1978, 1–2). Smith felt that the egalitarian values of Gilbertese society were inconsistent with retaining the monarchy, acting through a governor-general after independence. The chief minister was also concerned about the lack of support for government on outer islands, so he and the governor called a constitutional convention, preceded by the circulation of discussion papers on the issues it would consider.

In the scattered archipelagos of Melanesia and Micronesia and in the PNG Highlands, the touring committee was used to gauge and influence public opinion. PNG's Constitutional Planning Committee convened five hundred discussion groups, circulated six discussion papers, visited every subdistrict in the country, and held meetings attended by an estimated sixty thousand people (Goldring 1978, 21). In Solomon Islands a parliamentary select committee toured the country, held village meetings, heard submissions, and reported to the legislature. The reports of these meetings tended to be edited and used selectively. Often they were politely set aside or treated as a symptom of the need for downward "political education" that would better align popular opinion with the views of leaders. In Solomon Islands, local concerns about restricting freedom of movement or deferring to chiefly authority were regularly set aside.

The results were not simply an expression of internal compromises. The final form of the Solomon Islands constitution was the result of negotiations held in London between British ministers and officials and a Solomon Islands delegation that included opposition and independent members. There were sharp differences between Britain and Solomon Islands over the future citizenship of government-sponsored settlers from the then Gilbert and Ellis Islands. These differences were not resolved until the negotiations in London. The outcome was influenced by the application of pressure through the shape and increased amount of the financial settlement that Britain would make at independence. Solomon Islands was not a trust territory, but Britain reported to the UN on its progress with decolonization—UN agreement was needed for a former colony to become admitted as an independent state.

Fiji's 1970 constitution was settled behind closed doors in London. Its successor was put in place in 1990, following two coups in 1987, though its designers did canvass popular opinion. New methods of transfer were introduced in the external pressure to reform Fiji's postcoup constitution. The first was the establishment of an NGO, the Citizens' Constitutional Forum (CCF), with funding from Conciliation Resources, a conflict-prevention NGO based in London. CCF held workshops designed to explore and gain support among the elite for constitutional change. The 1998 constitution was developed after an elaborate process of international comparisons. Its travel was funded by an external donor, Australia. During the 1990s, human rights and other international concerns have come attached to trade agreements, particularly with the European Union, as part of a more explicit insistence on external standards of good governance.

Who

The most influential nineteenth-century constitutional advisers were Wesleyan missionaries, particularly the Reverend Shirley Baker. Later they were often lawyers and academics. The Reverend Shirley Baker's friendship with Tonga's King George would be a prototype for many other friendships between local leaders and foreign advisers. According to Latukefu, Baker "was not highly educated, but was gifted, vigorous, full of enthusiasm and drive, and was also very ambitious" (1975, 33).

King George also received unsolicited advice and public criticism from a *Sydney Morning Herald* journalist, Charles St. Julian, who was also consul for Hawai'i. St. Julian first wrote to King George in 1854, encouraging him to adopt a constitution and enclosing a copy of Hawai'i's as a model. He then published an article sharply critical of King George's governance, complaining that "with the true feeling of a semi-barbaric chief, he obstinately resists all improvement" (quoted in Latukefu 1975, 31). Nevertheless, the king gradually introduced much of what St. Julian had urged. Baker arrived in Tonga as a missionary in 1860 and helped draw up the 1862 legal code that became the basis for the 1875 constitution. Baker claimed, "Most of the new laws are the result of my conversations with the King. I wrote them and they were printed almost exactly" (ibid., 33).

In the 1870s, Baker became a close adviser to the king, who had decided to introduce a constitution. Baker drafted it on the basis of the Hawaiian constitution of 1852 and the example of New South Wales legislation. He also promoted the idea of a constitution in the monthly newspaper *Koe Boobooi*. He went on to help the king achieve international recognition, by negotiating a treaty with Germany that they hoped would provoke similar recognition from Britain. Instead, it provoked the British to press the Wesleyans to recall Baker, though he returned to Tonga as the king's premier and minister for foreign affairs and lands. Baker pressed amendments to the constitution and other reforms that provoked local business and missionary interests, and after a series of rows he was deported by the British in 1890 (Latukefu 1975, 56–63). The British then found a replacement for Baker as adviser to the king. Basil Thompson reformed public finance and introduced a new code based on an Indian model (ibid., 66–67).

The most widely influential twentieth-century constitutional adviser has been Yash Ghai, who has advised in PNG, Solomon Islands, Vanuatu, Samoa, Kiribati, Fiji, and Cook Islands. His role was not simply to provide technical advice on constitutional law. He played a much more active entrepreneurial role, acting as advocate for national delegations in constitutional negotiations and negotiating on their behalf. He is also an active researcher, and the solutions he transferred were more creative and drawn more widely than the typical Commonwealth precedents—he invented as well as transferred. He was trusted in part because of his personal qualities: warmth, intelligence, and stamina. He himself came from a developing country (Kenya), so the transfers could be seen as South-South borrowings rather than impositions from the North. In Fiji he went further, supporting a pressure group to bring the government to accept the need to review the 1990 constitution and later advising the opposition political party on its submission to the review committee.

Secessionists in Espíritu Santo and later on in Bougainville did not have access to sources of technical assistance available to internationally recognized governments. So they had to turn to the private sector. In Vanuatu, American property developers who had bought up plantation land for residential subdivisions became alarmed at the prospect of losing their land at independence. Some had links to the Phoenix Corporation, a Far Right organization in Arizona that was promoting "new countries" (Doorn 1979; Oliver 1968). They supported a rebellion against the new national government in Vanuatu, providing it with a constitution that would have protected freehold rights. The rebellion was put down with military assistance from PNG, Australia, and Britain, allowing the official constitution to abolish freehold and return land to customary ownership. Later, the Fiji government, under international pressure, had to turn to private overseas constitutional advice in drafting its 1990 constitution.

There was substantial overlap between constitutional advice and advice about democracy until the 1990s, when new NGOs were established to promote democracy in developing countries. These included the Institute for Democracy and Electoral Assistance (IDEA) and Conciliation Resources, which supported the Citizens' Constitutional Forum in Fiji. These new NGOs were often funded by governments in developed countries but worked at arm's length from them. Similarly, AusAID funded a Centre for Democratic Institutions at the Australian National University (ANU) to provide workshops, training courses, and study tours. Consultants included Donald Horowitz, who advised the Constitution Review Commission (CRC); Roland Rich, who headed ANU's Centre for Democratic Institutions; and Ben Reilly, formerly of IDEA, who specialized in electoral systems.

What

The nineteenth-century constitutions were partly what political theorist James Tully (1995) characterizes as treaty constitutions, which recognize the prior existence and continuity of indigenous forms of government. These constitutions also sought, in a more modernistic way, to transform what they found and thereby make it acceptable to the progressive thinking of the day. One common characteristic among the constitutions was impermanence. Samoa produced constitutions in 1873 and 1875, before it came under German rule in 1900 (Latukefu 1982, 28). In Fiji, the Kingdom of Bau produced a constitution in 1867, and the Lau federation did the same in 1869, before they both came under British rule (Routledge 1985, 111–116). Hawai'i produced four. The first incorporated a Bill of Rights, created a House of Nobles, and, for the first time, provided for the election of a House of Representatives. The bill was drawn up with American advisers, "who came as close as they dared to marrying a republican system of government to a monarchy" (Meller 1982, 52). The Hawaiian monarchy fell to a settler coup that was intended to facilitate U.S. intervention. Tonga's constitution—which provided for a king, nobles, and an assembly containing members elected by adult male suffrage—survives until the present.

The nineteenth-century constitutions had differing and contradictory purposes. Leaders of newly centralized governments wanted to make them more modern and democratic. Others, such as Hawai'i's Kamehameha IV, wanted to use the constitution to protect the monarchy against the liberal ideas of their predecessors. Constitutions were devised to maintain local independence against growing encroachment by Western powers and to protect the interests of powerful settler groups—the latter conspiring to depose Queen Lili'uokalani, declaring a republic, and inviting American annexation in 1898 (Latukefu 1982).

Traditional authority became an issue again during decolonization. In the early 1960s, Samoa's election laws provided for two election rolls: one of individuals, mainly "Europeans" and their descendants, who elected five members; and one "Samoan" list, which consisted of *matai*, who elected forty-one members. The Working Committee designing the constitution that Samoa would adopt at independence wanted to replace categories of race with categories of citizenship, but it was reluctant to go all the way to universal adult suffrage and a common electoral roll for all citizens. The issue of suffrage was controversial even within Samoa. A constitutional convention had debated it in 1954, deciding to retain *matai* suffrage "for the time being" (Davidson 1967, 327–328). In the following Legislative Assembly election, only 5,030 *matai* out of more than 94,000 Samoans were registered to vote (ibid., 336). The Working Committee on the constitution believed that extending the franchise to non-*matai* was not "immediately desirable," but it kept the possibility open by recommending that qualifications for electors be left to legislation rather than entrenched in the constitution itself (ibid., 375, 377). The tension between international expectations of universal suffrage and the actual domestic reluctance and disagreement resulted in a paradoxical plebiscite conducted under universal suffrage, in which 83 percent voted in favor of the constitution and 79 percent for independence.

The objects transferred included legislation and the apparatus for holding a general election—voter registration, polling, and counting votes. In the 1990s, international attention turned to voting systems, particularly alternatives to the first-past-the-post (FPP) system (in which the individual who receives the most votes is elected) for Fiji and PNG (Reilly 2001).

From Where

In the nineteenth century, British and U.S. models influenced Hawai'i, which in turn became a model for Tonga. During the period of decolonization, models were drawn mainly from within the Commonwealth, including India, Pakistan, and East Africa. The advice to the rebels in Vanuatu was from North America. Fiji's Constitution Review Commission looked for lessons from Nigeria, Malawi, Northern Ireland, Sri Lanka, Mauritius, and South Africa.

More generally, the Greek city-states provide Western political theory with its basic political ideas (Held 1987). These city-states also inspire some Tongan intellectuals. The 'Atenisi Institute, which "places criticism at the very heart of education," was so named "because its philosophy of education passionately embraces both the scientific and democratic ideals advanced by the ancient Greeks" ('Atenisi Institute 2002). The Bible was influential on constitution makers in Hawai'i and Tonga, and PNG's Constitutional Planning Committee was also said to have been influenced by liberation theology from Latin America.

Results

A constitution was successfully put in place in each country that became independent or entered into a compact of free association (COFA) with New Zealand or the United States during the 1960s and 1970s. The last to become independent was Vanuatu in 1980. Table 5 shows the date of adoption of Westminster-style constitutions. Table 6 shows the date of adoption of universal suffrage by a wider group of countries, under different types of voting systems—AV (alternative voting), PR (proportional representation), FPP (first-past-the-post), single nontransferable vote, and two-round runoff. Westminster constitutions began to be transplanted in

TABLE 5. Westminster Constitutions in the Pacific Islands

Country	Date of adoption	Comment
Tonga	1875	Adopted to centralize, modernize, and stave off colonial rule
Samoa	1962	Adopted at independence from New Zealand
Cook Islands	1964	Adopted on entry into COFA with New Zealand
Nauru	1968	Adopted at independence from Australia
		Crisis in 2004 led to agreement with Australia to provide a financial secretary and a commissioner of police
Fiji	1970	Adopted at independence from UK
	1990	Adopted after 1987 military coups
	1998	Adopted after international and domestic pressure to review 1990 constitution
		Reaffirmed by appeals court after civilian coup in 2000
		General elections in 2001
		Supreme court ruled in 2003 that Qarase government must follow power-sharing provisions of constitution
Niue	1974	Adopted on entry into COFA with New Zealand
Papua New Guinea	1975	Adopted at independence from Australia
Solomon Islands	1978	Adopted at independence from UK
		Police coup forced change of government in 2000
		Parliament appointed a Review Committee in 2000 to identify a "homegrown state government" system
		Australian-led Regional Assistance Mission intervened in June 2003 to restore law and order
Tuvalu	1978	Adopted after separation from Kiribati and at independence from UK
Kiribati	1979	Adopted at independence from UK. The Beretitenti (president) is popularly elected from a short list of MPs
Marshall Islands	1979	Unlike other former U.S. territories, Marshall Islands adopted a parliamentary executive at self-government. It then entered a COFA with the USA, effective from 1986 (and renegotiated in 2003)
Vanuatu	1980	Adopted at independence from UK and France

TABLE 6. Representative Democracy

Country	Universal suffrage achieved	Voting system
Guam	1931	FPP
French Polynesia	1953	PR
American Samoa	1957	FPP
Cook Islands	1957	FPP
Nauru	1957	AV
New Caledonia	1957	PR
Niue	1960	FPP
Tonga	1960	FPP
Wallis and Futuna	1961	PR
Fiji	1963–1987, 1992	FPP until 1997
		AV after 1998
Papua New Guinea	1964	AV until 1972
		FPP since 1972
		Limited AV from 2002
Federated States of Micronesia	1965	FPP
Marshall Islands	1965	FPP
Northern Mariana Islands	1965	FPP
Palau	1965	FPP
Kiribati	1967	Two-round runoff
Solomon Islands	1967	FPP
Tuvalu	1967	FPP
Vanuatu	1975	Single nontransferable vote
Samoa	1991	FPP

Sources: Larmour 1994; Ben Reilly, pers. comm.

the nineteenth century. The phrase "foreign flower" was originally applied to democracy by the *Fiji Times* in 1987. Voting systems have more recently become objects of deliberate transfer.

Not all of the constitutions listed in table 5 have survived. There have been coups in Fiji—the first in 1987 (followed by further military intervention) and the second in 2000, led by a civilian, George Speight. The first led to the abandonment of the 1970 constitution, but the second was followed by high court and supreme court decisions that involved overseas judges and reaffirmed the validity of the 1998 constitution and the holding of new elections under its provisions. The Solomon Islands constitution was shaken by a police-led coup in 2000 that forced the prime minister to resign and installed a more pliant successor whose government presided over a breakdown in law and order and a collapse in the economy. In December 2000 a task force was appointed to recommend a new "homegrown state government" system, a federation in which "each respective province would become a State with its own State constitution."

Security forces also made a number of challenges to constitutional government in PNG and Vanuatu. In PNG, senior officers were close to deposing the cabinet after it sacked their commander because of talks he had held with rebels in neighboring Indonesia. Troops later converged on Parliament over a pay claim and demonstrated over proposals to reduce the size of the military. In Vanuatu, troops kidnapped the finance minister until their pay demands were met. Each of these challenges to the government grew from grievances internal to the military, but they created opportunities that opposition politicians could exploit.

These events are not directly about transfer, though constitutional crises reflect back on the wisdom and foresight of the designers and their advisers. Of Solomon Islands, for example, we could, with hindsight, ask if more attention should have been paid to providing for ethnic balance in the police service, to establishing a more federal system of government, and to enacting gun control.

Transfer issues were more directly raised in the cases of Samoa and later PNG, over the discretion allowed to the head of state to select the prime minister, and in the case of Fiji, over its Constitution Review Commission, which recommended a deliberate attempt at institutional engineering.

Choosing the Head of Government in Samoa

The designers of Western Samoa's constitution saw it as adapting the Westminster model to Samoan circumstances. The terms of this adaptation have shifted in several ways since 1962. There has been legal and political argument about the way the head of state chooses the prime minister. There has also been a major national debate about *matai* suffrage, culminating in a referendum and a change in the electoral act toward universal suffrage.

A defining characteristic of the Westminster system—distinguishing it from Washington, or presidential, systems—is the selection of the prime minister from Parliament. If a political party has a clear majority in the Parliament, the choice is easy. If parties are weak or multiple or a number of MPs are unaffiliated, then the choice is harder. In Samoa the head of state was to be elected by the Legislative Assembly. The two most important chiefs—*tama aiga*—were initially nominated to hold the position jointly for life.

Following Westminster traditions, the Samoan constitution provides that the head of state selects as prime minister that MP "who commands the confidence of a majority of the Members of Parliament." In the absence of strong political parties, it may be difficult to decide who that person is. So in 1972 the Parliament decided to take a vote to produce a nominee for the job of prime minister.

Three years later, however, when the prime minister died suddenly, the head of state used his discretion, without a ballot, in appointing a successor. Parliament then appointed a select committee to review the procedures and accepted the attorney general's advice that the head of state had a right to use his discretion in this way. Part of the attorney general's argument was an appeal to British constitutional practice (which does not require a ballot).

The discretion of the head of state was also an issue in constitutional changes in PNG in 2000. The new Organic Law on the Integrity of Political Parties and Candidates required the head of state to invite the political party that had endorsed the largest number of elected candidates to form a government together. In a fluid political situation, this change reduced discretion, favored parties, and gave the advantage to the first mover—as Sir Michael Somare discovered.

Constitutional Engineering in Fiji

The Alliance Party held power in Fiji under the 1970 constitution for seventeen years. The Alliance was formally a coalition of ethnic organizations. Though it was dominated by its Fijian wing, it always attracted a substantial Indian vote. It faltered briefly in 1977, when it narrowly lost a general election. However, the opposition were so divided that they could not form a government, and the Alliance was restored with a large majority in a second general election held later in the year. It faltered fatally in 1987, when the opposition coalition briefly took office before being removed in a military coup.

In 1987 a coalition of the National Federation Party and the Labour Party won four more seats than the ruling Alliance Party. Dr. Timoci Bavadra replaced Ratu Sir Kamisese Mara as prime minister. Both were indigenous Fijians, but most of the coalition's electoral support was non-indigenous. A month later the new government was deposed by a military coup. A second coup, later in the year, forestalled a political compromise between party leaders. The country was declared to be a republic and left the Commonwealth. The former governor-general became president and established an interim government. A new constitution was drawn up to replace the one adopted at independence in 1970. Its preamble explained that the "events in 1987" had been "occasioned by a widespread belief that the 1970 Constitution was inadequate to give protection to the interests of indigenous Fijians, their values, traditions, customs, way of life and economic well-being."

The new 1990 constitution contained provisions that its designers believed would protect and promote the interests of indigenous Fijians, including disproportionate parliamentary representation, more influence for the Great Council of Chiefs, affirmative action in the public service, and the reservation of the office of prime minister for indigenous Fijians. Its affirmation of indigenous rights attracted much sympathy from governments elsewhere in the region. The constitution was also criticized, mainly from outside the region, for its impact on nonindigenous Fijians, particularly the descendants of Indian indentured laborers and settlers who had come to the country during colonial rule. Emigration increased, and investment fell. Constitutional change became the test for investor confidence and a return to the Commonwealth.

Steady international pressure on the coup leader, Sitiveni Rabuka, who had become prime minister, led to a change of heart. As we have seen, some of that pressure was applied through the Citizens' Constitutional Forum, an NGO that held workshops on constitutional issues in an effort to change elite and popular opinion. I participated in a number of these workshops.

The 1990 constitution contained provisions for its own review within seven years (section 161). The review was eventually commissioned in March 1995 and reported in September 1996. Its terms of reference began: "The commission shall review the Constitution promoting racial harmony and national unity and the economic and social advancement of all communities and bearing in mind internationally recognised principles and standards of individual and group rights" (Fiji Constitution Review Commission 1996, 754).

The chairman of the commission was Sir Paul Reeves, a former archbishop and governor-general of New Zealand. Its members were Tomasi Vakatora, an indigenous businessman, and former cabinet minister Dr.

Brij Lal, an Indo-Fijian academic historian (now professor) at the Australian National University.

The commission traveled widely overseas, as well as consulting local opinion. Its terms of reference gave priority to ethnic reconciliation. The commission was particularly impressed by the arguments of Donald Horowitz that in certain conditions a system of alternative voting can encourage candidates to adopt more cooperative and moderate positions on ethnically sensitive issues and can appeal across the ethnic divide (Fiji Constitution Review Commission 1996, 310–329). The commission recommended AV for its potential to encourage ethnic moderation in campaigning. So Fiji's new electoral system became a kind of deliberate experiment in institutional transfer, first tested in the general election of 1998. A similar system was adopted in PNG in 2000, for use in the next election but one.

The Fate of Alternatives

Some politicians were given a chance to consider alternatives to Westminster. In Kiribati, which adopted a kind of presidential system, three MPs in a new parliament are nominated by their fellow MPs to be candidates in a subsequent popular election.

Nauru, which became independent from Australia in 1968, inherited Australia's system of the alternative vote in national elections. However, Nauru then went on to "reinvent" a system first proposed by Charles de Borda, a French scientist, in 1781 (Ben Reilly (2002). It involved assigning numerical weights to the first, second, and other preferences expressed by voters and declaring the candidate with the highest weighted score as the winner of the election. Apparently it was intended as a simplification of the system of counting votes inherited from Australia and was proposed by the Nauru secretary for justice, Desmond Dowdall. According to Reilly (ibid., 366), it is unclear if Dowdall was aware of Borda's writings, but if not, it is a neat case of reinvention. What is called in Nauru the Dowdall system has in any case survived through twelve national elections. It is also used in Kiribati to select the three candidates for the presidential election (ibid., 367).

Ghai describes how, as a consultant to the Constitutional Planning Committee in PNG, he canvassed alternatives to Westminster. He found some support for a presidential system, but the CPC saw a parliamentary executive as more participatory and as under the control of the elected legislature. The alternatives, he said, were also abstract and difficult to imagine (Ghai, interview with author, 14 April 1999). Ghai also floated a committee system for Cook Islands, in the latter stages of the 1998 political review. He suggested that the present Westminster system might make more use of committees or that "government by committee" might actually "replace the Westminster system." The main aim would be "to significantly reduce the role of parties, and to provide for the role of all MPs in policymaking and administration" (Cook Islands Commission of Political Review 1998). The commission had found that 72 percent of the people it polled wanted participation by all MPs in government, but it decided to leave the question of government by committee to a future review. However, the recommendation was not pursued, in part because the possibility was introduced late in the review committee's discussions and in part because the politician who chaired the commission lacked enthusiasm for it.

The most sustained attempt to construct a more "appropriate" alternative to Westminster took place in Solomon Islands before independence but was later rejected by the legislature in favor of a more conventional Westminster system. In 1968 the colonial government set out the reasons it thought that Westminster might be unsuitable for an independent Solomon Islands: scatteredness of islands, poor communications, shortage of qualified people, small population, diverse cultures, lack of national unity, and dependence on foreign aid (Saemala 1983, 3). Ironically, the British colonial government argued against Westminster, noting that "the Westminster pattern of government has either failed or had to be substantially modified to meet the political needs of some developing countries in the Commonwealth" (ibid.).

A review committee came up with an alternative system: a Governing Council in which executive functions were distributed among five committees. All members of the council sat on one or another of the committees, which also included some senior public servants. The council sat in public, as a legislature, whereas the committees sat in private as executives. The system was said to be less divisive than Westminster, as it did not need political parties, it provided opportunities for learning, and it embodied Melanesian traditions of consensus. It was not, however, entirely innocent of transfer, for it was said to have been adapted from models in British local government and the island of Jersey.

The Governing Council system ran in Solomon Islands from 1970 to 1974, but according to Francis Saemala, then a senior public servant, "many leading Solomon Islanders felt that the system was not as simple and cheap as expected" (ibid., 4): "The meeting of the whole Council in private aroused suspicion regarding the role of elected representatives. Trying to understand the functions of the committees and the council, in public and private, caused more confusion. The system neither provided for leadership by an individual, nor was it conducive to its creation" (ibid.). Some also felt that the Governing Council was somehow "second best," so in 1974 the country reverted to a more conventional Westminster system, with a chief minister, an opposition, and an "Independent group" of MPs, with clearer lines drawn between the cabinet, senior officials, and the legislature.

Apart from the monarchies, the only long-term alternatives to democracy have been at the local level, where colonial governments often ruled through local chiefs of various kinds. During decolonization and since independence there has been continuing debate in many parts of the region about the appropriateness of elections at the local level. Proposals to introduce local-level democracy in PNG provoked one of the most threatening political movements against it, the Mataungan movement. It had racial overtones, as local democracy would have given nonindigenous voters a say in local politics. In Kiribati, local and traditional groups of elders *(unimane)* have contested power with elected councils and in one case deposed a council. In Samoa, increased democracy at the national level was accompanied—and perhaps compensated for—by increased autonomy for unelected village *fono*. Some went on to embarrass the government by meting out punishments to people who wanted to introduce a new religion or who otherwise challenged their authority. In 1993 a successful businessman, returned from New Zealand, was accused of failing to participate properly in village life and, in particular, of not paying a fine imposed by the *fono* (assembly). He was shot and killed, and his property destroyed. His killer was found guilty of murder, and six senior *matai* were found guilty of incitement to destruction of property but were excused from prison sentences (Va'a 2000). By contrast, attempts by the Solomon Islands government to do away with elections at the area council level, which is below the province level, were contested in the courts and found to be unconstitutional. However, there is not much reason to think that an elected local government would be any less willing to exceed its powers. In any case these conflicts between traditional and democratic forms of political organization seem likely to persist at the local level throughout the region.

6 Public Sector Reform and Anticorruption

The end of the cold war witnessed a growing international debate about the use of loan conditions to achieve policy transfer. Donor governments and private foundations also funded international NGOs that promoted reform in developing countries. International rankings and so-called peer reviews brought a new kind of indirect pressure on recalcitrant governments. Neither loan conditions nor NGO nor peer pressure is completely new, but each was deployed more widely and in pursuit of good governance. In this chapter these events are analyzed as examples of policy transfer, and in chapter 8 we will look at ways in which they involve an exercise of power, both direct and indirect.

Loan Conditions

The World Bank typically attached conditions to loans for particular projects. The International Monetary Fund had typically set precise targets for money supply and deficit limits, before extending credit to members in crisis. In the 1980s the World Bank started to lend for programs rather than projects, with conditions that were broad, often qualitative, and economy-wide (Mosley et al. 1991, 27–29). Structural elements also became more important in IMF lending in the 1990s (International Monetary Fund 2001, 2). As we saw in the introduction to the present book, Malaysia's former prime minister, Mahathir, was particularly critical of the standard, off-the-shelf quality of the conditions the IMF set in its loans. Mahathir's complaint was later echoed by Joseph Stiglitz, then chief economist at the World Bank, who criticized the IMF for its "one-size-fits-all" reports (Stiglitz 2000, 48). The advice in the East Asian crisis of 1997 was not only standardized but also wrong. The IMF recommended fiscal austerity to countries that already had budget surpluses and tight monetary policies (ibid., 104–113).

The World Bank had begun to use loan conditions to achieve public sector reform in PNG in the 1980s. In the mid-1990s the Asian Development Bank used loan conditions in a broader and almost simultaneous program of public sector reform in six of its member countries.

International Nongovernmental Organizations

International nongovernmental organizations have often drawn attention to the abuse of power by governments at home and abroad. In the nineteenth century they campaigned against slavery, and they now campaign against other abuses of human rights. Their numbers had grown from about two hundred in 1900 and eight hundred in 1930 to nearly four thousand in 1980 (Boli and Thomas 1999, 14). NGOs try to "to make rules, set standards, propagate principles and broadly represent 'humanity' vis-à-vis states and other actors" (ibid.). Without resources or the legal authority to enforce their views, they use the media to embarrass governments and press them to reform. During the 1990s, aid donors began to fund NGOs in their campaigns for good governance. Transparency International, for example, was set up by disaffected World Bank officials who were concerned about the bank's complicity in corruption in Africa. TI initially campaigned against bribery in international business dealings, through, for instance, an Organisation for Economic Co-operation and Development (OECD) convention that banned the bribery of foreign officials. TI also began publishing the Corruption Perceptions Index, which, by ranking countries from best to worst, aimed to shame their governments into reform. TI is an NGO, but roughly half of TI's income comes from governmental institutions, including foreign affairs ministries and aid agencies in the Netherlands, the United Kingdom, the United States, Canada, Norway, Germany, Sweden, Finland, Denmark, Switzerland, and Australia. The main function of TI is transfer. Its founders come from the world of international development. While breaking older diplomatic taboos against talking about corruption, they also talk of local solutions and reject "best practice" in favor of "best fit."

Peer Pressure

Peer pressure is a familiar technique in international relations, where countries are jealous of their sovereignty and formal equality as independent states. In the absence of a central authority to monitor and enforce agreements, governments may agree to monitor each other's performance and—through publicity—to shame each other into sticking to agreements they have made.

Since 1997 the Secretariat of the South Pacific Forum, a regional intergovernmental organization which was renamed the Pacific Islands Forum in 2000, has convened annual meetings of its members' economic ministers to pursue a common action plan, including the adoption of principles of accountability and transparency, and to report to each other on their progress. The forum's Eight Principles of Accountability deal with budget processes, accounts, loan agreements, contracts, oversight, and the independence of the central bank. Its Code of Good Practices on Fiscal Transparency was devised by the IMF, and island members of the forum have come under strong Australian pressure to sign up to it.

When

Three overlapping periods of transfer of public sector reform are summarized in table 7. PNG's interactions with the international financial institutions (IFIs) began in the early 1980s. The second period began in the mid-1990s, with Cook Islands. Tourism was falling in Cook Islands, while government wages, welfare payments, and capital expenditures were growing. The government first resorted to taking money from government-owned enterprises, before turning to the ADB, which helped design an economic reform program. During the 1990s, the Solomon Islands government borrowed from domestic banks, and its debt grew to 30 percent of gross domestic product (GDP). Fears that the Vanuatu government might loot the personal savings in the National Provident Fund led to a riot, massive withdrawals, and a run on the currency. The third period was characterized by peer review processes and driven particularly by Australia, through the Forum.

Four periods of transfer of anticorruption measures are summarized in table 8. The first period, in the 1970s, was associated with decolonization in Melanesia. PNG's constitution makers were influenced by examples from Africa, particularly concerns about the rise of the "politician-businessman" and the effects of private interests of leaders. PNG's constitution provided for a Leadership Code, and Solomon Islands (advised by Yash Ghai, who had worked on the PNG constitution) and Vanuatu followed by adopting similar codes. The codes bound leaders, both elected and appointed, to avoid conflicts of interest and to disclose their assets. In

TABLE 7. Transfer of Public Sector Reform

When	How	Who	What	From where / to where	Degrees of transfer	Factors
1980s–2002	Loan conditions	World Bank and IMF	Downsizing Privatization	Argued from first principles rather than places/PNG	Staff reductions offset by new recruitment in 1991 2,750 of 4,568 staff reductions proposed in 1994–1995, achieved by 1997 1,181 of 7,000 staff removed in 1999 Only one privatization achieved (PNG Banking Corporation)	Support from finance departments Resistance from bureaucracies Army unrest
1990s	Loan conditions Technical assistance	Asian Development Bank	Downsizing Privatization Transition ministries	New Zealand/Cook Islands/Vanuatu/ Solomon Islands	Cook Islands: 57% of staff cut FSM: 37% cut Marshall Islands: 33% cut Solomon Islands: 6% cut Vanuatu: 10% cut	Asian financial crisis End of aid agreements Domestic support mustered through summits involving private sector and NGOs
1997–2002	Annual ministerial meetings	Economic ministers of Pacific Forum and Secretariat (16 countries)	Action plan Eight Principles of Accountability IMF Code of Good Practices on Fiscal Transparency	First principles, IMF/island ministers	Commitments to implement, but FEMM Stocktake found little action[a] Social impact assessments often not carried out	Countries at different stages of reform Inadequate legislation Dependence on OFC revenues Political resistance to external pressure

[a] Pacific Islands Forum Secretariat 2002.

TABLE 8. Transfer of Anticorruption

When	How	Who	What	From where / to where	Degrees of transfer	Factors
1970s	Constitutional Planning Committee	University of PNG Law Faculty Sir Anthony Siaguru Gang of Four	Leadership Code	Tanzania/PNG PNG/Solomon Islands PNG/Vanuatu	Watered-down proposal in PNG constitution Stronger version withdrawn in 1978 Numerous reports and some successful prosecutions	Radicalism of Constitutional Planning Committee Resistance from businessmen–MPs
1990s	Memorandum of understanding Technical assistance training	Simon Pentanu Marie-Noelle Ferrieux Patterson Peter Kape	Operational issues in Leadership Code	PNG/Vanuatu	Vanuatu established in 1995, but government and Parliament tried to stifle it Nearly 80 reports published in 1996–2000, but only 10 percent of recommendations acted upon	Change of government in Vanuatu Personal interest of PNG prime minister, Sir Julius Chan
1990s	Visits and workshops	Peter Rooke Sir Anthony Siaguru	Local chapters of Transparency International	TI Berlin and Australia/NGOs in Pacific Islands	Chapters established: PNG, 1997 Fiji, 1999 Vanuatu, 2001 Solomon Islands, 2003 PNG chapter active in electoral reform	Capacity in local civil society Sandline crisis in PNG Popular outrage at corruption
2000s	Self-assessment, peer review, blacklisting, countermeasures	Financial Action Task Force	The Forty Recommendations	G7/Nauru, Cook Islands, Marshall Islands, Niue	Marshall Islands and Niue taken off blacklist in 2002 Cook Islands and Nauru legislate but still on blacklist in 2004	Dependence on international banking links

PNG and Vanuatu, to reduce the number of new agencies created, the Leadership Code was to be administered by the Ombudsman Commission, which also carried out the more traditional ombudsman function of acting on public complaints against maladministration. In PNG, future prime minister Julius Chan and others had opposed the Leadership Code, and a compromise version, to be implemented by the Ombudsman Commission, was included in the new National Constitution. In 1978 a group of leaders dubbed the Gang of Four had tried to introduce a stronger code but failed to get support.

Vanuatu did not actually set up its Ombudsman's Office until 1995, when the international climate was more concerned with good governance, and after the Anglophone Vanua'aku Pati, which had brought the country to independence, finally lost office to a Francophone government. The office was set up with technical assistance from PNG, a rare example of transfer between developing countries in the region (Barcham 2003). PNG's prime minister, Sir Julius Chan, was interested, having been prime minister in the fateful period just before Vanuatu's independence, when PNG troops were brought in to repress the rebellion on Espíritu Santo and Tanna. Technical assistance—such as help with drafting and temporary staff from PNG—provided a practical embodiment of political claims about Melanesian solidarity.

The 1990s also saw the rise of Transparency International and rich countries' concern with tax evasion. The PNG chapter of Transparency International—TI (PNG)—was formally established in January 1997 (Larmour 2003; Siaguru 2001). Its immediate origins lay in a forum entitled "Ethics in Business," which was convened by the Business Council of PNG and the PNG Institute of National Affairs in July 1996. It quickly gained prominence "against a backdrop of private deals and questionable activities involving senior public officials that ultimately came to be known as the Sandline Affair" (Siaguru 2001). Sandline was a British company of mercenary soldiers secretly contracted by the PNG government to bring an end to the long-running Bougainville rebellion. There were suspicions of corruption in the award of the contract, and, ironically, the PNG officer who raised the alarm was himself found to have received payments from another overseas arms company. The Sandline revelations precipitated a profound political crisis, in which some of the founders of TI (PNG) were closely involved—though not the organization itself. The crisis ended with public demonstrations protected by parts of the army, forcing Sir Julius Chan to step down as prime minister and creating an impression of the power of "civil society" to bring nonviolent political change.

The activities of TI (PNG) have since been influenced by the rhythm of national elections. Founded a few months before the general election in July 1997, TI (PNG) campaigned to have candidates sign a National Integrity Pledge, in which they promised to declare their interests and expenditures and to eschew political interference in public administration. Bill Skate replaced Sir Julius Chan as prime minister in 1997 and introduced a regime of more overt corruption and eventual conflict with the World Bank. The general election in July 1999 brought to power a reformist government headed by Sir Mekere Morauta and provided TI with a new opportunity to press its agenda, particularly in relation to Morauta's plans for privatization. TI national chapters were formally established in Fiji in 1999, in Vanuatu in 2001, and in Solomon Islands in 2003.

Pacific Islands countries had been setting up financial centers since the 1970s, often with encouragement from or acquiescence of donor governments, which saw these centers as an opportunity to raise revenue (Hampton and Levi 1999). The globalization of the international economy in the 1990s, and specific concerns about dirty money coming out of Russia, led to international concern that the Offshore financial centers (OFCs) were undermining metropolitan tax regimes, providing opportunities for organized crime, and, incidentally, corrupting officials and politicians in tax-haven regimes.

The Group of Seven set up a Financial Action Task Force (FATF), housed in the OECD Secretariat, in 1989 and an Asia Pacific Group in 1997, based in Sydney. The FATF consisted of twenty-nine rich countries; the Asia Pacific Group, sixteen. However, the countries that these organizations targeted were generally not members. The organizations attempted to persuade the governments that sponsored OFCs to regulate them more closely. They became more forceful after the terrorist attacks of 11 September 2001. Among the targets were OFCs in Cook Islands, Marshall Islands, Niue, Nauru, and Palau (Financial Action Task Force 2003). They were particularly concerned about money laundering, which was defined as "the process of converting cash, or other property which is derived from criminal activity, so as to give it the appearance of having been obtained from a legitimate source" (Asia Pacific Group on Money Laundering 2003).

How

Ideas about public sector reform entered into the relationship between IFIs and developing countries in several ways. Economists in the IFIs favored market-based solutions. Countries facing fiscal problems were often forced to sell off companies they owned to pay debts and employees' wages. Privatized companies in the West, such as water utilities, saw possibilities for investment abroad. Privatization in the West had also produced a group of freelancing consultants who knew about the process.

These tendencies were brought together when governments in developing countries turned to IFIs for loans to tide them over during fiscal crises. Postindependence aid agreements and prudent financial management had allowed the countries to avoid the structural adjustment programs visited on Africa in the 1980s. But in the 1990s, PNG entered into a period of fractious negotiations with the World Bank, and the ADB attached public sector reform conditions to a series of loans it made to six countries in the mid-1990s.

The ADB saw the provision of loans and technical assistance as an opportunity to reduce the size of the public sector and encourage the growth of a private sector. Bilateral donors, particularly Australia and New Zealand, were ready to step back and let the bank take the lead—and any political heat—in reform. The island countries were members of the ADB, with representation on the board, which could provide a channel for appeal against conditions. In a short period the ADB made six program loans, each conditional on public sector reform. The conditions in Cook Islands drew particularly on New Zealand experiments in new public management and were transmitted to Vanuatu, as the same consultants moved from one job to the next.

The loan negotiations were a complex multilateral process. The banks worked with each other and with bilateral donors. The government dealt with parastatals, the private sector, unions, and other NGOs. Who should be involved could itself become an object for negotiation. The ADB, for example, favored national summits that would bring the local private sector and NGOs into the process of deciding reform and thereby legitimate the outcome. Cook Islands held a three-day brainstorming retreat, involving the Public Service Association and business leaders. Vanuatu's national summit in June 1997 involved chiefs and NGOs as well. Marshall Islands did not convene a summit until 1998, after donor pressure. In Cook Islands, continuing consultation with business was meant to be institutionalized in a National Development Council, formed in late 1996, but the council was not included in the loan conditions and has proved ephemeral.

Neither side was unitary. The interests of elected politicians on the national side were different from those of their own civil servants. They had to face the electoral consequences of reform, though they found that the consequences could be positive as well as negative. Their own privileges were also under threat. Their numbers, allowances, and rights to appoint junior ministers were threatened in Cook Islands. In Solomon Islands and Marshall Islands, privatization of public enterprises threatened powers of patronage to the boards of public utilities, such as those providing electricity. For politicians, turning to IFIs was electorally tricky. There was often domestic political support for reform of some kind, as well as domestic lack of sympathy with the privileges of politicians and civil servants.

Public servants were threatened with layoffs. Revenue-raising departments, such as finance, had interests different from those of spending departments, such as health and education, and efforts were made to quarantine some departments from cuts. Sometimes collusion occurred between finance departments and the banks, in agreeing to conditions that either had already been met or could be met easily. Some conditions had, in fact, already been completed (twenty-five of sixty-five in Solomon Islands' case). The banks themselves had a strong interest in making loans and rolling them over. Banks hated to foreclose on a loan and typically would give another loan to pay back the first. Mosley et al. (1991, 166), for example, note that the World Bank foreclosed only twice on loans in the 1980s: to Senegal and to Argentina. Finance departments were often sympathetic to bank demands for cost cutting, and the real action was taking place between finance and spending departments. The IFIs could serve as a useful scapegoat.

Leadership codes had been transferred through constitutions, of which they were a part. The methods used in the next wave of transfer were quite different, as Transparency International supported the establishment of autonomous national chapters in PNG, Fiji, Vanuatu, and Solomon Islands. TI also targeted the aid donors that were influential in the region to support its efforts.

TI (PNG) drew on its founders' personal networks among business leaders in government and in the private sector. These networks were institutionalized in the Institute of National Affairs (founded in 1976); in professional associations, like the Institute of Accountants; and in peak bodies (publicly sanctioned and recognized representatives and advocates), like the National Council of Women. The founders of TI (PNG) lobbied officials, gave lectures, and held and attended workshops. They tried to reach out beyond the Port Moresby elite through regional visits, a newsletter, and a Web site, but they were fighting against the limits of high transportation costs and low levels of literacy, newspaper readership, and Internet usage. TI (PNG) worked through various fronts and coalitions, with overlapping memberships drawn mainly from the political and business elite. Its board represented big business: two from mining companies, two from banks, and three from law firms, plus one each from the National Council of Women, a radio station, and the University of Papua New Guinea. Its coalition extended its reach into the Trade Union Congress and government agencies dealing with corruption. It also developed anticorruption material for use by teachers that was distributed through teachers colleges, potentially multiplying its influence beyond the limits of face-to-face lectures and lobbying.

The most sophisticated campaign, drawing on public relations expertise, was the Electoral Reform Project (ERP), carried out during 2001–2002 with two government bodies, the Constitutional Development Commission and the Electoral Commission. It was intended to persuade members of Parliament to strengthen political parties by amending the constitution and enacting electoral legislation and to replace the first-past-the-post electoral system with a limited preferential system. The campaign would then move to educating voters about the new system, which would take effect after the 2002 general election. The first part of the campaign included radio talk shows, television and newspaper advertisements, and posters and flyers such as one setting out "the ten commandments of PNG democracy," including "Thou shalt not vote for self-interest." The campaign was funded largely by the European Union.

The OECD used the threat of adverse publicity, ostracism, and blacklisting to press island governments to clean up their financial center legislation. It started with a process of "self-assessment," in which members filled out a questionnaire about their implementation of antilaundering techniques. This self-assessment was then peer-reviewed by a team of representatives from at least three other governments. Countries that were "noncooperative" were then listed in press releases and on the Web, alerting other members to "give special attention to business relations and transactions" with them, and—if those business relations and transactions had "no apparent economic or visible lawful purpose"—to investigate their background (recommendation 21). If listed countries continued to fail to cooperate, the FATF could take additional countermeasures. Members dealing with noncooperative countries could be required to insist on more stringent procedures for identifying clients, reporting, and establishing subsidiaries from noncooperative countries, and members were expected to warn businesses about dealing with the noncooperative countries.

Who

The consultants on public sector reform were recruited by the international financial institutions. Lloyd Powell was influential in Cook Islands, then Vanuatu, and then Solomon Islands. A. V. Hughes, a former financial secretary in Solomon Islands, was influential throughout the region, under the auspices of the UN Economic and Social Commission on Asia and the Pacific (UNESCAP) and then the ADB. The most controversial was Pirouz Hamidian-Rad, who had been the leader of the PNG "country team" at the World Bank. He went over to the other side of the negotiations and negotiated a deal in which he would supply economic advice to the PNG government, reportedly at a cost of $7 million over two years. The World Bank then refused to deal with Hamidian-Rad, and his removal jokingly became the "forty-first condition" of the loan, which had forty official conditions. Hamidian-Rad meanwhile drew up the savage 1999 budget, which Filer characterizes as "structural adjustment without the loans" (2000, 70). A later World Bank adviser, Dan Weise, defected for different reasons. Believing that the World Bank, under Australian pressure, had gone too soft on enforcing conditions on the Morauta government, he blew the whistle during an Australian television program on current affairs (Australian Broadcasting Corporation, *Four Corners*, 24 June 2002).

PNG's Constitutional Planning Committee and its academic advisers in the early 1970s knew about conditions and debates about corruption in Africa. The committee was worried that leaders would compromise the ambitious goals they had set for PNG "by accumulating personal wealth, by collaborating with foreign or national businessmen, or by accepting bribes" (Constitutional Planning Committee 1974, 3/2). In an influential article on corruption first published in 1962, political scientist Colin Leys had compared the history of Western countries with those of developing countries and wondered "where the puritans are to come from in the new states, with their prevailing lack of economically independent professional and middle classes and corresponding weakness of the puritan ethos" (2002, xx). Leys' "puritans" emerged both from among the staff of international agencies and from among middle-class citizens of developing countries acting as "civil society." They often were the educated sons and daughters of a first generation of leaders who had become middle class through politics and business. Both staff and citizens had become disgusted by Western complicity in corruption among the politician-businessmen and soldiers who ruled in many developing countries. The groups came together in Transparency International.

Consultants were less influential in the transmission of TI's ideas, which were promoted in this region particularly by Peter Rooke, TI's Australian executive director, through visits and regional conferences and workshops. The founder and chairman of TI (PNG) was the late Sir Anthony Siaguru, a key member of PNG's nationalist elite and a droll commentator on its political affairs in the national press. He had extended his international networks as deputy secretary-general in the Commonwealth Secretariat in London, so he was well placed to knit domestic and international coalitions together in an energetic, somewhat patrician style. TI is housed in the offices of the Institute of National Affairs, a business-oriented think tank run by Mike Manning, a similarly energetic and patrician naturalized citizen. The budget of TI (PNG) in 2001 was about kina 163,000 (US$50,000), mainly funded by subscriptions and donations.

What

After governments facing financial crises had borrowed or simply took as much as they could from local banks or provident funds (social security systems), they were compelled to sell assets to meet their obligations to pay public servants. Calling those asset sales "privatization" or "public sector reform" helped present them in a more rational, forward-looking way. The phrase "new public management" (NPM) crystallized around a wider set of reforms that were packaged together and made more coherent in the 1990s. They included privatization but drew on management literature and public choice theory. NPM advocates had a suspicion of state intervention and the motives of bureaucrats, as well as a positive preference for private ownership and markets. The OECD took an active role in standardizing these ideas and disseminating them through conferences, publications, and an annual report on developments. NPM ideas were originally justified in terms of the special conditions of Western Europe and the United States: complex liberal economies that could no longer be regulated by command and control; and sophisticated users of public services, who wanted to exercise choice. Nevertheless, NPM's critique of insensitive and inefficient state planning and of self-interested officialdom had intuitive appeal in many postcommunist and developing countries.

Loan conditions typically repeated or highlighted the basic documents of a reform program already drafted, often with technical assistance from the IFIs or other donors, such as the Economic Reform Project in Cook Islands or the Public Sector Reform Program in the Federated States of Micronesia. The reforms typically included asset sales, downsizing, the introduction of value-added taxes, and budget reform. Existing heads of department were to be removed, and their jobs advertised, though most in Cook Islands got their jobs back. New consultation and accountability mechanisms were to be introduced, such as national summits with the private sector and NGOs.

Leadership codes were mainly aimed at reducing conflicts of interest between the public positions of senior officials and the private business interests of the officials and their families. TI (PNG) promoted a wider range of ideas. In 1997, as mentioned above, it promoted a National Integrity Pledge, and legislation set up the Independent Commission Against Corruption. TI (PNG) has also developed curricula for teachers. In 1998 it sorted its activities into four program areas: promoting legislation designed to increase transparency and accountability in government; education and community awareness; codes and integrity pacts in the private sector; and monitoring corruption (Siaguru 2001, 3–4). In 1999 it worked to get the Electoral Reform Project funded, and after the election of the Morauta government it tried to get the new Privatisation Commission to adopt the idea of integrity pacts.

TI's *Source Book*, published on the Internet, was a summary of best practice, organized around the idea of pillars of a national integrity system (Pope 1996). The idea of integrity pacts was to avoid a "prisoners' dilemma" in which companies feel compelled, against their own best interest, to offer bribes because of fears that their competitors would gain advantage by doing so. The pacts, in which competitors agreed not to offer bribes, could be introduced ad hoc without national legislation and enforced as conditions in contracts. In 2000, TI (PNG) held a workshop with the Institute of National Affairs to look at privatization, a long-standing issue in PNG public policy, and at ways in which integrity pacts might be introduced into the process, which was otherwise vulnerable to corruption. The workshop offered a model set of procedures, designed by TI, and case studies of efforts to apply integrity pacts and more transparent forms of public contracting and privatization in Ecuador, Panama, Brazil, and Colombia. PNG's National Capital District Commission, notorious for corruption in its contracting and hiring, claimed then to have introduced integrity pacts (Transparency International PNG and the Institute of National Affairs 2000), but it did not succeed.

TI (PNG) also picked up on an earlier enthusiasm of its chairman, Sir Anthony Siaguru. The idea of preferential voting, or alternative voting (AV), is an idea recovered from PNG's past rather than imported from abroad. Until 1972, voters in PNG listed candidates in order of preference, ensuring that—after the preferences of low-scoring candidates were distributed—the winner would have a majority. That system was replaced with a first-past-the-post (FPP) system, for reasons of simplicity, at independence. When large numbers of candidates ran for a position, FPP could deliver victory to a candidate with a very small percentage of the total vote. It also gave little incentive for candidates to reach out beyond their core support. Sir Anthony had been a longtime supporter of the revival of AV, but it came back on the agenda in the 1990s as part of a broader international campaign and with more elaborate theoretical justification.

The Financial Action Task Force tried to get governments to adopt what it called the Forty Recommendations, which it said were a complete set of countermeasures against money laundering that were "designed for universal application." The recommendations included obligations to criminalize the laundering of the proceeds of serious crimes, to require financial institutions to be able to identify their clients, and to report suspicious transactions. Governments were to introduce systems for controlling financial institutions and to enter into treaties allowing international cooperation.

From Where

Ideas about new public management were transferred from New Zealand to its former colony, Cook Islands, and then by New Zealand consultants to Vanuatu. Ideas about leadership codes were transmitted to Papua New Guinea mainly through lawyers recruited from East Africa to staff the Law Faculty at the University of Papua New Guinea. According to Siaguru (2001, 2), the National Integrity Pledge, like the original Leadership Code, came from Tanzania. The idea that a group of companies would sign an anti-bribery pledge, forming an "island of integrity," was attributed to Robert McNamara, a former World Bank president (Lundberg 2002, 15). Independent commissions against corruption (ICACs) came from Hong Kong, by way of Sydney. Other ideas, such as whistle-blowing and freedom of information, are best practice ideas that have circulated internationally. The Pacific Islands Forum's Eight Principles of Accountability are a kind of distilled best practice, shorn of any national origins, whereas the Code of Good Practices on Fiscal Transparency is attributed to the International Monetary Fund. Similarly the Financial Action Task Force's Forty Recommendations were from no particular jurisdiction but were adopted by the group in 1990 and updated as patterns of money laundering changed.

Results

Papua New Guinea has had several successive engagements with the IMF and the World Bank. Each was more intense and longer-lasting than the previous one. PNG's first financial crisis came in 1981, six years after independence. The Central Bank of PNG suggested borrowing from the IMF, but the government decided to make cuts in public expenditure on its own. The next crisis came in 1990, after rebels closed the Bougainville copper mine, which had been contributing 20 percent of government revenue. The government devalued the currency, cut public expenditure, froze wages, and tightened credit. It borrowed from the IMF and the World Bank in 1990. Phase two of PNG's borrowing was planned to include longer-term structural adjustments directed at improving growth in the nonmining sector. A long list of measures included "human resource development; investment deregulation; trade policy reforms; privatisation and commercialisation of government parastatals," and so on (Kavanamur 1998, 104). Significantly for the next episode, it included "policies to improve land administration."

However, the economy stabilized quickly, and the government went ahead with a supply-side policy of cutting wages and taxes, the deregulation of business, and the promise of eliminating primary school fees. Cash flow problems then brought the PNG government back to the IFIs in 1994. The first portion of a loan was released in 1995, but negotiations over conditions for the second tranche dragged on with increasing bitterness until it was released in early 1997. The most violent points of contention involved land and forestry policy.

In 1999 the new prime minister, Sir Mekere Morauta, a former secretary for finance well regarded by the donors, proposed his own structural reform program. Its objectives were familiar: promoting good governance, sustaining macroeconomic stability, improving public sector performance, and removing barriers to investment and economic development. In March 2000 the government signed a letter of intent with the IMF that contained six "quantitative benchmarks" for public expenditure and seven "structural benchmarks" relating to privatization and reform in the public and financial sectors (Curtin 2000, 30).

With regard to forestry policy, the new government reinstated the previous export regime for logs, funded an inspection service, and declared a moratorium on new permits. It also promised to require more transparency from the Forestry Board. A $90 million loan from the World Bank contained four new second-tranche conditions about forestry. Meanwhile, Hamidian-Rad had been arrested on charges of tax evasion.

However, relations broke down again in February 2001 when the PNG government canceled the visa of the World Bank's resident coordinator, accusing him of having "seen fit to interfere in the domestic affairs of PNG," including being involved in a "campaign to have senior officials removed from office" (*Australian Financial Review*, 9 February 2001). The influence of the World Bank and other donors was an issue in an army mutiny the following month. The soldiers were opposed to the recommendations of a Commonwealth-sponsored Eminent Persons Group, adopted by the PNG government, that the army be halved in size. The soldiers' petition was more widely targeted, demanding that "all representatives of the World Bank, the IMF and all military personnel from Australia or New Zealand leave this country immediately" (*Canberra Times*, 23 March 2001). The government backed away from its plans to reform the army, and the soldiers handed back their weapons.

The World Bank's relationship with PNG intensified over several loans, but the Asian Development Bank's program had quite a different shape (Knapman and Saldhana 1999). A common element—and a test of performance—was cuts in the number of civil servants. In Cook Islands the public service staff was reduced by a startling 57 percent in one year. Table 9, drawn from the ADB's own review of the bank's activities, summarizes the results.

PNG's Ombudsman Commission achieved an impressive record of activity and independence, and engaged in transfer itself, when it provided technical assistance to the establishment of Vanuatu's Ombudsman Commission. In the late 1990s, for example, it had uncovered corrupt investments of PNG's National Provident Fund money in an office block in Cairns in North Queensland, which had become a popular location for holidays and investment by PNG's elite. However, supporters of PNG's Ombudsman Commission perceived gaps in the Leadership Code legislation. In particular, leaders under investigation were able to resign and thereby avoid being brought before a tribunal.

TABLE 9. ADB Loans for Reform in the South Pacific

Country	Population (thousands)	Loan date	Loan size (millions of US$)	Number of loan conditions	Conditions fulfilled by 1999 (%)	Reduction in public service (%)
Cook Islands	18	1996	5	110	86	57
Federated States of Micronesia	100	1997	18	122	78	37
Marshall Islands	48	1997	12	59	56	33
Samoa	160	1998	8	62	65	Not available
Solomon Islands	319	1998	25	65	59	6
Vanuatu	147	1998	20	46	57	10

Source: Knapman and Saldhana 1999, tables 1.1 and 1.2 and appendix 1.

Through workshops and the media, TI devised and pressed a broad agenda for PNG, including the creation of an Independent Commission Against Corruption (ICAC), a national integrity pledge that candidates were challenged to sign, and electoral reforms, a longtime concern of TI's chair. But fourteen years after independence, Vanuatu's first ombudsman had still not been appointed. Marie-Noelle Ferrieux-Patterson, a naturalized citizen of French descent, had to start her work in that position in 1994 without the benefit of detailed legislation until the Ombudsman Act was passed in 1995. She produced a stream of hard-hitting reports detailing corruption, mismanagement, and incompetence among politicians and senior officials. In 1997 she won two High Court cases: one against an attempt by the Council of Ministers to dismiss her, and another from the board of Air Vanuatu, then under investigation, that the Ombudsman Act was invalid. A report in January 1998 found that the National Provident Fund had been improperly giving loans to politicians. Protests and a run on savings invested in the fund led to riots, looting, and the declaration of a state of emergency.

So forceful were her reports that Parliament moved to silence Ferrieux-Patterson. The 1995 act was repealed in 1998, and a new Ombudsman Act of 1999 reduced the independence of the office to hire its own staff, prohibited allegations of criminality without providing details and evidence, and eliminated the power of the ombudsman to enforce recommendations if the executive failed to do so. From then on, the ombudsman could only recommend or mediate. At the end of her five-year term, Ferrieux-Patterson was replaced by Hannington Alatoa, an indigenous citizen. There were concerns he would take a softer approach.

The Solomon Islands Leadership Code commissioner deliberately took a more conciliatory approach than his counterparts in PNG and Vanuatu. The original Leadership Code Commission (LCC) legislation, passed in 1981 and 1983 but strengthened in 1999, required all leaders to make a biannual declaration of their assets, directorships, and so on, as well as those of their spouses and children over age eighteen. A four-page form—inviting officials to list their directorships, shares, gifts, assets, and business transactions involving more than SI$500 (US$67)—was distributed to the estimated ten thousand people covered by the act, including all public servants. The act specified that leaders who accepted personal benefits by reason of their official position, or bribes, were guilty of "misconduct in office." So were leaders who faced a conflict of interest over their shareholdings. Leaders had to get permission from the LCC if companies they owned were to hold contracts with the government.

The first Leadership Code commissioner was Leonard Maenu'u, a former departmental head. He took the position that it was necessary to be realistic about the business interests of leaders (Larmour 2000b). Salaries were low, he said, and extended families put demands on them. The act allowed the LCC to take into account "the value to the development of Solomon Islands as a whole of the investment the leader has made" in deciding if a conflict of interest might occur. Shortages of skills —for example, in surveying—might make it appropriate for government professionals also to operate privately. If the lifestyles of leaders suggested that their expenditures were higher than the income they had declared, the commissioner could question them. As of 2000 the LCC had taken only six leaders to court, with several being acquitted and the others receiving fines of less than the SI$1,000 (US$134) maximum provided by the act.

The Financial Action Task Force published annual lists of "non-cooperative" countries, starting in 2000. The United States also sharply increased its own pressure on the offshore financial centers, as part of its counterterrorist activity after the attacks on 11 September 2001. Among South Pacific countries, Cook Islands, Marshall Islands, Niue, and Nauru appeared on the first FATF list. Being listed invoked countermeasures, including warning nonfinancial businesses dealing with listed countries that transactions might run the risk of involving money laundering. In December 2001, FATF members agreed to apply additional countermeasures to Nauru for its failure to abolish four hundred shell banks, which had no physical presence in the country.

Australia then found itself in an awkward position. Nauru had agreed to act as a processing center for intercepted asylum seekers heading for Australia—what the Howard government called the Pacific Solution. In exchange, Australia had offered aid and help in lobbying to have Nauru taken off the FATF blacklist (*Sydney Morning Herald*, 25 June 2002). A spokeswoman for the Australian foreign minister stated that the government would continue to support Nauru's anti-money-laundering capacity, while implementing the countermeasures.

As of March 2004, and in spite of passing domestic legislation against money laundering, Cook Islands and Nauru remained on the FATF blacklist, but Marshall Islands and Niue had been removed.

The Fate of Alternatives

It is hard to find local or indigenous alternatives to the reform programs promoted by donors and international agencies in the 1990s. The reform programs filled the policy space, and opposition or independent politicians offered no alternatives. However, PNG did experiment with "adjustment without loans." Under the proposals made by a former World Bank consultant, public funding was to be terminated for research, training, and other statutory institutions, and university funding was to be cut by 20 percent. Twenty-one national government departments were to be restructured, central and provincial staff were to be reduced by 20 percent, and police and defense staff were to be cut by 10 percent (Curtin 2000, 3). A layoff program covering about seven thousand staff members was supposed to start on 1 January 1999 but was repeatedly delayed as costs of implementing the layoffs increased to 150–200 million kina ($US46–62 million), without prospects of funding. The government also tried to boost log exports, while budget cuts limited the Forest Board's ability to supervise extraction. Its final effort was to send a delegation to Taiwan, offering recognition in exchange for credit. On 14 July 1999, after days of bargaining among MPs and last-minute switching of support, Mekere Morauta replaced Bill Skate as prime minister. Morauta then went back to negotiate with the World Bank.

7 Determinants of Transfer

What determines if transfer takes place? Here we sift through the episodes already recounted to see if patterns emerge. In the next chapter we will work more deductively, using concepts such as specificity and ownership. We will also go on to look at how transfer involves an exercise of power.

Timing and Crises

In each case that has been discussed, except perhaps customary land registration, the transfer was associated with a particular coming together of domestic and international circumstances. Two clocks were ticking, one domestic and one international, and they were only loosely connected. Influential external events included the collapse of the Soviet Union and the terrorist attacks on the United States on 11 September 2001.

In each case the transfer of institutions was associated with a crisis or perceptions of one. Yet a crisis is not self-evident. It may need to be talked up. PNG's first financial crisis, in 1981, was precipitated by a combination of external shocks and internal leaks of information. Political scientist David Kavanamur describes how PNG ministers had to be convinced that there was a crisis by the use of strong words like "bankrupt" in briefing papers (Kavanamur 1998, 112). The Asian Development Bank listed four triggers for its loan programs, which were made conditional on public sector reform. Two of them involved crises: Asian financial crises, and domestic fiscal crises caused by "overwhelming debt burdens and a ballooning public sector." Perceptions of crisis might precipitate transfer but also might make it more difficult to achieve. A 2002 report on the action plan of the Pacific Islands Forum economic ministers found that urgency caused countries to avoid making social impact assessments of economic reform (Pacific Islands Forum Secretariat 2002). Actions taken to resolve a fiscal crisis sometimes had unintended and negative consequences on recovery and reform. Governments in crisis were almost by definition unable to judge the quality of the proposals being pressed upon them, sometimes as a condition for the loans that would ensure their political survival. The better public servants might then accept retrenchment packages offered as part of public sector reform and return to the public employment as more expensive consultants. Further on, loan repayments might put a drag on recovery.

Proponents of policy transfer sometimes regretted the end of the crisis. PNG recovered so quickly in 1991 that the International Monetary Fund criticized the government for dragging its feet on drawing down the loan. But it was no longer needed as revenue grew from mining and exploration projects. Kavanamur concluded, "Whilst it is easy to stabilise PNG's economy, it is often difficult to sustain structural adjustment" (1998, 115). In 1995 what were then called the South Pacific Forum finance ministers (1995) agreed among themselves that "mechanisms are also required to protect the reform process from being undermined by temporary improvements in economic circumstances." Crisis was the occasion and the opportunity to slip in a much broader, but politically unpalatable, reform agenda.

Techniques and Processes

The transfer of constitutional ideas has tended to take place within political and legal elites and to rely on conference papers and journal articles (typically in English). The transfer of public sector reforms has been more combative and adversarial in style. Lines were drawn between the old and the new, with public administration academics often finding themselves among the defensive skeptics. Public sector reform has been spread through traditional conferencing and elite networking, but also through newer think tanks and consultancies and by the international financial institutions. Transparency International has two quite distinct styles of transfer. One style involves lobbying among governments and international organizations ("the suits"). The other is a more grassroots, populist style ("the streets") that relies heavily on the Internet for diffusion.

The transfers that were backed up by loan conditions or sanctions were somewhat coercive. Irrational mimetic transfers also took place—for example, in the adoption of Westminster constitutions. We also find many examples of the significant role of professions in transmitting their norms in relation to surveying, law, accounting, and economics.

In every case we find a mix of techniques: copying of laws; loan and aid conditions; consultancy; study tours; and training, workshops, and conventions. The range of practices is in fact quite limited. Beyond copying a law, making a loan, hiring a consultant, providing training and study tours, or holding a workshop or convention, there is not a lot that aid agencies can do. This is not to belittle what are complex and difficult tasks—except that they sometimes seem belittled in comparison with the grandiose programs to which they are attached. Nevertheless, operational technologies are not perennial. Each particular technique of government has its own history. We have seen that the first study tour in the South Pacific was the Tongan king's visit to New South Wales in 1853. The idea of national conventions, used in Hawai'i in the mid-nineteenth century, was influential in the constitutional negotiations of the 1960s and 1970s and resurged in the Asian Development Bank's public sector reforms in the 1990s. NGOs like Transparency International have introduced new techniques, drawn from the world of lobbying and public relations (table 10).

In chapter 3 we found reasons to think that transfer might not be an entirely rational process. Commissions of inquiry were tasked with considering alternatives and making recommendations about the best way of dealing with a problem or achieving an objective. The Commission of Enquiry into Land Matters and the Constitutional Planning Committee in Papua New Guinea had a rational style. So did Fiji's Constitution

TABLE 10. Transparency International's Techniques of Transfer

Technique	Method of transfer
Corruption Perceptions Index	Media
Bribe Payers Index	Media
Convention on bribing foreign officials	Lobbying
Successor to Lome Convention	Lobbying
Integrity Pact	Lobbying
National strategies	Workshops
Establishing national chapters	Handbook, training manual, workshops, seed funding

Review Commission, which made worldwide comparisons and explained its recommendations as means to achieve the end—particularly racial harmony—as set out in its terms of reference.

The decisions on what to adopt, however, were made elsewhere, and the results, as Peter Fitzpatrick (1980) complained of the Constitutional Planning Committee report, were surprisingly ordinary, in spite of the fuss. The Allan Commission on land tenure in Solomon Islands in 1957 recommended that customary land be registered as individually owned freehold, in the same way as alienated land had been. PNG's Commission of Enquiry into Land Matters recommended a qualified version of the Kenyan model that had outraged members of Parliament a few years earlier. For the constitutions, the Solomon Islands governing council system reverted to the Westminster type, and Cook Islands retained its Westminster constitution after a review in 1998.

Commissions did lead to some constitutional innovation, such as Kiribati's presidential/parliamentary hybrid, the land groups legislation in PNG, and the provisions for decentralization in Melanesia. But the search for innovation was confined within a perimeter of professionally acceptable thought. The virtues of land registration, constitutions, democracy, public sector reform, and corruption prevention were generally accepted as a given.

That rationalistic mode of transfer by commission of inquiry did not apply to public sector reform in the 1990s nor to Transparency International's transfer of anticorruption ideas. With regard to public sector reform, the banks, finance departments, and their consultants were confident they had the right answers. In any case, the atmosphere of crisis that brought them in did not lend itself to the creation of a commission of inquiry. The money was about to run out. Payrolls had to be cut, and government assets had to be sold to pay back the debts. Yet the rational consideration of means and ends was not completely set aside. The banks and donors funded a series of studies and consultancy reports, though decisions were not necessarily based on them. The banks and donors talked in a language of means and ends. And they were often willing, after the event, to evaluate what they had done and admit they had gotten it wrong.

TI's style differed from that of the commission of inquiry in another way. TI's was driven by anger at corruption and by impatience with rationalization. TI deferred to national differences and national initiatives, but it also had assembled its own body of doctrine, embodied in its *Source Book* and made available on the Internet (Pope 1996, 2000), and had devised new techniques, such as integrity pacts. Anticorruption campaigns are vulnerable to millenarian calls for national renewal and zero tolerance. Those calls may be right, but they are not rational in the sense of means/end calculations.

March and Olsen's research on policy making (1976, 1989) found policy makers reaching into a metaphorical garbage can for the first solution that comes to hand. More broadly, March and Olsen found that solutions were being produced independently of problems and that the links between problems and solutions depended on timing and opportunity as much as choice. Solutions ended up looking for problems to attach themselves to. The international financial institutions in this sense have been a storehouse of conventional ideas. They have had the opportunity to implement these ideas when countries in crisis have come to the institutions for a loan. TI has similarly been a storehouse of bright ideas about what to do about corruption. It has promoted its ideas laterally, by lobbying among international organizations. TI has also promoted its ideas with and through national chapters, which have lobbied their own governments from within. A similar sense of "solutions looking for problems" has surrounded customary land registration and public sector reform. Local crises provided the opportunity for solutions already in circulation to gain a foothold. The solutions were already there, on the shelf, waiting for a problem to arise. And although they may have been good ideas, it is not clear why they happened to be chosen—except that they were available, conformed to conventional wisdom, and were in good standing among the professional communities and consultants promoting them.

The list of solutions set out in reform programs and loan conditions have something of this garbage-can logic. These solutions include value-added taxes, output budgeting, and land registration. They are all perfectly good ideas, but they are only loosely linked to prior diagnoses. They might be the right ideas, but there is a weakness in the mechanisms used to test them and, just as important, to reject those found to be irrelevant. Research tends to come after the event, but even then it has little effect on professional support for conventional wisdom. Research on new public management in Brazil, for example, cast serious doubts on the relevance of NPM to developing countries (Tendler 1997). Research on land registration in Africa cast serious doubts on its ability to deliver development in the way that proponents of land registration had said it would (Platteau 1996). And practically no independent research has been conducted on the efficacy of TI's proposals for corruption prevention.

Behind this garbage-can process is the power of professional doctrine. In the case of land registration, the professionals were surveyors. In the case of Westminster constitutions, they were usually constitutional law-yers, but historians have also been influential in the South Pacific. Fewer professional interests have been at stake in the promotion of democracy, but the highly technical debate about voting systems may be a sign of growing professionalization among specialists on electoral systems. In the case of public sector reform, the professionals were accountants. TI in many ways has cut across the professions hitherto dominating the discussion of corruption and its control—the police and lawyers. TI's populist approach is antiprofessional, though TI draws on the emerging professions of media management and lobbying to get its points across.

Objects of Transfer

In chapter 3 we adopted a model of policy transfer, reserving the word "institution" for the intended results. Of the five cases examined, land registration is probably the one most easily understood as a policy—a rationalized account linking a recognized problem (land disputes and insecurity) with a proposal to solve it (registration) that nevertheless faced severe problems of implementation (funding, staffing, local resistance, sustainability). Public sector reforms were also presented as manifestations of considered judgments, at least after the first panicked responses to fiscal crises. Some anticorruption measures also had the character of policies. The world of aid in which those measures operated also demanded that government activity present itself as policy. Much effort and money were spent on producing written diagnoses of problems and formal statements of purposes.

Legislation was copied in each case. Land registration and the Westminster constitutions were explicitly legal projects. New accountability legislation was introduced as part of reform in Cook Islands (borrowing from New Zealand), and new ICAC legislation was proposed by Transparency International in PNG (borrowing from Hong Kong and Sydney).

The transfer of customary land registration was particularly legalistic. One of the reasons it failed was the absence of the administrative and commercial infrastructure necessary to make the law do the things it was supposed to. There were also transfers of laws in the constitutional negotiations, but for many years some parts of the constitutions—for example, leadership codes and rules governing political parties—were not legislated for. Changing the law was not easy, particularly in countries where the government was a coalition or a minority in the legislature. Changing the law was nevertheless often easier than making newly established agencies work or ensuring compliance.

Dolowitz and Marsh suggested that the thing transferred was "knowledge about policies, administrative arrangements, institutions and ideas" (2000, 5). Doctrines or counterdoctrines were embodied in texts, which were circulated at the time of the transfer or later, as justification of it in retrospect. Alan Ward's article on the "agricultural revolution" (1972) was particularly timely and influential in blocking land legislation in PNG. Ideas in transfer were often part of a broader framework that gave particular events and issues salience and meaning. Indeed, alternative frameworks could interpret the same events quite differently. Customary land tenure, for example, could be seen alternately as "evolving" or as "breaking down."

Shifting frameworks of meaning were involved in the transfers of public sector reforms. Put simply, the sale of government assets to pay debts and the dismissals of public servants to save salaries were presented as forward-looking policies of privatization and public sector reform.

Ideas of public choice and privatization were not simple and discrete. They amounted to quite elaborate bodies of doctrine that highlighted some issues as worthy of importance (unemployment, say, or inflation) while downplaying others. Each framework gave different meanings to the same event: a budget deficit might be explained and justified as necessary to maintain demand in a downturn in the business cycle. The same deficit might be explained and criticized as a result of rent seeking or a symptom of fiscal indiscipline. The government might continue to run deficits, however they were interpreted. The government might, for example, lack the capacity to monitor its spending, or it might be buffeted by external events. What was transferred was simply a way of explaining what was already happening for quite other reasons.

The cases also showed a vulnerability to panaceas. Historian Sione Latukefu (1975) faulted the Tongan king and the Tongan missionaries for believing that the constitution was a "magic wand" for Tonga's problems. Now changes in the electoral system—from first-to-the-post to alternative voting—are expected to diminish deep ethnic divisions. The cases also showed an unmet demand for "new ideas" that will cut through difficulties and leapfrog over problems, such as reengineering and reinvention. There has also been an excess of ideas. Pacific Islands economies have been thoroughly and repeatedly analyzed, often on the basis of shaky data, and island governments have tired of the succession of visiting missions and their demands for information.

Sources

The archaeology of the policy is only part of the story. Policies are transmitted through intermediate places and broader networks. Tonga's constitution borrowed from Hawai'i's, which in turn drew on those of the United States and the United Kingdom. There was greater interest in intraregional comparisons and solutions during the period immediately after independence. The academic consultants to PNG's Commission of Enquiry into Land Matters looked to New Zealand. Public sector reformers borrowed ideas more generally from OECD countries. In particular they looked to New Zealand, which was an extreme exemplar of public sector reform in global terms and in a strong position to influence its former colonies in the South Pacific.

Most of the cases of transfer were accomplished through complex networks rather than through a simple bilateral link. These networks had central places—London for the British Empire, Manila for the Asian Development Bank, Berlin for Transparency International—but the transfers did not only radiate out from these centers. Rather the network facilitated sideways, or South-South, transfers. The ideas about customary land registration that originated in the Sudan were developed in Kenya before being picked up in Melanesia.

As well as spreading outward along spokes of a wheel, there were transfers around the rim. PNG's Commission of Enquiry into Land Matters influenced its Solomon Islands counterpart in the mid-1970s, when consultants with experience in PNG and Solomon Islands influenced the development of policy in Vanuatu in the early 1980s. There was transfer round the rim when PNG provided technical assistance to Vanuatu to set up its first Ombudsman's Office. Indeed the Torrens title system on which it was based was invented in another colony, South Australia, and transferred to Britain only in the early twentieth century. The South Pacific was decolonized relatively late, so many of the constitutions that were used as models were from former colonies in Africa and Asia. Notably, the Leadership Code provisions were based on East African constitutions.

The imperial system became a looser network, the British Commonwealth, within which professional associations helped shift ideas, particularly about Westminster constitutions. Membership in international organizations like the World Bank and the Asian Development Bank tied independent states into networks of doctrine, best practice, and advice. TI self-consciously tried to create such a network, before going on to establish, or franchise, local chapters in particular countries. It used the Internet to coordinate its potentially diffuse activities and source book.

The networks were sustained by brokers and consultants. In relation to land tenure they formed a series of exclusive epistemic communities, recommending each other for jobs and promoting distinctive ideologies. The most significant professional group was lawyers, and law was particularly mobile. Economic ways of thinking influenced proposals for land registration in the 1980s and public sector reform in the 1990s, and they continue to influence thinking about corruption prevention. Accountants were just as influential in public sector reform. Academic historians were also influential in constitutional transfers.

Melanesia has a long-running pattern of borrowing from and comparison—positive and negative—with Africa. Ideas about land registration, as we have seen, were deliberately copied from Africa. So were constitutional innovations, such as leadership codes. Tanzania's constitution influenced PNG's (Goldring 1978, 19–20). Decolonization and subsequent financial crises came later in the South Pacific than in Africa, and both positive and negative references to African experiences were made during constitutional debates in the South Pacific and later with regard to structural adjustment and public sector reform. At other times the comparisons were negative and disparaging: it was said that the region was "not like Africa" and "would not go down that path."

Scholars sometimes also saw Melanesian institutions through an African lens. I am guilty of that too, drawing the idea of institutional transfer from Apter's writing on the Gold Coast. Of the ideas about politics discussed in chapter 1, only the cargo cult is a Melanesian original, now gone global. The homegrown constitution was devised to protect the Pacific Islands from what were seen as the problems Africa had faced with the Westminster model. Theories of the postcolonial state and models for a leadership code came from East Africa. Several of Hobsbawm and Ranger's invented traditions (1983) were African. MacWilliam's research on indigenous capital (1986) draws explicitly on African models. The World Bank first used the word "governance" in a report on sub-Saharan Africa, and the structural adjustment programs visited on PNG and ADB's island-members in the 1990s were first tried in Africa in the 1980s. Anthropologist J. A. Barnes (1990) questioned the use of "African models in the PNG highlands." He was not against comparison, but he faulted his colleagues for comparing the "muddled configurations of actual alliance, cooperation and conflict observed in the field" with highly abstract and simplified models derived from African research. In doing so, Barnes asserted, they had missed "distinctively non-African characteristics of the highlands" (ibid., 45), including the multiple allegiances of individuals and the high value placed on violence. Political science in the South Pacific has continued to turn back to Africa for ideas about "weak states" (Dauvergne 1998), "indigenous capital" (MacWilliam 2002), "criminalisation of the state" (Dinnen 2001, 2002), or simply "Africanisation" (Reilly 2000). However, Denoon (1999) describes the Sandline mercenaries as finding that the South Pacific was "not like Africa" after all. There is now some flow in the opposite direction, with adviser Anthony Regan bringing his PNG constitutional experience to bear on Uganda.

Borrowing from Nowhere

Place-to-place transfers were combined with "placeless" sources in texts and arguments from first principles. Knetsch and Trebilcock's report on land policy (1981) influenced PNG government policy in the early 1980s. Although the authors drew on research on American Indian land tenure, their argument proceeded from the universal assumption that farmers made rational choices. The Tongan constitution drew on the Bible as well as Hawai'i's constitution, and Latin American liberation theology influenced PNG's Constitutional Planning Committee. The constitution written for the Nagriamel rebels in Vanuatu was published in Amsterdam and devised from libertarian first principles. The academic advisers to Fiji's Constitution Review Commission based their arguments on the evidence of the application of alternative voting in other countries, but they also relied on arguments from first principles about how rational candidates would respond to the incentives that the electoral system presented to them. Transparency International's *Source Book* cited examples from particular places but also proposed new doctrines of its own, such as integrity pacts.

Arguments from first principles were buttressed by anecdotal evidence from a particular country. Or a particularly national experience was generalized into an abstract principle. The idea of "international best practice" combined place and nonplace.

In Fiji the arguments from first principles were subsequently reinforced by advice from a particular place, Australia. Its Australian provenance was not strongly emphasized by the Constitution Review Commission, except to reassure against criticisms of exoticism. Once the constitution was implemented, however, the Labour Party in Fiji turned to its counterparts in Australia for advice, in particular about the effects of distributing preferences.

The involvement of international organizations in the transfer of ideas, policies, and institutions contributes to their placelessness. The British Empire facilitated lateral transfers, as well as implanting English institutions in colonized countries. The Commonwealth now promotes good governance. The Organisation for Economic Co-operation and Development has promoted ideas about public sector management and, more recently, reforms against money laundering. The World Bank casts itself as an "ideas bank." Its annual *World Development Report* sets the agenda for thinking about development. Countries wishing to join the European Union must first adopt its institutions. The World Trade Organization encourages its members to adopt more liberal economic policies. In the South Pacific, Australia has pushed the Pacific Islands Forum finance ministers to adopt a set of principles about accountability and to review each other's performance in achieving them.

Corruption prevention is the most extreme example of reforms devised and driven by an international organization. Whereas the World Bank and the ADB became vehicles or conduits for transfers among their members, Transparency International was set up as an international non-governmental organization precisely and only to promote reform. Its earliest targets included other international organizations (OECD, EU), as well as national governments. It has its antecedents in the churches, missions, and abolitionist societies of the nineteenth century, which also argued from first principles in the Bible and promoted ideas that had not yet been tried anywhere.

Borrowing from the Past

Transfer depended on prior conditions, but the burden of history seems to have been different in each case. Timing mattered, and exhaustion with older policies created opportunities for newer ones. The countries in the South Pacific are not only peripheral but also relative latecomers to human settlement, colonization, and decolonization. They could thus learn from their predecessors, if channels were available and they wanted to do so.

The history of land alienation in PNG, Solomon Islands, and Vanuatu created a strong distrust of government motives in customary land registration. The Melanesian constitutions' provisions about land, for example, allowed the legislature to reverse colonial legislation and return some alienated land to its traditional owners.

The constitutions inserted themselves into a game that had been under way for some time. Almost everywhere in the Pacific Islands, colonial bureaucracies and legislatures were already well established. The transfers were incremental. The constitutions reframed the relationship between the bureaucracies and the legislatures and added new elements to it. In a sense the bulk of the institutional transfer had already taken place. And in their land provisions, the Melanesian constitutions sought to create opportunities to reject or reconsider the transfers that had already taken place. They aimed to reverse history.

History is often conceptualized as a conservative force setting constraints on choices, as when institutional economists talk about path dependency. In the cases in the Pacific Islands, the past was also seen as something to be rejected or improved upon. In Solomon Islands and PNG the turn to the Kenyan model was driven by a recognition that existing legislation was not working. The alternatives promoted by the Institute of National Affairs in the 1980s and the land registration legislation drafted for East Sepik and East New Britain were also conscious of past failures. The independence constitutions were generally built on the frameworks of late colonial constitutions, but the orientation was toward the future and toward imagining difficulties that might come up.

For public sector reformers and anticorruption activists, the past was something to push against: "The basic machinery of economic management with which [the Pacific Islands] came to political and economic independence stagnated during the 1970s and 1980s, concentrating on managing aid programs, and compiling detailed (but little used) development plans, and becoming increasingly out of touch with political and commercial reality" (A. V. Hughes 1998a, 51). Public sector reformers did not show much interest in learning from past attempts at reform. The new public management generally takes an adversarial stance toward the past and is suspicious of public servants' ability to reform their own activities. Its impulse in Cook Islands and Vanuatu was partly a radical rejection of the past—it traded on popular understandings that "we can't go on like this."

Issues of timing and sequencing were important in transfer, as well as who got there first. In these cases, the Westminster model had the clear advantage of being there first.

Borrowing from the Future

Early versions of customary land registration were strongly forward-looking, imagining a common future in which indigenous farmers and settlers would share a common tenure system. The idea of customary land registration was sometimes presented as "evolutionary," assuming that changes were taking place that the law might anticipate and channel. However, Ward (1972) later warned against the Kenyan model as an "agricultural revolution."

Borrowing from the United States (or, until 1989, the Soviet Union) meant, for many countries, to borrow from their own future to some extent. For colonies the highest form of modernity was often vaguely represented by the metropolis, perhaps London or Australia's modernist capital, Canberra. Because such metropolises were also real places, it was possible to see how ideas borrowed from them actually worked in practice. The king of Tonga, for example, was shocked by the poverty he found in New South Wales.

The nineteenth-century Tongan constitution looked toward the future in its grant of adult male suffrage and the transformation of land tenure that accompanied it. Yash Ghai (1997) described how the PNG constitution was meant to create the new conditions for its own success. Although the constitution failed, it paradoxically survived: "The system which it intended to create did not exist but had to be called into being" (ibid., 312).

Fiji's Constitution Review Commission had similar ambitions. The public sector reforms promoted by the ADB were couched in forward-looking terms—they were sold as once-and-for-all reforms that would clean up government. Transparency International's approach also borrowed heavily from the future. The downside to these utopian aspirations was pervasive disappointment, as well as elite calls for more "political education" to align popular aspirations with their own.

What Makes Transferred Institutions Stick

Sideways relationships with other institutions seem to be as important as downward relationships with clients and society in making institutions stick. A system of land registration, for example, needs to mesh with the existing system of courts and agricultural extension services, as well as to have something to offer its clients.

The persistence of constitutions in the South Pacific, and their restoration when overthrown, depended as much on sideways pressure from other states as on domestic pressure from below. The regime in Fiji needed international recognition, and the process of designing what became the 1998 constitution was funded by foreign aid. International pressure on Solomon Islands, along with guarded support for Manasseh Sogavare's government, kept up an appearance of constitutionalism after the coup in 2000.

The leadership code commissions took different approaches to seeking support and survival of their constitutions. PNG's commission took politicians to task in a series of reports and legal actions. Solomon Islands saw itself providing confidential advice to politicians and avoided soliciting popular complaints. Vanuatu's commission took a very public, confrontational role, so that Parliament eventually clipped its wings.

The survival of the constitutions—and, more generally, of democracy —and the fate of public sector reform suggest that it is not simply popular support that matters, but also a specific compact or political settlement between powerful social forces. The word "compact" was used by Fiji's Constitution Review Commission to describe the underlying agreement between ethnic groups upon which a constitution might be built. The Tongan constitution embodied such a settlement between the king and the other chiefs he had triumphed over, who were embodied in the constitution as "nobles." Another part of that settlement was the introduction of a new force into the political arena, that of commoners, whom the constitution enfranchised. Independence constitutions in Melanesia embodied settlements between regions—for example, in the Bougainville Agreement that ushered in provincial government in PNG and in provincial government in Solomon Islands. In Vanuatu, by contrast, a brief civil war at independence defeated secessionists in Espíritu Santo and Tanna, so constitutional commitments to decentralization were weaker. These compacts or settlements stabilized institutions for periods of ten to twenty years but were vulnerable to erosion or sheer mismanagement. Fiji's 1970 constitution embodied an agreement between leaders of ethnic groups, and no stable successor has yet to emerge.

Corporatist pacts between the government, peak organizations in the private sector, and NGOs were part of the Asian Development Bank's approach to public sector reform. Transparency International promoted a coalition-building approach to corruption prevention. Both approaches depended on a capacity for self-organization among the groups. The collapse of efforts to register land in PNG in the 1970s also led to a corporatist response from the private sector through its think tank, the Institute of National Affairs, which promoted reform. Governments tried to organize the private sectors—for example, by setting up chambers of commerce in Vanuatu. An autonomous "civil society"—existing somewhere between the government and family or clan-based organizations—may in fact depend heavily on government recognition and support.

The military and (in Solomon Islands) the police and militia were the greatest threat to constitutionalism in Melanesia. In PNG, military interventions tended to protect the institutional interests and autonomy of the armed forces—their pay and living conditions and (in Lae) the control of an airfield. PNG troops also mutinied over public sector reform, particularly a proposal to downsize the army. Troops then explicitly complained about the role of the World Bank. Similarly, the police in Vanuatu, in pursuit of the resolution of a pay dispute, kidnapped a minister.

In Solomon Islands and Fiji, military intervention has been directed for or against wider compacts or political settlements. In 1987 the army in Fiji acted against a change of government that upset the army's understanding of the balance of ethnic power established with independence in 1970. The army also showed little enthusiasm for suppressing the civilian coup of 2000, which challenged the new compact supposedly established by the 1998 constitution. In Solomon Islands, Malaitan elements in the police intervened to depose Ulufaʻalu on the grounds that he was not sufficiently defending the regional balance established at independence, which had allowed Malaitan settlement on other islands. That 1978 settlement was under pressure, as Guadalcanal people began to evict Malaitans from their land in the 1990s.

Determining Factors

Sometimes factors facilitating or constraining transfer were expressed negatively, as the absence of factors supposed to be important in the West. Thus Bale and Dale argued that developing countries should be cautious of borrowing the New Zealand model of new public management because it depended on the prior existence of "a tradition of politically neutral, relatively competent civil service; little concern about corruption or nepotism; a consistent and well-enforced legal code, including contract law; a well functioning political market; and a competent, but suppressed, private sector" (1988, 116). There is some truth in this picture of New Zealand, but also a danger of idealization. A country's self-image is used as the objective standard for judging another: "you are not like what we like to think we are." And difference is automatically turned into deficit.

Factors facilitating or constraining transfer were sometimes anticipated as risks to a program. In both the Federated States of Micronesia and Marshall Islands the ADB correctly anticipated risks in a lack of domestic capacity, a loss of political will, and a failure of the private sector to take up the opportunities presented to it. PNG's Forestry Conservation Program also accurately identified risks to its implementation. It saw a high risk that representatives of existing landowner companies would undermine the more participatory machinery proposed under the program, and a modest risk that "inappropriate changes" would be made to forest policy, presumably by the government (Filer 2000, 52).

Geographical Conditions

Islands are not necessarily isolated. They stand in a medium of communication. Sociologist Epeli Hau'ofa (1993) has asserted that "isolation" is a convenient external perception that fails to see the ocean as linking rather than separating. The ocean was the medium through which Polynesian chieftaincy was diffused and through which the islands were linked into the world economy by maritime trade. In World War II the islands became stepping-stones along which social changes and cargo cults were transported.

Smallness also tipped the islands toward regional institutions that provided networks through which ideas could be diffused. The colonial South Pacific Commission provided the prototype. The University of the South Pacific was set up as a regional institution, because each member state was regarded as too small to justify its own. It was modeled on a similar university in the Caribbean. Once in place, USP became a useful network through which ideas, particularly about land registration, could be transmitted. However, the costs of joining regional organizations, and suspicion of oversight, deterred Nauru and Tonga from joining the United Nations. Nauru proved adept, however, at joining the international network of shady banking when the country became a tax haven.

Social Conditions

The transfer of customary land registration was based on the evolutionary theory that social conditions were flowing in the direction of the introduced policy. Custom was breaking down and becoming more individualized: the introduced legislation would encourage this process, as much as drive it.

Explaining the success of the Pacific model of constitutionalism in the early 1980s, Greg Fry (1982) identified several reasons why force had not been used to change governments, including the absence of military forces (outside Fiji and PNG) and the persistence of chiefly authority in Polynesia. Most important, Fry believed, was the proliferation of ethnic groups, so that they had to form coalitions in order to achieve power and ensure that no group felt it might be permanently excluded. By the same token, Fry presciently concluded that the threats to constitutional changes of government would come from the development of political out-groups based on ethnicity or region. The exceptions, since Fry's writing, have to some extent proved the rule. When the military intervention of 1997 and George Speight's civilian coup of 2000 took place in Fiji, the country was divided between two large ethnic groups, one or the other of which feared permanent marginalization. Similarly, by the time the Malaitan Eagle Force aligned itself with the police to compel a change of government in Solomon Islands in 2000, ethnic politics had become polarized around Malaitans versus Gwale. There was probably also a demonstration effect, as militants in Solomon Islands took their cue from Fiji's coup several months before.

The comparative work on the social conditions of democracy by Rueschemeyer, Stephens, and Stephens (1992) did not include the South Pacific, but their conclusions can explain something of the pattern of democracy's emergence and setbacks in the region. The authors (henceforth abbreviated as "RSS") start with landlords whose labor-repressive systems of agriculture, RSS argue, make the landlords hostile to democracy. RSS show that the push for democracy tends to come from the new working classes, which (being small) need allies. Thus RSS disagree with those who see the middle classes as bearers of democracy: the middle classes may jump either way, based in part on their perception of longer-term threats from the working class. Parties play an important role in moderating perceived threats. Perceived class interests and allegiances are socially constructed, and what happens in one place may provide a model for others. Once a particular pattern is established, it may be hard to shift, so conditions for the establishment of democracy may be different from those for its maintenance.

Thus RSS explain the correlation between democracy and development in terms of relative class power. Capitalist development tends to open up spaces for democracy and creates new classes to press for its realization or frustration. These democratic opportunities, however, are also determined by state, and interstate, structures of power. History matters in the sense that the outcome depends on the sequence of the interaction. Existing patterns constrain future possibilities, but institutionalization takes time to achieve. RSS's three factors involved in the success of democracy—relative class power, relative autonomy of the state, and international circumstances—and their interaction and sequencing provide a framework for considering the social bases of democracy in the South Pacific.

In RSS's analysis, landlords will be more antidemocratic "the more they rely on state-backed coercion rather than on the working of the market" to control their labor force (ibid., 60). The landlords are also under threat from peasants with small or no landholdings "because they demand land more frequently than workers insist on control of the means of production" (ibid.). There are two typical candidates for labor-repressive landlords in the South Pacific: chiefs and big plantation owners.

In the more extreme forms of precontact Polynesian chieftaincy, particularly in Hawai'i, chiefs dispossessed kinship groups and claimed to own the land themselves. Stratification was also taking place in Tonga. Elsewhere in Polynesia, kinship, the need for popular support in competition with other chiefs, and the possibility of popular rebellion kept relationships between chiefs and commoners more even and interdependent. Tribute was repaid in various ways, and chiefs could not in practice dispossess those who failed to pay (Kirch 1989).

Paradoxically, the earliest form of adult male suffrage emerged from one of the more stratified traditional systems in Tonga. Clearly it was part of a (continuing) struggle in which the king must often appeal for popular support against the nobles who might challenge him again. Although chiefs in the systems in Samoa or Fiji may claim some of the systems' product, they do not own the land and they cannot dispossess people from it nor alienate the land itself.

The second typical candidates for antidemocratic landlords were the big plantation owners: Unilever in Solomon Islands, the Colonial Sugar Refining Company in Fiji, the Société Française des Nouvelles Hébrides, and so on. Their political power was based not on feudal hangovers but on their centrality in the early colonial political economy, particularly as a source of government revenue. However, like feudal landlords, the plantation owners had little interest in expanding democracy to include representatives of labor, the landless, or smallholders.

There is a faint relationship between the extent of alienation and the lateness or failure of responsible government (Larmour 1994). Generally, countries with less alienated land achieved universal suffrage in the 1960s and responsible executives in the 1970s. In the countries with more alienated land, responsible executives were achieved relatively late (Vanuatu) or interrupted (Fiji, which also had the most alienated land). However, two of the countries with the most alienated land also achieved universal suffrage relatively early: Guam in the 1930s and New Caledonia in the 1950s. The reasons there lie in metropolitan rather than local circumstances.

The other side of relative class power is the working class, defined in terms of its reliance on selling its labor to subsist, without the guarantees provided by membership in a landholding group. This working class grew in plantations and mines, which provided both the circumstances and opportunity to organize for narrowly industrial goals and for wider political goals such as democracy (which may then be instrumental in promoting industrial goals like minimum wages and health and safety legislation).

In addition to relative class power, RSS propose two other factors to explain the success of democracy: the relative autonomy of the state, and international circumstances. A state highly dependent on landowners, for example, will be more resistant to democracy. Landowners in Fiji, for instance, had a relatively privileged place in the state and saw their interests as intertwined with the state. In other parts of the region, colonial states listened closely to the views of settlers or of large plantation or mining interests. Elsewhere colonial states acted relatively autonomously. The postwar international climate was sympathetic to democracy, particularly after the end of the cold war. The United Nations promoted decolonization and supervised elections—for example, in PNG and the U.S. Trust Territory of the Pacific Islands (which became Palau, the Northern Mariana Islands, Marshall Islands, and the Federated States of Micronesia). U.S. strategic interests still set ultimate boundaries on the exercise of democracy in Micronesia.

RSS identified the social conditions for democracy, but their concern with the balance of domestic forces and the role of international factors also helps make sense of anticorruption activity. TI's doctrine assumes the existence of a middle-class civil society, with the time available to act as volunteers, critical of the government and driven by moral outrage. Such a civil society emerged briefly in PNG over the Sandline affair and was visible in support for the Citizens' Constitutional Forum in Fiji. This sort of civil society depends crucially on international support, as well as on technological developments like the Internet that allow international support to be mobilized. It is also fluid and unevenly developed.

Organizational Conditions

A policy of customary land registration depended in the first instance on the existence of a government lands department, able and willing to carry out surveys and fieldwork. The absence of such a department at independence meant that Vanuatu, for example, could not implement customary land registration even if it wanted to—there were surveyors and a land registry, but no capacity to carry out sustained investigations of ownership. The presence or absence of a legal profession also had an important impact on the implementation of many provisions of the independence constitutions.

Constitutional provisions requiring that Parliament vote for the head of government were designed to overcome what was thought to be a gap in the organizational conditions for success of the Westminster model—the absence of strong political parties. In Kiribati, for example, politicians were elected "on the basis of personal achievements rather than as representatives of any party, organisation, policy class or ideology" (Macdonald 1996, 6). Hence there was a high turnover of members of Parliament, who were acutely conscious of the fickle moods of their electorates, and governments were loose coalitions of individuals, without distinctive or long-term commitments to particular policies. Nevertheless Macdonald saw evidence of parties evolving (ibid., 24). Legislation in PNG in 2000 tried to strengthen parties.

The proponents of alternative voting in Fiji had been quite specific about the conditions under which they expected AV to lead to accommodative behavior in which leaders took into account the interests and feelings of ethnic groups other than their own: ethnically heterogeneous constituencies; multiple parties, within and cutting across ethnic groups; and electoral incentives. The Constitution Review Commission had sought to ensure the first by providing for large, multimember constituencies. But experts canvassed at a workshop held at the ANU in Canberra were concerned about whether AV would act as predicted in multimember seats (Lal and Larmour 1997). In the end, the seats were single-member, and after the election there was some disagreement about whether they had been sufficiently heterogeneous. However, there was certainly a proliferation of parties.

Public sector reform was based on a fatal reliance on the institutions it condemned: those institutions most in need of reform were, by that token, the least able to deliver it. Consultants filled the gap, sometimes with their own transferred ideas. Other institutions that were invoked—such as the private sector and NGOs—were also often weak or under stress. In relation to public sector reform, the ADB concluded that it had been "unduly optimistic" about the capacity of the private sector: "Contraction of the public service has led to contraction of the private sector" (Knapman and Saldhana 1999, 77).

Implementation

A policy may fail for many reasons other than its foreign origins. The most often cited factor constraining transfer was lack of skilled, qualified, and motivated staff. The assessment made for the Pacific Islands Forum economic ministers also found a shortage of human and financial capacity to be an important barrier to implementation.

Even homegrown policies have faced problems of implementation: lack of resources, lack of attention, official misinterpretation, and so on. The alternative approaches to customary land registration adopted in Solomon Islands and Vanuatu are hard to staff and resource. Similarly, transferred policies may be welcomed but may fail for reasons other than their origins. There might be no nationalist objection to an ombudsman (the persistence of the Swedish term for the position suggests that its foreignness was not something to be disguised). But the official in charge of the leadership code might interpret the role as to be privately supportive of politicians rather than publicly critical of them, as happened in Solomon Islands.

We could dissolve the problem of institutional transfer into a more general theory of implementation. In this sense, introduced policies failed because all policies failed. Poor countries lacked the ability to implement policies, wherever they came from. Conditionality was found to work best if the government (or at least the finance department) was committed to reform. Institutional strengthening worked best for already strong institutions. But the argument tends toward redundancy—transfer worked best when there was no real need for transfer.

Where introduced institutions survived, it was often by coexisting with indigenous ones rather than replacing them. Introduced systems of land tenure, for example, coexisted with indigenous ones in Melanesia. They extended only over parts of the country, which remained divided into two classes of land, one of which remained customary. The research on customary land registration in Solomon Islands, for example, also found that indigenous ways of doing things persisted even when the land was registered. Unregistered dealings took place, and the register increasingly diverged from what was happening on the ground. In Vanuatu—and to a lesser extent in Solomon Islands, PNG, and Fiji—alienated land was returned to traditional ownership after independence.

Tonga was exceptional in thoroughly reforming its tenure system in the nineteenth century. Yet even in Tonga there were debates about how to deal with custom in the legal system. Elsewhere an uneasy formal dualism persisted. Samoa was the pioneer, but in the 1990s Samoan intellectuals began to question the 1962 constitution as "unfinished business." Malama Meleisea (1987) pointed to opportunistic appeals: defeated in the traditional arena, a person might turn to introduced ones, and vice versa. Yet it is probably unrealistic to imagine a single moral community that is fully "traditional" or fully "modern." In addition, most countries in the world are now multicultural, and Samoans themselves are minorities in New Zealand, Australia, and the United States. Living in several worlds is now a common condition, and Tully's discussion of "treaty constitutions" (1995) suggested ways in which indigenous constitutions may be relevant to the contemporary dilemmas of multiculturalism.

Consistency with Local Values

Legislation to individualize land tenure clearly and deliberately challenged some local attitudes and values about land. Student leaders and NGOs in PNG easily appealed to attitudes and values against private and foreign ownership in 1995, forcing the government and the World Bank to back away from the Land Mobilisation Programme. Mistrust was also amplified by the history of registration, which up until then had been reserved for settlers on alienated land and seemed only to confirm the loss of land. Registration also showed that a gap might exist between attitudes and behavior—land use was often individual rather than communal, and there was a clear backlog demand from individuals for lease-leaseback arrangements that would effectively register their ownership.

Barrie Macdonald (1996) found that indigenous values in Kiribati affected politics and government in many ways. A low-key, egalitarian, and consultative style of leadership was favored, and the high cultural value put on personal independence and self-reliance made negotiations about aid conditions particularly embarrassing (ibid., 16–17, 33).

Fijian nationalists argued that attitudes of deference to chiefs and of racial solidarity would undermine the new constitution. Widespread consultation about a constitution did not necessarily, in and of itself, lead to distinct or indigenous outcomes. It might simply serve to explain the values of an introduced constitution and inculcate them in the committee and the population. A frequent criticism of representative democracy was that it restricted participation to election campaigns and allowed representatives to live in the capital while ignoring their constituents. This style of government was contrasted with the more participatory style of face-to-face village meetings, when leaders lived among their followers and were subject to sanctions, even assassination, if they failed to perform.

Provisions for stronger local government, procedures like referenda, and (in Kiribati) the requirement that national legislation be considered on outer islands before being put to a final vote were designed to increase participation. Parliamentary committees that toured the country, holding meetings in every village, were another attempt to increase or restore participation.

Some current local values were themselves introduced. The reports from Vanuatu's ombudsman commissioner typically began with a quote from the Bible. Kalev Crossland, first counsel to the commission, commented that "while it may sit oddly with western audiences," the use of biblical metaphors and moralistic judgments were an appropriate reflection of the Christian context of Vanuatu (Crossland 2000).

It was also possible for people to share quite inconsistent values—and for transfer to take advantage of this. In Kenya, Jean Ensminger's research (1992) had found that old men, for example, might hold comfortably to patriarchal attitudes, except when their daughters were affected. Farmers might believe in communal ownership and the emotional security it provided, while at the same time being irritated by the demands made on them by their kinsfolk. One of the difficulties with anticorruption programs was that people might be in favor of their MPs spending money on a local project or helping their relatives get a job, yet at the same time be strongly opposed to "corruption."

Subjective attitudes and values were not necessarily immutable. TI cheerfully confronted the argument that corruption is an expression of traditional values and focused its campaigning and media skills on changing attitudes. PNG's draft 1998 ICAC legislation, a result of pressure from a local TI group, includes a section entitled "Custom Not to Be a Defence" that says bluntly: "In any proceedings for a relevant offence, it shall not be a defence to show that corruption is customary in any profession, trade, vocation, calling, area of the country, or tribal or family group."

Reformers in PNG and the Pacific Islands also drew on attitudes of cynicism and disillusionment with politicians (so, over the PNG land conditions, could the critics of reform). There was also cynicism about advisers, promoting "reforms" that their consultancy company was well-placed to provide.

Radical Ambition

Socialist traditions of transformation were influential in some parts of the region. Trades unions flourished for a time in Kiribati, Fiji, New Caledonia, Cook Islands, Solomon Islands, and PNG. Liberation theology and progressively minded constitutional advisers were influential in the making of the PNG constitution, which included radical, transformative goals, partly borrowed from Tanzania.

Yash Ghai's gloomy assessment (1997) of PNG's constitution showed that the possibility of transfer also depended on the degree to which a constitution aimed simply to reflect local conditions or rather to reform or transform them. Writing about Ethiopia, Rene David (1963), a specialist in civil law, criticized what he called the sociological approach to law, which specified that the law must be aligned with local customs. Instead, he said, Ethiopians were living in a revolutionary period, looking for "a total renewal of the basis of their society": "[Their new Civil Code] aims at the perfection of society, and not only to a static statement of behaviour observed by a sociologist. For these reasons it is apparent that it was doubtlessly necessary to take customs into account, but it was necessary to keep this accounting limited, and not to fear changing them" (ibid., 194).

PNG's founding fathers gestured in this direction, seeing their constitution as contributing to a wider and more fundamental process of "integral human development." The Vanuatu reforms were self-consciously "comprehensive" because a combination of policies could be "mutually reinforcing." "Reform" became a popular slogan, open to many interpretations but signaling a comprehensive break with the past.

(Mis)Understanding

Constitutional provisions—for example, those dealing with human rights—might be adopted without a full understanding of their implications. The ADB's review of its public sector reforms found "no real understanding of the program" in the Federated States of Micronesia (Knapman and Saldhana 1999, 62). Joan Nelson's study of political commitment to economic reform (1984) paid particular attention to the economic doubts of local leaders as well as their political fears. The problem was not simply that leaders lacked an understanding of economics but that the ideas themselves were often counterintuitive. Exchange rates, for example, were regarded as values to be politically determined rather than prices that should be set at a market-clearing level. More generally and throughout the developing world, Nelson noted, "most officials and intellectuals and much of the public tend to doubt that the profit motive can be socially constructive, view middlemen as unproductive and exploitative, and place considerable confidence in the efficacy of state economic controls to pursue national goals" (ibid., 988).

Suspicion of markets and belief in government controls certainly underlay resistance to land registration. Journalist Rowan Callick criticized NGOs for the "aggressive disinformation campaign" they spread concerning the land conditions in PNG (Filer 2000, 35). Elites in the South Pacific were often quick to recommend "political education" when the masses were unconvinced. Yet the masses' fears were not unrealistic. Early versions of customary land registration promoted in Melanesia were frankly individualistic and were seen as a way of tipping rural institutions in favor of energetic entrepreneurs. That was a perfectly justifiable program, but it should not be surprising that it was opposed by people who saw themselves as losing out. An early scheme in Solomon Islands, for example, strengthened the position of a group of in-migrants against the claims of the traditional owners who had granted them permission to farm —and it aroused bitter resistance from the owners' spokesmen (Maenu'u 1979). Behind that was the not unreasonable fear that land would be alienated and consolidated—that is, after all, what the early reformers wanted. Similarly, popular questioning of the need for a national constitution, its relevance, or its specific provisions, such as guarantees of freedom of movement, were not necessarily signs of ignorance but signs of disagreement with a project that clearly meant a lot to politicians and officials in the capital city but had little immediate local relevance.

Individual Interpretations and Refusals

Research on land registration found individuals routinely ignoring the register. Yet there was a continuing demand for registration by individuals in PNG. In many cases the personalities of individuals who interpreted the offices or roles prescribed by constitutions strongly determined the results. In interpreting the role of a leadership code commissioner, Leonard Maenu'u, for example, was much more sympathetic to politicians in Solomon Islands than Marie-Noelle Ferrieux-Patterson was of politicians in Vanuatu. Sir Mekere Morauta was much more attractive to bankers than was his predecessor, Bill Skate. The World Bank's consultants in PNG occasionally defected or blew the whistle.

Sometimes proponents of reform seemed surprised at the motives of the individual actors they had prescribed institutions for. Supporters of transfer often called for a revolutionary change of heart to support the institutions they commended. Brij Lal concluded, "The 1997 constitution did not fail. The people of Fiji failed the constitution" (2002, 161). Anti-corruption reformers sought to induce radical changes in individuals—through integrity pledges and awareness campaigns—that would complement changes in institutions. New types of people would be required before new institutions could work.

These individual interpretations and refusals suggest that images of foreign flowers or constitutional engineering may grant institutions too much solidity, organic or inorganic. The fate of customary land registration, constitutions, and public sector reform showed institutions to be quite ephemeral and personal, like the script of a play that has to be enacted and reenacted by unruly groups of actors. The particular group of actors may be preoccupied with existing private and family matters and thus find it hard to concentrate on the script. The language may be unfamiliar. The actors may not necessarily believe the lines they are saying and may behave in unscripted ways. Or they may not understand the script fully. The script is easy to publish, like a law, but harder to get people to adhere to, day in and day out. Actors interpret their roles differently, as leadership code commissioners did in Solomon Islands, and ombudsmen in Vanuatu. The actors may simply walk off the stage, like the registered landowners who don't use the register. The fate of constitutions in Fiji and Solomon Islands also showed the actors' vulnerability to personal violence and intimidation.

Combining Effects of the Factors

Customary land registration was burdened by the history of land alienation, which made people suspicious of government intervention. Nevertheless, the social conditions of agriculture, particularly in coffee production, created a local demand for registration. It was, however, difficult to muster political support in the face of suspicion. The policy was sustained by a series of networks: colonial and academic networks, think tanks, and the World Bank. The internal characteristics of the policy were generally conducive to transfer. It was available off the shelf. Lands departments were already in place to carry it out, except in Vanuatu. It had been tested in other places, though research in Africa was beginning to question its usefulness. It began with the ambition to individualize tenure or to support an individualization that was thought to be happening anyway. To that extent, it was inconsistent with local values (though not necessarily local behavior). It was also radical and was criticized by Alan Ward (1972) for being "revolutionary." Later versions were less ambitious, aiming to reflect existing group ownership rather than transform it.

The Westminster constitutions were also available off the shelf and had been tested elsewhere. However, some of their features fitted uneasily with local social conditions and values, which were in any case often fluid or emergent. There were continuing conflicts with traditional leadership and conflicts over human rights. Although there were many arguments for having a constitution—and these arguments were made by constitutional planning committees—they were complicated and often had little impact on everyday life. There was no single coherent statement of doctrine.

Representative democracy faced slightly different tests from constitutionalism. Chiefly political traditions in much of Polynesia were unsympathetic to it, while there was nostalgia in Melanesia for a more participatory, face-to-face style of government. Working classes were small, except in Fiji, where ethnic divisions reduced democracy's chances. Representative democracy depended on international support—most visibly, for example, in the foreign aid that flowed toward constitutional change in Fiji in the 1990s. Yet democracy expanded its reach in Samoa, and a pro-democracy movement established itself in Tonga, getting some support from overseas NGOs.

Public sector reform faced a generally negative set of conditions, though it could trade on a history of dissatisfaction with the performance of existing public services. Arguments for a smaller state had little popular appeal in countries dependent on government provision of services, particularly in rural areas and outer islands. Politicians used employment and services as a form of patronage. Public servants resisted downsizing. The radicalism of the proposals appealed to some, like those in Vanuatu who favored reform, but it alienated others. It was, however, available off the shelf. It was being tried in a number of Anglo-Saxon countries, particularly New Zealand, though (as with customary land registration) research was beginning to question its effectiveness in other contexts (Tendler 1997).

Finally, anticorruption policies faced difficult conditions: social conditions and values favored support for kin and patron-client relations with politicians and officials. Politicians saw elected office as a route into business. Officials resisted oversight by new agencies. But the historical growth of corruption created popular sympathy for cleaning up government. The radicalism of the reforms worked both ways: enlisting support and crystallizing opposition. Some anticorruption tools were available off the shelf, like ICACs, but others had to be invented, like TI's integrity pacts. Similarly, some had been tested empirically elsewhere, but others were quite new inventions.

Each transfer benefited from location in a network. The networks were of different kinds—official or academic. They were institutionalized in universities, think tanks, consultancy firms, and the network of national chapters that TI deliberately set out to create. Radicalism seems to have worked both ways—appealing to those who wanted change and frightening those who did not. There were deliberate attempts to tone down the radicalism of customary land registration and of the recommendations of the Constitutional Planning Committee in PNG. But the new public management and anticorruption policies were intrinsically adversarial.

As Latour (1996) argued, projects create their conditions, political and technical, and have to sustain them. Implementing a transfer is a social and political process of convincing key individuals and sustaining coalitions— a process well-understood by the Asian Development Bank, for example, in its insistence on coalition building on behalf of reform. So having isolated a number of conditions, we will try to avoid the temptation of adding them up or treating them as a checklist. Instead, we will ask how the results can be explained by more elaborate theories about policy transfer and the exercise of power.

8 Explaining Transfer

In his study of the World Bank's institutional strengthening projects, Arturo Israel (1987) was unimpressed by the explanations for success that were offered by the bank's staff. These were "exogenous factors; outstanding individuals; effective planning and implementation; effective application of management techniques; adequate relative prices; and sufficient political commitment" (ibid., 31–32). Some of these explanations, Israel said, were commonsense. Others were linked to each other—political commitment to a project ensured that it got the best managers and protection from exogenous shocks. So Israel went on to look for more fundamental and intrinsic characteristics that determined the performance of institutions and (by extension) institutional development programs.

In chapter 7 we looked inductively for factors that might explain whether or not transfer took place. Here we work more deductively, asking if the outcomes in the Pacific Islands can be explained by theories of specificity and competition, ownership, political will, or the acceptability of ideas. We then consider the role of power in transfer and the different types of power—direct and indirect, positive and negative—that are deployed within transfer.

Specificity and Competition

Anticipating the thinking behind the public sector reforms of the 1990s, Israel (1987) looked at the incentives acting on individuals within organizations. "Specificity" referred to

> the extent to which it is possible to specify for a particular activity the objectives to be attained, the methods of achieving those objectives, and the ways

of controlling achievement and rewarding staff; and the effects of the activ-ity—their intensity, how long it takes for them to become apparent, the num-ber of people and other activities affected, and the practical possibility of tracing the effects. (ibid., 4–5)

"Competition" was external, from other organizations offering similar services, but also included three internal surrogates: "pressures from clients, beneficiaries, or suppliers; pressure from political establishment and regulatory agencies; and managerial and organizational measures that create a competitive atmosphere among units and individuals within the institution" (ibid., 5).

Specificity was intrinsic to the activity, operating almost automatically and quite apart from the internal management structure and external com-petitive environment. Specificity determined how easy it was to reward or punish individuals for their performance. In high-specificity activities, the objectives were clear, as were the means of achieving them. The results of nonperformance were intense, immediate, and easy to attribute to a par-ticular individual. Israel's example was maintaining a jet engine. In low-specificity activities, by contrast, the objectives were multiple and unclear. There were disagreements about how to achieve them. The results of non-performance were diffuse, took a long time to become visible, and were not easy to attribute to individuals. Israel's example was educational coun-seling: each student was different, there was no consensus on objectives and methods, and the effects of bad advice might not turn up until years later. Consequently, it was hard to tell who was a good or bad education counselor.

Customary land registration was fairly specific, in Israel's terms. It promised an increase in agricultural productivity and a reduction in dis-putes, which could in principle be assessed (and the Solomon Islands Land Research Project eventually began to do so). But it was less clear who was responsible if these results were not achieved—farmers typically blamed the government for failing to follow through with extension services, credit, and improved transportation. There were some opportunities for competition as an alternative to specificity—governments might decide to promote registration in areas where people clearly wanted it and to refuse to do so in areas where there was lack of enthusiasm. Teams could com-pare their performance with each other's.

The objectives of constitutions, by comparison, were vague and mul-tiple, and their results long-term. If things went wrong, there were many people to blame—present leaders, founding fathers, and their advisers. There was scope for competition in federal constitutions; it was possible to compare the performance of different states and of other countries.

Public sector reform was more specific in its objectives and responsibilities. As promoted by the international financial institutions, it had a simple, measurable goal of cuts in public service costs and staff numbers. Responsibility, however, was somewhat diffused between central agencies and departments themselves. There were also opportunities for competition in comparing the relative successes of departments in achieving cuts.

Anticorruption activity promised long-term changes, and, as with crime, it was hard to assess the underlying rate of corruption against which successes could be measured. PNG's Ombudsman Commission, for example, was highly active, but in a climate of steadily worsening corruption. Responsibility could be shifted home to anticorruption commissions or the police. TI's doctrine, however, tended to diffuse it among civil society and a popular change of heart.

Israel's analysis might predict a relatively successful transfer of land registration and public sector reform and less successful transfers of constitutions (nonspecific, low competition) and anticorruption reform (nonspecific, diffused responsibility).

Ownership

The concept of ownership was developed by Johnson and Wasty (1993), who reviewed the results of a number of World Bank structural adjustment loans. They found a strong correlation between satisfactory outcomes (as assessed in the bank's internal reports) and borrower "ownership," as assessed in terms of the degree of borrower (as opposed to donor) initiative in designing and implementing the adjustment program; the level of conviction among borrower policy makers about the degree of crisis and the need for reform; the degree of public support that local leaders gave to the program; and the efforts they put into building consensus for the program. For the ADB, the biggest lesson was the importance of local ownership and local champions and of attention to timing and sequencing that produced early, positive results. The reforms in Samoa were said to be "designed, owned and driven by Samoans," unlike an earlier agriculture sector loan (Knapman and Saldhana 1999, 105).

Killick's research on conditionality also endorsed the importance of ownership, though pointing out that ownership was "ad hoc, not set within a theory of government" (1998, 91). Killick developed such a theory in terms of conflicting interests of donors and governments, including "resentment of foreign intervention and of the apparent erosion of national sovereignty that results from conditionality" (ibid., 93).

Comparing our four cases, local political ownership was lowest for customary land registration. Nationalist legislatures rejected late colonial models, and commissions of inquiry proposed their own alternatives. Touring committees and national conventions were used to build ownership of constitutions. TI also tried to create popular constituencies against corruption.

The relationship between transfer and ownership is tricky. If a program is initiated locally, with conviction, support, and efforts to build consensus, then little transfer seems to be involved. Can ownership be transferred? The difficulty points to a larger issue about paternalism, trusteeship, and acting on behalf of others that we will return to later in the chapter.

Political Will

The standard, somewhat circular, ad hoc explanation for success or failure in transfer is political will. For example, Sir Anthony Siaguru (2001), the chairman of TI (PNG), clearly identified "fundamental self interests," "vested interests on the part of many political leaders," and the absence of "political will" as factors in Parliament's failure to proceed with an ICAC. He also worried that the successful integrity legislation might yet be subverted for "Machiavellian purposes." TI (PNG) recognized, behind the absence of political will, a need for voters to become more demanding of their leaders, and thus the publicity campaigns of TI (PNG) are directed at the voters. This shifts the question one step back: why are voters not more demanding?

As Joan Nelson noted, political will is not something simply present or absent but "a variable on which outside agencies can have some influence" (1984, 984). It is a matter of commitment, but it also involves capacity to implement and the response of influential private and nongovernmental interests to government initiatives. Mosley, Harrington, and Toye's research on policy reform (1991) tried to look behind the phrase and identified four possible explanations for government commitment, which the authors then tested against their evidence from Africa, Asia, and the Caribbean (but not PNG and the Pacific Islands).

First, there was the old argument that authoritarian regimes find it easier to reform than democratic ones. Our cases allow comparison between colonial and democratic periods, and the example of customary land registration shows that newly elected legislatures in PNG and Solomon Islands closed off reform. After independence, each of the countries we have been comparing became a parliamentary democracy, but differences between them seem to have had some impact on political will. Most Melanesian governments, for example, have been unstable coalitions, with frequent changes of prime minister on the floor of the house between general elections. They have therefore found it difficult to muster and sustain support for reform. In contrast, a long period of single-party government and a somewhat authoritarian style toward criticism allowed Samoa to sustain economic reform. Cook Islands was governed by a single party through its traumatic reforms in the mid-1990s. Fiji also adopted radical economic policies in the years following its first coup d'état: this adoption was partly driven by necessity but facilitated by the absence of parliamentary opposition. However, it is also possible for leaders to be excessively preoccupied with reform. A.V. Hughes (1998b) suggested that Solomon Islands' coup d'état may have happened because the government was too preoccupied with economic reform and not paying attention to its political support. A liberal political atmosphere, like that in PNG, is also necessary for political will to be driven by civil society, as Transparency International envisages.

The second argument was that new governments find it easier to reform than governments that have been in power for a long time. Ulufa'alu's coalition, acting as a new broom in Solomon Islands, is a good example. So is the Morauta government in PNG. However, there were also examples that stable leadership provided a better context for development. For instance, with the same government in power since 1988, Samoa has often presented itself as a model of reform.

The third argument emphasized learning: either the success of earlier reforms increases the prospects of later ones, or failure reinforces failure. Some kind of positive feedback seems to have taken place in Samoa, whereas PNG's cycles of engagement with the World Bank may have had a negative effect, encouraging cynicism. However, learning implies the existence of memory. The turnover of officials on both sides and their lack of interest in earlier episodes suggest that organizations may be systematically forgetting inconvenient or awkward precedents or alternatives (Douglas 1986). As we saw in our discussion of the conditions for reform, history can work both ways: as something to constrain choices, as in the idea of "path dependency"; or as something to push against, expressed, for example, as "we can't go on like this." The latter role of history seems to have been important for public support for reform in Cook Islands and Vanuatu. Rejection of history also drives popular support for anticorruption reforms.

The fourth argument pointed to the struggle between interest groups and, as such, was potentially circular. We need to look deeper and ask how these interests are mobilized or repressed and how institutions may muffle, amplify, or modify their effect. A powerful interest group in each case has been the public service itself, either directly or indirectly, through its unions. Politicians had a collective interest in the constitutions that entrenched their authority and dominance over the public sector. The personal interests of politicians, rather than their political interests, also seem to have been important in their push for land registration in spite of popular hostility in PNG and in their opposition to tighter controls on forestry. It is these personal and business interests that the leadership codes were directed at. Anticorruption campaigns often forced politicians to make difficult choices between their political interests (to restrict corruption) and their personal ones (to condone it).

Moving outside politics and the public service, we see the organization of private sector interests in the creation and sustained funding of the Institute of National Affairs in PNG. Opponents of land registration saw the World Bank as acting in the interests of foreign companies.

The ADB's reforms in the South Pacific were based on a strong theory of interest groups. On the one hand, the ADB encouraged and pressed governments to step outside Parliament and incorporate the private sector and NGOs in national summits. The ADB also saw the need for some interest groups, such as public service unions, to be bought off with transition grants and retrenchment packages. Transparency International also made public-private-NGO coalitions part of its reform doctrine.

Constitutional law talks of the significance of the Grundnorm, the fundamental or basic rule of a legal system. There are also pre- and extra-constitutional premises on which the written constitution is based. These premises may refer to the territories and people to be included or excluded—something that has to be decided before those included can vote to adopt a constitution. They may refer to a minimum of shared values, or they may refer to a political settlement—an acceptance, even if formal or tactical, by relevant and powerful interest groups of the basic terms of their relationship. Such a settlement may be between classes, regions, or ethnic or gender-based groups. At the time the constitution is being drafted these groups may be fluid and emergent, but in the absence of such a settlement the constitution, whatever its content, may not stick. In Melanesia, provisions about land tenure and decentralization in particular seemed to embody wider political settlements between racial groups (over land) and regions (over decentralization). Politics since have often shown some settlements of this sort to be imaginary or transitory.

The architects of Fiji's constitution were mandated by their parliamentary terms of reference to subordinate its provisions to the wider ethical principle of improving race relations. This led the Constitution Review Commission to recommend a system of alternative voting rather than proportional representation. The commission conceded that the latter might be more democratic, but AV promised to encourage ethnic conciliation and therefore trumped democracy (Fiji Constitution Review Commission 1996). This principle was more than a norm to be embodied in the constitution or an aspiration to be achieved through it. The possibility of order in Fiji, constitutional or not, was thought to depend on harmonious relations between indigenous citizens and Indo-Fijians, and so other goals of the constitution had to be subordinated to that end. The constitution, for example, refers to an underlying compact among the different ethnic groups in Fiji and claims to be built upon that compact (ibid.). The constitution also refers to the aspiration of interracial settlement, based on a degree of mutual recognition and mutual interdependence.

The evidence for each of the explanations we have considered so far—specificity, competition, ownership, and political will—is summarized in table 11.

Acceptability of Ideas

To explain why ideas are accepted or rejected, Peter Hall's study of the international spread of Keynesian economic ideas (1989) identifies three perspectives. Each sees Keynesianism as "a doctrine for solving puzzles"—puzzles for economists in economic theory, puzzles for officials in public administration, and puzzles for politicians in putting together coalitions (ibid., 13). Hall's framework links ideas to politics in a structural way that avoids the voluntarism of ideas about political will and the circularity of arguments about interest groups.

The first, economist-centered approach focuses on acceptance or rejection by the profession, which is assumed then to influence politi-

Table 11. Explanations for Success or Failure of Transfer

	Specificity	Competition	Ownership	Political will
Customary land registration	Some observable short- and medium-term effects on farming	Some pressure from clients	Colonial models rejected by nationalist legislatures	Opponents easily mobilized
Westminster constitutions	None: responsibility diffuse and impacts hard to assess	Federal	Popular support enhanced by touring committees	Constitutions enhanced position of politicians
Democracy	Impacts on development indirect	Some international pressure	Unevenly held: conservative and some middle-class opposition	Support could be mobilized in streets and among trade unions
Public sector reform	Cuts measurable, and agencies could be made responsible	Some pressure from private sector	Public service predisposed against cuts to its numbers	Politicians happy to curb officials
Anticorruption	Impact and responsibility often unclear	Some competition between agencies	Enhanced by NGOs	Intermittent: politicians targets as well as sponsors of reform

cians. In this perspective, Keynesian ideas might offer better solutions to problems puzzling economists or might provide opportunities for the practice of new techniques by younger scholars. Its strength is the force it gives to the ideas themselves, but its weakness lies in the assumption that economists will influence governments.

The second, state-centered approach casts its net more widely and asks if and how officials might be receptive to Keynesian ideas. There might already be regular communication between the government and the economics profession in the treasury or the reserve bank. Or the government may already have experience with policies that Keynesianism proposed. However, this approach ignores the role of politicians.

The third, coalition-centered approach looks beyond economists and officials to the broader constellation of political actors and social forces that may be predisposed for or against Keynesianism. Coalitions of trades unions and sectors of industry, for example, may be able to give support for a policy, and the absence of support may doom it. For example, the Pacific Islands Forum *Stocktake* noted that "community groups tended to be more organised in talking to government than business and are more structured in their approach" (Pacific Islands Forum Secretariat 2002, 28).

In table 12, "Keynesianism" has been substituted with the five transferred good governance policies we have analyzed, and the results have been summarized. The second column in the table lists the professions involved in transfer. Surveyors were strong advocates of land registration, but they also supported the alternative customary land records in Solomon Islands. Politicians were advocates for democracy—at least when they were winning elections. The local legal profession, or the absence thereof, was an important factor in the acceptance, rejection, and implementation of constitutional ideas promoted by consultants like Yash Ghai. Accountants and management specialists were sympathetic to the reforms being pressed on the Cook Islands government. The police were vital to the adoption or rejection of anticorruption reforms, while auditors have promoted better "corporate governance."

The third column in table 12 points to the links between professions and the predispositions of state officials to act or not on new ideas. For example, lands departments resisted or occasionally embraced reform, and finance departments pressed the economic and budgetary reforms recommended by the IFIs.

The final column in the table points to the broader societal conditions that might be mobilized for or against new ideas. For example, we saw the importance of trades unions in allowing public sector reforms to go ahead.

We also saw the active use of summits and national conventions to create coalitions in favor of reform. TI's theory talks explicitly of public-private-NGO coalitions.

Hall's analysis (1989) broadened from the ideas in good standing within professions to include state officials and the political coalitions that support ideas. It clarified the links between knowledge and power and explains why some ideas prevail and others are ignored. It highlighted the influential role of professional groups and the links between academics and bureaucracies, through think tanks and consultancies. Hall's arguments about acceptability pointed to the links among professions, sympathetic officials, and external political conditions in sustaining support for Keynesian ideas (and, by extension, for their successors). Latour (1986)

TABLE 12. Explanations for Acceptance or Rejection of Transfer

	Profession-centered	State-centered	Coalition-centered
Customary land registration	Surveyors	Lands departments	Links to business and agricultural entrepreneurs Rural revolts
Westminster constitutions	Legal profession	Attorney generals	Opponents and proponents of independence Secession
Democracy	Politicians	Legislatures and electoral commissions	Class and racial alliances/conflicts
Public sector reform	Accountants and management specialists	Public service commissions and finance departments	Trade unions and labor parties
Anticorruption	The police and auditors	Independent audit and ombudsman commissions	TI's coalitions with private sector, NGOs, and IFIs

described how projects had to whip up support for themselves, including the project of transfer. His word "interest" captured both the cognitive and the instrumental aspects of the process—powerful actors had to be made to pay attention (be interested), and the project had to offer something to them (appeal to their self-interest). Ideas in good standing among the professions did not get anywhere without official and political support. Officials in developing countries have been particularly suspicious of economic ideas.

The cases are good examples of attempts to construct these linkages around reforming ideas. The Institute of National Affairs in PNG was successful in bringing private sector interests to bear on officials and politicians and helped achieve a sea change in official ideas about customary land registration (though without building the political support, which collapsed in the face of student and NGO protests). The ADB in the South Pacific was canny in insisting on national summits that brought together peak private sector and NGO interests behind reform (though parliaments were often resentful).

Successful transfer did not depend only on capturing the interest of elites. The Ethiopian research (Beckstrom 1973) also showed the importance of individual calculations of convenience and relevance to everyday life (which economists call transaction costs). Traders were ignoring commercial law because it was easier to use custom. Similarly, the research on land registration in Solomon Islands (Heath 1979) found farmers grumbling about the inconvenience of registered land boundaries and their irrelevance to the kind of agriculture the farmers wanted to practice. Many of the complaints about constitutions had to do with their complexity and their irrelevance to practical purposes, rather than their inconsistency with values and beliefs.

Nevertheless, Hall's model (1989) is a highly state-centered one—as befits the Keynesian ideas that it deals with, which assume an active, capable state ready (if necessary) to intervene to manage demand in a national economy. A characteristic of many of the states we have been comparing is their weakness and their openness to international economic pressures. The influential professional groups are often overseas, in the IFIs, while local bureaucracies lack the capacity to deliver any kind of policy, Keynesian or not.

In the absence or weakness of the state, we are forced to look more widely and deeply at the kinds of power being deployed in transfer (summarized in table 13). Sociologist Bertrand Badie noted that whereas Western political ideas and institutions have been carried by colonization and

TABLE 13. Forms of Power in Transfer

Form of power	Explanation	Examples
First dimensional	A gets B to do what B would rather not do	Land and forestry conditions
		Finance vs. spending departments
		RAMSI
Second dimensional	A sets the agenda for negotiations with B	Broadening of economic agenda to include Green and public sector reform conditions
		World Development Reports
Third dimensional	A's ideology prevents B from seeing B's real interests	Economic orthodoxy
		Nationalism
		Interpellation of subjects
Infrastructural	Capacity to implement	First tranche payouts
		Technical assistance
		Implementation issues
		RAMSI
Elite theories Totalizing	Power concentrated in educated, business, or expatriate elite Overriding indigenous autonomy, history "Seeing like a state"	Nonimplementation of land policy and leadership codes
		Radical constitutions
		Land tenure conversion
		Some anticorruption rhetoric
Weapons of the weak	Prudent indirect challenges to the force behind the dominant ideology	Demonstrations, expulsions, "letter rather than the spirit"
Market dominance	Rent seeking; monopoly and monopsony	World Bank monopoly of data
		Donor coordination
		Appeals to Taiwan or China
		Incentive funds
Governance	Indirect use of peer pressure	Pacific Islands Forum finance ministers' meetings
		National summits
		Development forums
		TI's rankings
		FATF listing
Disciplinary	Power enhances capacities through people taking responsibility for themselves	Training and technical assistance
		Donors seek self-discipline, responsibility, and ownership of projects
Power/knowledge	Power linked to knowledge and expertise	Consultancy reports, consultants' expertise, and Web sites
		Role of professionals and epistemic communities

conquest, "the most effective exportation has often been the most diffuse, carried by the configuration of power that has structured a worldwide, international order since the end of the eighteenth century" (2000, 7). What forms has this configuration taken, and what kinds of power have been deployed?

Power in Transfer

Coercion is only one of the many types of power at work in transfer (see table 13). The types of power are not entirely commensurate. They draw on different assumptions about what can be known and seen and about methods. Some people see power in a negative light, a few see it positively, and Foucault (1980) saw it as simply pervasive and inevitable.

First Dimensional

The simplest kind of power is the ability to get someone to do something he or she would rather not do. This is the view taken by Mosley, Harrington, and Toye in their book, *Aid and Power* (1991). The authors positioned themselves between what they saw as two naive views. On the one hand were the apologists, who saw conditionality in the "mutual interest of donor and recipient," and on the other hand were those who saw it as a form of imperialism and "necessarily coercive" (ibid., xiii, 67–68, 87). Similarly, Killick (1998) asked if conditionality is "co-operative or involuntary" and concluded that it was "essentially coercive." This led him to distinguish between "pro forma" conditions, which both sides readily agree to, and "hard-core" conditions, which were made only at the lender's insistence and "would not otherwise be undertaken" (ibid., 9–11). Killick then compared conditionality with economic sanctions.

Examples from PNG's negotiations with the World Bank in the late 1990s show that conditionality is not simply or only consensual. Some conditions were strongly resisted and were clearly an exercise of power, in which the government did things it would otherwise not have done. The bank tried to have a condition about land registration written into a loan, students rioted, and ministers backed down. In that case the bank lost, but it did win on changes to forestry policy, against strong government opposition. The conditions would, in summary, have required the government not to amend the Forestry Act, which reserved decisions about licensing to a statutory Forestry Board; to introduce restrictions on logging under existing permits; to introduce a revenue system that would provide more benefits to landowners and the government; and not to starve the Forest Authority of funds (Filer 2000, 28–32). International environmental NGOs were putting pressure on the World Bank in Washington. A well-established timber industry was pressing the government in Port Moresby. Customary landowners did not necessarily welcome intensified government regulation; conservation would stop them from selling their timber. Individual ministers and politicians had been doing well personally as intermediaries between landowners and timber companies. (The man who became PNG's minister of forests in 1994 was the director of a landowner company.) There was the possibility of an uneasy alliance between the World Bank and NGOs against the PNG government.

A showdown took place in 1996, during which the PNG prime minister told the bank to "go to hell" and the Parliamentary Privileges Committee found the bank guilty of contempt (ibid., 41). But the prime minister backed down, and the second tranche of the loan was eventually released in January 1997. The struggle continued with a new government elected in August 1997.

Second Dimensional

The view of power as the ability of one side to get the other to do what it otherwise would not may be insufficient (Lukes 1974). Political scientist Stephen Lukes (1974) called it one-dimensional and identified another, two-dimensional view that included the ability to control the agenda: to decide what is important and should be talked about, as well as what is unimportant and should not be talked about. For example, why did so many of the well-thought-out initiatives of TI (PNG) not succeed? Some seemed to drift into a kind of "fog of war" where it became unclear what had happened to them. As Sir Anthony Siaguru (2001), the founder and chairman of TI (PNG) noted, the ICAC proposal "was not presented to Parliament for reasons we could not quite fathom," and the Privatisation Commission rejected the advice for "technical reasons which we could not fully understand or accept."

Killick was talking "two-dimensionally" about agenda setting when he criticized the proliferation of loan conditions as a "Christmas tree" that tried to incorporate the agendas of different branches of the World Bank (1998, 108). Agenda setting was also involved when consultants promoted a single model of best practice in a number of countries (Dolowitz and Marsh 2000, 10).

The World Bank typically sets international agendas for development. It does so narrowly, in the sense that economic issues have tended to be included more easily on the agenda than others, and broadly, in the sense that noneconomic issues taken up by the World Bank (corruption, the digital divide, and so on) tend to overwhelm others. The annual *World Development Report* aims to set and reset the agenda. Important bank publications have been carefully edited to reflect particular institutional lines (Wade 1996, 2001). The bank's ability to set the agenda is determined by a combination of its ability to hire talent, its command of data, and the resources and effort it puts into disseminating doctrine, whatever that doctrine happens to be. In the past the IMF and the ADB have been less interested or skilled in controlling the public agenda, but they are becoming more aware of it. Meanwhile, each agency is more narrowly involved in controlling the agendas of the negotiations it holds with governments. These agendas are reflected in the conditions of the loans each agency makes.

The things that are termed conditions seem to have changed. The "new" World Bank applied Green (environmental) conditions in PNG with at least temporary success. The PNG government seemed to be committed to more regulation of the forestry industry than would have taken place in the absence of the conditions. The second-dimensional power to set the agenda was often seen as a restrictive one, keeping awkward subjects from being discussed. The World Bank used to be criticized, for example, for the narrowly economic focus of its agenda and for its ability to squeeze social and gender issues off the agenda. Later, agenda control seemed to work the other way. In those cases, it seemed that the power of the World Bank was used to introduce environmental issues, when the government might have preferred simply to talk about money. Similarly, the ADB's widening of its scope brought public sector reform into a hitherto economic agenda.

Third Dimensional

Lukes (1974) also proposed a third-dimensional view of power, as ideology or the ability to control thoughts and desires. Those subject to the third-dimensional exercise of power were not necessarily aware they were being influenced. (Those subject to second-dimensional power, by contrast, know that their issues are not on the agenda, but they are not able to do much about it.) Ideology is embedded in the language used to talk about development and in the kind of data that are collected, tabulated, and reproduced. The existence of an ideology is hard to prove, although an ideology is sometimes made obvious in advertising, training, or propaganda. An ideology becomes more noticeable when it is in motion, as in Killick's remark about the bank's knowledge: "The bank knows best, but what it knows varies over time" (1998, 94). A good example of an ideology is what was called the Washington consensus, a belief in the virtue and inevitability of representative democracy and free markets that emerged in the early 1990s. Fukuyama's *End of History* articulated it. Right or wrong, its third-dimensional quality lay in its claim to be a consensus from which no one could sensibly dissent. Lukes' implication was that people might not recognize where their real interests lay, and that others—foreign experts, technocrats, a revolutionary party, or the World Bank—might be able to see through the veil of ideology and decide what was best for them (West 1986).

The third-dimensional role of ideology, as we have seen, is in principle hard to detect. In PNG and the Pacific Islands members of the ADB, little substantive dissent about the economic remedies was proposed. Unions in Solomon Islands and Cook Islands acted to protect the interests of their members against layoffs, rather than to challenge the ideology upon which reform was based. Morauta's economic orthodoxy in PNG quickly attracted international support. However, there had been signs of dissent from IFI orthodoxy before. In the early 1990s, PNG had taken an expansionist, supply-side approach to economic policy (Kavanamur 1998, 104–106). The activists who took to the streets against the land conditions had broader ideological differences with the bank.

Other kinds of ideology were also at work, some supporting transfer and others resisting it: nationalism; calling forth the beneficiaries of a policy; and the role of economic ways of thinking.

Nationalist Ideology

Nationalist ideology seems to have been more influential than dissent from economic orthodoxy. It was certainly strong in the resistance to reforms and in the general hostility toward foreign advisers and consultants expressed in the army mutiny in PNG. Yet nationalism has an ambiguous relationship to policy transfer. As we saw in the discussion of "nation making" in chapter 1, nationalists claim distinctiveness in order to have the right to a state like everyone else has. Nationalism is a universal doctrine that respects the rights of others to have nation-states of their own (though it is less tolerant of its own minorities). Many nationalists' claims to peculiarity are like those of others, and to that extent they are self-refuting. Political scientist Stephanie Lawson (1991), for example, has shown that indigenous Fijian arguments for political hegemony are very similar to nineteenth-century European conservative reactions to the Enlightenment.

Ideology and Identity

Transferred policies often contain an image of the ideal recipient— for example, the progressive farmer as the ideal recipient of agriculture extension. As Marxist theorist Louis Althusser (1971) noted with regard to ideology, policies interpellate—"hail" or "call forth"—their recipients. A Marxist party calls on people to see themselves as workers, for example, whereas a conservative party may call on the same individuals to see themselves as nationalists or mothers. Some institutions speak only to men, others only to women, and still others are indifferent to gender. Dedications in books sometimes spell out whom they are calling out to, or interpellating. Robert Doorn's *A Blueprint for a New Nation* (1979), for example, set out the terms of the libertarian constitution it was offering to rebels in what became Vanuatu in 1980. It was dedicated "to those individuals who are fighting Communism and Big Government, which kill individualism and free enterprise." Modern institutions call upon people as individuals, while traditional institutions may call on them as members of a family; but the individuals called upon are the same.

Each of the policies analyzed calls upon different kinds of people to receive them. The ideal client for land titles, for example, was a male farmer who wanted to plant cash crops but was inhibited by insecure tenure. Constitutional adviser Jim Davidson, writing about proposals for land reform in Samoa in the 1960s, referred to the figures of the "progressive planter" and his opposite, the "landless proletariat," who might be created by reform (1967, 393–394). Land reform spoke less to other clients. It was also unclear how many people of these other clients there were in any concrete situation, relative to other claimants on land. In arguments about land registration, women were neither addressed nor heard as such.

The ideal clients for a Westminster constitution were partisan politicians, loyal to leaders and anxious for preferment. Elections spoke more widely to people as voters or party members (in Fiji, particularly, as Indians, Fijians, or general electors). Fiji's AV system was designed precisely to encourage candidates to call out across the racial divide rather than interpellating people as "Indians," "Fijians," or others. Meanwhile communal seats ensured that people of one ethnic group called for support only from each other and could put ethnicity aside as something taken for granted.

Promoters of the new public management had clear ideas about the types of people who inhabited the world of their institutions: public servants were rent-seeking opportunists, and their clients were like consumers, making the kinds of choices they did in supermarkets. Whether these types existed or not, as well as their preponderance in the population, may have determined whether or not the calls for NPM were heard.

Finally, Transparency International's anticorruption strategies spoke to people outside government—in the private sector and civil society. Again, these presumed constituencies did not always recognize themselves as being spoken to or heard and may not have even existed in any numbers.

Economic Ideology

Economic ways of thinking pervaded the arguments about customary land registration, constitutions, public sector reform, and corruption prevention. These ways of thinking were of different kinds. Sometimes they were formal—borrowing from economics the model of the rational actor, who makes choices in situations of scarcity. Sometimes they were substantive, concerned with the effects of a policy on economic growth. On occasion they drew on older meanings of "economical" more familiar to accountants than to economists, that is, as avoiding waste and reducing expenses. The alternative of rule by committee, proposed by the late colonial government in Solomon Islands, was justified on grounds related more to accounting than economics, such as frugality and avoidance of waste, as well as being consistent with Melanesian traditions.

The Institute of National Affairs' interest in PNG land tenure in the 1980s was driven by the substantive commercial and economic concerns of its business members and the government. It also drew explicitly on ideas from institutional economics and treated landowners as calculating, rational actors.

Economic arguments were not so obviously made over independence constitutions. However, substantive economic concerns featured in arguments about compulsory acquisition and the constitutional protection of private property rights, in particular against the claims of traditional owners over alienated land. The worry was that returning land to its traditional owners would affect "the economy."

Formal rational-choice assumptions underlay Michael Oliver's constitution for the Nagriamel rebels in Vanuatu in the late 1970s. It would have limited government to protection of individuals against force and fraud, mandated a gold standard (so governments could not debauch the currency), and prevented governments from creating the kinds of public enterprises that public sector reformers in the 1990s came to see as an instrument of political patronage.

The interests of politicians and parties were also crucial to the Fiji Constitution Review Commission's scheme of enlisting the self-interest of politicians to the achievement of accommodative behavior in Fiji. Heterogeneous constituencies and alternative voting guided the vote-maximizing politician to take the interests of other ethnic groups into account. The CRC's scheme assumed that at least some politicians were rational, in the sense that they calculated the best way of maximizing their votes and chances of reelection (even if this involved their appealing outside their ethnic group). Donald Horowitz (1997) believed that the scheme would work if just some politicians were rational, hewing to the center while leaving the fringes to the fundamentalists. The plan also assumed a kind of rationality among voters—in the outcome it was clear that some voters simply wanted to punish some parties rather than wanting others to succeed.

The review of the Cook Islands constitution in 1998 was explicitly linked to ADB-supported public sector and substantive economic reforms. Popular opinion was mindful of the costs of MPs' salaries and allowances and was in favor of reducing their numbers. Concern with being economical—minimizing costs and reducing waste—also drove the public sector reforms, which were possibly at cross-purposes with longer-term substantive concerns with economic development. As the ADB noted, less public expenditure might mean less growth in the private sector, which depended on government contracts and the salaries of people employed by government.

The new public management that was embodied in some of the Cook Islands reforms was based not only on the economic idea that markets were more efficient than states. It also followed public choice theory by extending formal economic modes of thinking to the state itself, conceptualizing officials as self-interested rent seekers. Its resulting suspicion of state activity justified arguments for privatization, deregulation, and downsizing. NPM had some resonance in postcolonial states where politics and public service became an avenue to business. The leadership codes introduced from Tanzania in the 1970s had in mind the politician-businessman.

The anticorruption doctrine of TI and other international organizations drew heavily on Robert Klitgaard's work (1988). Where economists had occasionally been tolerant of corruption, as oiling the wheels of otherwise rigid economies, the new wave of anticorruption activity in the 1990s was driven both by estimates of the cost of corruption and its distortionary effects on national economies and by a more institutionalist concern with transaction costs (Kauffman 1998). Klitgaard drew particularly on institutional economic ideas about principals and agents and the difficulty of trusting others to act on one's own behalf. He also drew on accountants' professional concerns with transparency. Generally, the ideas and values associated with transfer, and with aid in general, were more broadly utilitarian than strictly economic.

Infrastructural Power

Looking at the power of states, sociologist Michael Mann (1986) distinguished between despotic and infrastructural power. Despotic power was the ability to act arbitrarily, without negotiation. It was zero-sum—A's power was at B's expense. Mann's example was Lewis Carroll's Queen of Hearts, who was able to shout "Off with his head!" and have the whim gratified immediately (ibid., 113). This kind of power was nasty, but avoidable if one kept one's distance. Infrastructural power was the ability to implement policy at a distance, through other actors, and over a long period. It was variable-sum—A's power did not depend on B's not having power, and in some circumstances both A and B might benefit from its exercise. Infrastructural power was a characteristic of modern capitalist democracies.

It was precisely this infrastructural power that many developing countries lacked, and aid was often intended as "capacity building." Australia's RAMSI, with its soldiers and police, looks like a first-dimensional exercise of power. But it was invited and was also infrastructural in the way it strengthened the capacity of the Solomon Islands government and the state itself. Mann's ideas also pointed to the flow of resources in loans: to the check rather than the conditions. The loan was enabling as well as controlling. It got the government through a crisis, and at lower cost than without it. In Cook Islands the transition arrangements to resettle public servants weakened public service resistance to staff cuts. The government of Sir Geoffrey Henry presided through the crisis and, though newly hemmed in by machinery requiring greater transparency, survived until 1999. Without outside support, the government could have fallen. In the opposite direction, the Skate government imposed savage "structural adjustment without the loans" in PNG and fell.

It is often difficult to isolate the effects of transfer from more general problems of implementation, which typically involves acting through and negotiating with local "sovereigns" (Sabatier and Mazmanian 1976, 486). Policy is the result of an interaction between designers and deliverers, rather than the unfolding of a blueprint. The promoters of a policy may have formal authority but must in fact deal with, or get around, various informal sovereigns on the way. On the streets or out in the field, government officials treat policy as just one of multiple day-to-day pressures on them (Lipsky 1976). Implementation in developing countries may be particularly difficult. Resistance may come from within the bureaucracy or from riots in the street.

Transfer is in many ways a special case of more general problems of implementing laws and policies. The objectives of transfer are often unclear. Theories are untested. The transferred law is disobeyed. Implementers use their discretion to look after their own interests. Support from powerful sovereigns may be absent. Social change undermines the assumptions on which a policy is based. Much of this is common sense, as Israel (1987) remarked of the World Bank's own evaluations of institutional projects.

Among the cases analyzed here, for example, objectives were vague and shifting: was customary land registration meant to individualize titles, or was it meant to conserve group ownership? Did it in fact encourage investment? Owners in Solomon Islands often did not comply with the requirement that they register dealings in their land. Suspicion of official corruption had probably increased skepticism about the virtues of land registration. Parliaments in PNG and Solomon Islands rapidly backed away from land registration, and when students protested against the inclusion of land registration in the World Bank's loan conditions, finance ministers caved in. Social change undermined the policy if, for example, landowners chose to migrate to work in towns rather than develop their own registered land.

International implementation—and policy transfer—faces special difficulties. Unlike domestic policy, the conditions that a donor might impose on a client are not enforceable in any international court. The recipients are literally, not metaphorically, sovereign. All the donor can do, without much conviction, is threaten to go away. In practice, however, donors usually offer more. Donors face a double problem. They have to persuade recipient officials to want what the donors want. Then those officials have to persuade junior and local officials to implement what they have agreed with donors. Both types of encounters in practice involve interaction, complicity, and negotiation.

The problem of implementation also points to a central paradox in so-called technical assistance and policy transfer more generally. Those governments most needful of assistance are the least capable of using it. Israel's study of institutional strengthening found a high correlation between the existing effectiveness of the organization and the effectiveness of the strengthening program.

Elite Theories

Bertrand Badie's account of the imported state condemned elite hypocrisy, stating that it "often prevails over exportation, since the elite in Southern societies continue to borrow, even while loudly condemning the practice" (2000, 2). Richard Common's comparison (2001) of the introduction of the new public management into Hong Kong, Malaysia, and Singapore found that transfer is a political process manipulated by elites, who select those aspects of NPM that shore up their power and reject the others. Hall's argument about the acceptability of ideas (1989) suggested that the success of introduced ideas, like Keynesianism in its time or NPM in the 1980s, depends on bureaucratic and professional elites and on political coalitions with interest groups outside the state. Helen Hughes' critique of development aid in the Pacific (2003) was strongly antielitist, drawing on public choice theory's suspicion that public servants are simply self- interested rent seekers. Suspicion of public service elites has also been shared by Marxist critics, like Ian Frazer (1992), who saw the Solomon Islands public service elite as the indirect beneficiary, through taxation, of timber exploitation.

Jim Fingleton's explanation (1981a) for the failure to implement the recommendations of PNG's Commission of Enquiry into Land Matters pointed the finger at elite interests: those of expatriate officials, who were holding out against the new regime, and those of PNG politicians, who were anxious to gain ownership of plantations rather than divide them up among their traditional owners. Constitution making was a largely elite concern, though many Pacific Island governments tried to broaden participation by taking committees on tour throughout the countryside and the islands. The theory that Rueschemeyer, Stephens, and Stephens

(1992) presented about the social conditions of democracy noted the ambivalence felt by property-owning middle classes: they might be the champions of democracy, but they might also fear its effects on their property rights. Public sector reform was directed at the heart of the public service elite, which tended to dominate in small societies like Cook Islands and Vanuatu. The leadership codes were also directed at the public service elite, while TI combined, somewhat uneasily, an elite style of lobbying and engagement with big business with a streetwise style of mobilization and confrontation. In PNG, at least, the bias was toward the former style.

Barrie Macdonald's account (1996) of the Kiribati political process and its implications for aid donors compared traditional and modern elites. Traditional elites—older men *(unimane)* in meetinghouses *(maneaba)*— remained influential in local and outer island politics and controlled or vetoed the activities of legally constituted local government councils. National politics, however, was dominated by a Western-educated elite "characterised by residence on South Tarawa, high levels of consumption, ownership of motor vehicles, access to good educational and health services for their families, and the opportunity to travel beyond the country" (ibid., 15). This elite was small—Macdonald estimated that it consisted of about seven hundred people. It was somewhat self-perpetuating, given that entry to high school, though competitive, depended on English-language competency passed from parents to children. The educated and traditional elites intersected in the legislature. Voters learned the advantage of electing educated people to represent them in their dealings with the powerful colonial civil service. Village, clan, and religious loyalties influenced voting patterns, especially on outer islands, but successful candidates needed to demonstrate their ability to perform in the national arena and their possession of "a high standard of personal behaviour" (ibid., 16).

Weapons of the Weak

The ideological, or third-dimensional, view of power has been criticized from several directions. Arguing from the study of comparative politics, James Scott (1990) doubted that ideology could be so invisible. He pointed out that neither the powerful nor the powerless were completely convinced of the ideological justifications for the dominance of the powerful. Both sides recognized the violent basis on which it rested. The powerful kept their weapons handy, just in case. The powerless deployed "weapons of the weak"—jokes, playing dumb, minor sabotage—while dreaming of a "world turned upside down." Aid recipients had similar weapons at their disposal. They could drag their feet, play the fool, and sabotage a process they claimed to be going along with. Hau'ofa's jocular *Tales of the Tikongs* (1988) described the sophisticated weapons of the weak that Tongans had devised to bamboozle their donors. His Pacific Islanders were sly and calculating agents in a game they played with earnest, bewildered foreigners. They bent the rules, exploited donors' stereotypes, and played on donors' rivalries.

The weak also had weapons. Pacific Island governments could take symbolic hostages, like the biodiversity that, according to Filer (2000), drove the World Bank's Green interest in PNG. They could play on the IFIs' interest in making loans and desire to avoid foreclosure. They could go through the motions. They could delay, at least until the point that the money ran out to pay salaries. They could accept the general principle and drag their feet on the detail. Examples often did not show up in the diplomatic language of official reports, but the ADB's comment on Vanuatu's foreign investment legislation, fulfilling the letter but not the spirit of the conditions, was a good example of the irritating effect of the deployment of weapons of the weak (Knapman and Saldhana 1999, 157). So was PNG's expulsion of the World Bank's resident representative in 2001. In hiring Hamidian-Rad, however, Prime Minister Bill Skate might have pushed the World Bank too far, showing that weapons of the weak must be carefully calibrated not to precipitate a crackdown.

Market Dominance

The World Bank is a dominant producer, packager, and disseminator of ideas about policies and institutions. It has been criticized for relying on a narrow range of U.S. universities for its ideas. The bank is a sophisticated promoter of its ideas, using publications like the annual *World Development Report*, a Web site, and television advertising. Some bilateral donors promote particular institutions or restrict the trade in ideas to protect their own suppliers, universities, or consultants. Their clients, however, generally pay for errors in advice from donors—there is no consumer protection against bad ideas.

We can see transfer as the result of supply and demand for institutions. As soon as a parliament was put in place to express national demands in PNG, it balked at administration-proposed land legislation and proved reluctant to endorse alternatives. Yet proponents of land registration continued to argue that demand existed, expressed by foreign investors through the INA and by enterprising farmers at the local level. These demands combined in a proposal for sporadic registration, provided as and when particular farmers applied for it. The PNG government was already responding to sporadic demand by using an existing, legislated process called lease-leaseback. Governments in Melanesia also responded sporadically to demand from outside investors.

Local demand for constitutions was also limited and had to be stimulated by touring committees. These committees often uncovered demand for constitutional provisions that might have offended international norms.

Conditionality was meant to make up for—or to reinforce—deficient local demand for reform. Demand for NPM was particularly low among public servants, but ideas about smaller, more efficient government had support among the public, which was frustrated by bureaucratic inertia and corruption, as well as among businesspeople. Similarly, NGOs articulated a popular demand for anticorruption activity, against considerable official misgivings.

Before the end of the Soviet Union, small countries under pressure from the leaders of one bloc could, at least in principle, threaten to seek support from another bloc. Tonga, for example, played this game in achieving Australian funding for an airfield by threatening to turn to Russia. Vanuatu attracted considerable Australian and New Zealand attention through its Libyan connections. Thereafter, Western governments became less inhibited about insisting on good governance among those who depended on them for aid. There was greater donor consensus and fewer opportunities to appeal against downsizing. The proposals were developed by "national summits" but were also taken to "consultative groups" of donors. So it was not possible for a government to reject conditions applied by one donor in the hope of getting an easier ride from another. The only appeal available seems to have been to Taipei, which had a reputation of being generous to governments that recognized it, against the wishes of Beijing. Marshall Islands' commitment to reform, for example, weakened with the prospect of a loan from Taipei, whereas Solomon Islands got through an immediate crisis with grants from PNG and Taipei (Knapman and Saldhana 1999, 124). In 1999, the PNG prime minister, Bill Skate, visited Taiwan with an offer of diplomatic recognition in exchange for grants, loans, and technical assistance worth a

reported US$2 billion (Filer 2000, 74). The Sope government in Vanu-
atu also tried unsuccessfully to play a China card against the ADB reforms
it had inherited.

Governance

One of the several meanings of governance is the maintenance of order
without hierarchy, particularly the indirect use of peer pressure. Thus a
good governance agenda was advanced through the Pacific Islands Forum,
when its member governments adopted a common set of principles about
financial accountability and agreed to report to each other annually about
their progress toward its achievement.

TI's most influential technique has been the publication of an annual
Corruption Perceptions Index, which ranks countries according to how
corrupt they are perceived to be in surveys of businesspeople and other
influential entities. The index has been widely criticized, not least by the
governments of countries that find themselves perceived as quite corrupt
(particularly if they still garner this perception in spite of their efforts to
clean up their act). One criticism of the index is that it looks at only one
side of a corrupt relationship. Officials take money, but (it is argued) foreign companies offer it. In response, TI has produced a Bribe Payers
Index, ranking countries according to the propensity of their companies
to offer bribes. It has also lobbied the OECD and its members to outlaw
the payment of bribes to officials in foreign countries.

Controversy and embarrassment are, in any case, part of the point of
the Corruption Perceptions Index, which is a good example of institutional
transfer by naming and shaming. Indices like TI's are a characteristic technique of global governance. It is indirect. Unlike conditionality, which
tells governments what to do, ranking invokes shame and peer group pressure. The first such index was probably that of gross national product
(GNP) per capita, followed by the UN's more expansive Human Development Index. Ranking encourages the idea that countries are competing—for foreign investment in TI's case. Those with less desirable rankings are goaded into improvement. Because some country will always be
at the bottom, the struggle for improvement is never-ending.

TI's idea of integrity pacts has governance aspects to it: it seeks to
harness the self-interest of companies competing in a tender, each of
which agrees to eschew bribes if the others do. Their agreement is a condition of tendering. But the pact depends on the existence of central
authority in the background, to invoke sanctions on companies that break

ranks. However, this power is not invoked unless there is a complaint, and resolving the complaint might involve third-party arbitration rather than government sanctions. The system was proposed precisely to avoid the need for legislation and was resisted—by lawyers and bureaucrats more comfortable with legislation—for similar reasons.

Disciplinary Power/Knowledge

Michel Foucault (1980) asserted that power is everywhere, is unavoidable, and everywhere generates resistance. He saw Western thinking as preoccupied with the image of the sovereign, from whom power was thought to devolve (ibid., 121). In the way, for example, Western traders in the Pacific were often baffled by the absence of centralized authority and set about creating petty kingdoms from local materials. Instead, Foucault noticed the emergence in the West of new "disciplinary" forms of power, less centralized around the government, less easy to avoid, and relying on people to act responsibly and discipline themselves. They operated one step back, through the "conduct of conduct" (Hindess 1996, 96–136). Foucault saw these forms of power as something productive rather than inhibiting. They enhanced the capacities of those they operated upon, not necessarily at the expense of others. They were tied up with knowledge and expertise. In this way, power in the development business is often linked to professional knowledge and expertise; expressed in sets of data, reports, and publications; and applied through training and capacity building. The World Bank is trying to reinvent itself as an ideas bank (Stone 2000). Much aid activity consists of collecting and deploying information in the form of statistics, plans, and reviews. This is not a neutral, technical activity. Those institutions that are able to document their projects tend to succeed, and states that have this kind of information are better able to intervene in the economy and society.

Foucault also noticed that the exercise of power assumed the prior existence of freedom and never acted without some resistance, slippage, and reversal. None of the governments had to deal with the IFIs. Several governments had already begun their own reforms before they turned to the IFIs. "Discipline" is of course a favorite word among bankers, and—as Foucault envisaged—its preferred form is "self-discipline." Donors are not sovereigns in other countries, and they do not like to be perceived as pushing governments around. They seek influence rather than control. They want recipients to behave responsibly, to do the right thing because they want to do it. Donors also want a long-term relationship: the loan buys them a seat at the table, and they are usually happy to roll over another loan to stay in the game. Donor struggles to get recipients to take ownership of projects are a more complex example of a disciplinary exercise of power. It is like the power that a parent tries to exercise over a teenager or that a welfare officer tries to exercise over a difficult client. Donors want recipients to want what donors want. Development is shot through with these relationships of tutelage and trusteeship, of knowing what is best for the other. It is a story of welfare as much as banking. As we have seen, there are plenty of signs of resistance and slippage.

The cases we have examined show dense linkages between power and knowledge. The negotiations were conducted through endless reports and studies. Knowledge was embodied in the consultants who filled the gaps in local capacity, bringing their own ideas and experience from elsewhere. The ADB's review identified the risk that reform approaches were hostage to "the narrow experience of the long-term adviser" (Knapman and Saldhana 1999, 174). Different kinds of expertise were regarded as relevant, with the review concluding at several points that more expertise in public administration was required (ibid., 38, 64). There was criticism from local officials that their own local knowledge was pushed aside.

We saw examples of open resistance to institutions being imposed. But conditionality also involved complicity between finance departments and the IFIs. The World Bank could be a convenient scapegoat. Conditionality also started from freedom. We saw PNG swallowing its own medicine, without going to the doctor. So we should be worrying less about the exercise of power in institutional transfer. Conditionality is not exceptional, and its coerciveness is no greater than seemingly kinder and gentler forms of aid involving ownership, dialogue, and partnership. Each of those forms of aid also arouses resistance.

9 Evaluating Transfer

In a game, it makes sense to ask if the team has performed well and how its performance might be improved. In soccer the team exists to score goals, and it is easy to see when it fails. Better training, selection, or tactics might improve its performance. So might a new coach. We can easily judge the performance of a team. It is less easy to judge the performance of a game or a code. A team wins or loses. But does soccer, as an institution, win or lose? The subject is difficult and touchy. Evaluating institutions can quickly lead to accusations of impertinence, disloyalty, and lack of respect.

It is quite difficult, but not impossible, to judge the performance of the rules. We might ask if the rules allowed the game to proceed more safely, efficiently, or spectacularly. We might also ask how well the rules compared with other rules in some wider competition—against other games or codes—for spectators or sponsorship.

Institutions like the state or chieftaincy or big-man systems tend to bring their values with them. Those of us living in a state tend to accept the state's values, even if we are disappointed that particular leaders fail to live up to them. Similarly, chiefly systems of government have a different set of values—for example, hierarchy and lineage—that particular chiefs may or may not violate. Clastres (1971) warned against assuming that people living in "stateless societies" were therefore "missing something."

When David Apter (1963) returned to Ghana, he found that the result of what he called institutional transfer was a kind of limbo, neither introduced nor indigenous. Parallels between nineteenth- and late twentieth-century campaigns for good governance among the Pacific Islands also discourage simple views about progress. Samoa's national move toward universal suffrage was paralleled by a local move toward empowering village *fono*, some of whom revived traditional forms of punishment for non-conformity. The immediate future of Solomon Islands under RAMSI, for example, lies in the colonial past—in forms of "pacification" and rule by foreign officials.

Yash Ghai's evaluation (1997) of PNG's 1975 constitution concluded with a balance sheet. On the one hand, the constitution and the political system had survived: there were regular elections and changes of government; there was a free press; and the rule of law was more or less maintained. On the other hand, "almost none of the national goals has been achieved: there was persistent gender inequality, limited participation, low levels of accountability, high levels of corruption and a horrendous breakdown in law and order" (1997, 325). There was a paradox: "The Constitution works, but its primary goals are subverted" (ibid.). Ghai blamed the political and economic system in which the constitution was embedded: "At best a constitution can set up institutions and give them resources and competencies, but it can seldom infuse them with particular values" (ibid., 329). As Ghai suggested, the first, minimal test of institutional performance might simply be survival. Fiji's 1970 and 1998 constitutions failed that simple test of performance. Thus PNG can congratulate itself on achieving years of independence under the same constitution, whereas Fiji cannot.

Sometimes survival is taken for fitness, as if existing institutions have survived an evolutionary struggle. This notion can be comforting to their incumbents, who may feel they have gained legitimacy through surviving the test of time. But evolution remains metaphorical, until we can specify a mechanism equivalent to natural selection in biology (no known organizational process generates random changes and then selects survivors). In any case, evolution acts on populations rather than individuals (in this case, evolution would act on Westminster constitutions rather than particular constitutions, and it is true that this species of constitution is dominant). As North (1990) wrote, often some groups benefit from the survival of inefficient institutions and act firmly to conserve them. Such groups include what economists call rent seekers, who get paid more than a competitive market would offer them, and corrupt officials who benefit from the existence of regulations they can use to extract bribes. Lawyers may benefit from a complicated legal system that clients cannot navigate without professional help.

How can organizations fail and yet survive? Sociologists Meyer and Zucker (1989) found the reason in the disjunction of interests between the owners of organizations and the people who are dependent upon them. When organizations are succeeding, the interests of both parties are congruent. When organizations begin to fail, their interests diverge. Owners may want reform or termination. Dependents want things to continue as they always have. In any case, disagreement about which reforms are needed to regain success is likely. This internal political tussle can become permanent. Owners can increase their political power over dependents by privatization, which allows—indeed, requires—bankruptcy or by the segmentation of an organization into parts that can be more easily dropped if they fail.

The most pervasive assessment of performance in economic discussions is efficiency. We saw the *Sydney Morning Herald* castigating the Tongan government for its inefficiency in 1858. Efficiency links inputs and outputs: an efficient outcome is one that gets the most out of a given set of inputs. Yet an even simpler and earlier dimension is often applied by parliamentary accounts committees, auditors, and the IFIs. They ask if an institution is economical, in the sense of minimizing expenditure and reducing waste. Economizing was often the first step in a structural adjustment program: reduce expenditure, fire staff, and so on. This first step may prejudice later attempts to increase government efficiency and effectiveness.

In social and public policy, there is also concern with outcomes and impacts. As discussed above, Ghai assessed the PNG constitution in terms of its effectiveness in achieving the goals its founders had set it (and he found it wanting).

Finally, public organizations, because they are coercive monopolies and responsible to public opinion, are often subject to tests of justice and fairness. The cases considered in earlier chapters show several examples of ethical dilemmas. In one country the adviser became engaged in the politics of reform, helping set up a citizens' lobby group and advising the opposition party on its submission to the review commission. In another, the adviser resigned from the World Bank and contracted himself to the government the bank had been negotiating with. In none of these cases are the ethical issues easily anticipated or resolved—they involve genuine dilemmas, which would arise only for particular persons, but they are nevertheless important in determining the success or failure of transfers.

Aid relationships are also vulnerable to straightforward corruption. For example, a commission of inquiry into a World Bank–funded education project in Solomon Islands found that the permanent secretary in the education department had a close business relationship with the bank-funded consultant the government was employing (Larmour 1997).

Evaluation is often linked to questions of responsibility and blame. We saw in some cases of public sector reform that blame and responsibility were transferred, as IFIs were welcomed as scapegoats for difficult internal decisions. It was good to see the IFIs admitting their mistakes concerning public sector reform, but also slightly disquieting. The IFIs moved on, admitting their mistakes and writing up the lessons learned. The countries had to live with the consequences. Ethical issues are also raised by the whole concept of institutional engineering. How can we tell who is qualified to give advice? And who is responsible if the advice fails? Fiji's Court of Appeal began to get into the substance of the arguments for and against AV and criticized an academic whose work had been cited by one side of the case.

Courtlike processes pinpoint individuals, though they may also declare laws and policies invalid. Explanations based on social science tend toward the structural: "to understand everything is to pardon everything." In between are different kinds of audits and commissions of inquiry, which balance accounts of what has happened against recommendations to governments about what should be done. In some official inquiries, all parties are assumed to be doing their best in difficult circumstances. In others, there is a search for scapegoats as an alternative to making more difficult reforms of institutions.

The results of these separate tests of performance do not necessarily add up, and there are likely to be trade-offs between them. A single institution—say, a parliament—could be tested and judged differently on each of these dimensions of performance. The parliament might be wasteful and expensive, as voters complained in Cook Islands. It might be more or less efficient at turning inputs into outputs: bills passed per sitting, questions answered by ministers, and so on. It might be more or less effective —compliance with its legislation might be high. In turn, this compliance might affect economic growth or social justice. Finally, the parliament might operate more or less justly and fairly, in the way it treats women and ethnic minorities, for example, inside and outside parliament. Similar, internally contradictory assessments could be made of larger-scale institutions like the state. It could fail some tests, while passing others.

Self-evaluations

The constitutional advisers published explanations and self-justifications of what they had recommended. Jim Davidson's book *Samoa mo Samoa* (1967) was the first. Ghai (1993) reflected on the making of the Solomon

Islands constitution. Brij Lal (2002) has carried on this tradition in his reflections on his own role in Fiji's CRC. Anthropologist Asesela Ravuvu's research on Fijian culture (1991) preceded his involvement as chair of the predecessor to the CRC.

In PNG a government research institute commissioned research to evaluate customary land registration, as did a private-funded think tank. The Solomon Islands Lands Department initiated a research project that involved lands officers and university students (Heath 1979).

The IFIs looked back at their own performance in public sector reform. The ADB published an extensive and frank evaluation of its public sector reform program. The World Bank was briefer but also self-critical of its own role in PNG—as was one of its advisers, Dan Wiese. Sir Anthony Siaguru, the founder of TI in PNG, sought an evaluation of its impact by means of an "independent assessment from a person not involved" (2001, 1). Unable to find the funding for an independent review, Siaguru made his own extensive and self-critical assessment for the organization's annual general meeting in 2001.

These reviews were not completely internal—they were often public. Nor were they completely external—they included officials and advisers implicated in the activity they reviewed, or they were carried out by government agencies. They amounted to fairly frank, semipublic self-evaluations.

Evaluations of Customary Land Registration

Research carried out by lands officers and law students in Solomon Islands found customary interests persisting over registered land and development projects (Heath 1979, 352–372). One purpose of the so-called "land settlement" schemes had been to individualize title, but only half of the titles created were individual. The rest were registered under group names. The government's official handbook for registration teams said that the main aim of registration was "to help farmers develop the land," but the hopes for economic development were found by one of the scheme's architects to be "too optimistic" (A.V. Hughes 1979, 234). Development seemed to be going ahead, or not, irrespective of whether the land was registered. Those who had registered land were not making use of the titles they held. Few dealings were recorded on the register, and most dealings seemed to be going ahead without being registered.

A study of the Matakwalao land registration scheme for the government's Land Research Project found "widespread misunderstanding of the true nature of registration" (Fanegar 1979, 17). Dealings were "still on a customary basis," and not much development had taken place on the registered land after registration, simply because there was no more vacant land for development and expansion, because the area had already been under development before the settlement scheme (ibid., 17–18).

Neilsen's study (1979) of the Ndoma, Komuvadha, and Chuva schemes was rather more positive. Neilsen found that, because of meetings held by the Lands Division, people at Chuva and Ndoma "had a better idea of what land settlement was" (ibid., 23). Certain customary usages and dealings with land had been replaced through registration, and one man was selling parcels of land (ibid., 26). Lack of finance, lack of know-how, and shortage of land were inhibiting development, but nevertheless registered owners were satisfied with registration primarily because it had ended disputes over their land (ibid., 27).

The Land Research Project (Heath 1979) compared registration against its official developmental purposes. However, Leonard Maenu'u (1979), a lands officer himself, criticized the scheme at Fiu Kelakwai in more ethical terms. Registration had given greater security of tenure to incoming migrants than he thought it should have.

In PNG, as in Solomon Islands, systematic research tended to follow political decisions: it put nails in the coffin of schemes that had already lost support. Jim Fingleton looked at two schemes in PNG: a systematic conversion at New Warisota, near Popondetta, creating thirty-two titles carried out between 1965 and 1967; and fifteen sporadic conversions carried out in the Eastern Highlands, beginning in 1967 (Fingleton 1981a). Both of these schemes were carried out by the Land Titles Commission before the government turned to advice from Rowton Simpson, so they are not strictly evaluations of the results of transfer. Nevertheless, Fingleton's criticisms of them would also apply to the new legislation that Simpson had proposed, and they informed Fingleton's proposals for alternatives, such as land groups registration.

At New Warisota, Fingleton found the following: "All titleholders who were interviewed rejected the notion that they were free to dispose of their blocks. They regarded themselves as holding their blocks individually, but indicated that upon death their land would pass to their customary successors" (ibid., 27). In fact, "the economic effects of conversion were hard to distinguish from the effects of the state resources that were provided when the scheme was incorporated ten years later into a large oil palm project" (ibid., 28–29). In the Eastern Highlands conversions, Fingleton found that people other than the titleholder who were using or occupying the land had no formal rights in the land that protected their use of it; that the titles in such cases were affected by perceived interests in the land that were not shown on the register; and that tenure conversion had not in fact proved effective in abolishing customary interests. Assessment of the economic impact was difficult, Fingleton noted, as half the blocks were already developed before the registration application. Fingleton observed: "While some new development was no doubt attributable to tenure conversion, the extent of development on blocks since tenure conversion was in most cases unremarkable, and, when regard is had to the personal qualities and associations of the titleholders, it is likely that much of it would have occurred in any case, regardless of tenure conversion" (ibid., 50).

In both PNG and Solomon Islands, even if registration had not completely replaced customary methods of dealing and had not in itself encouraged development, it nevertheless satisfied its clients whose land became registered (sometimes leaving others, whose claims were rejected during adjudication, disappointed). Writing later about East New Britain, Fingleton asserted that systematic adjudication without tenure conversion—as provided for under the suspended Land Registration (Communally Owned Land) Ordinance—was also valued by its clients. He concluded that it was "unlikely that the final step of registration would have added much to the benefits gained from demarcation and adjudication" (1985, 255).

Evaluations of Westminster Constitutions

South Pacific leaders regularly criticize introduced institutions as inappropriate. Postcolonial constitutional reviews find popular resistance to human rights provisions—for example, those guaranteeing freedom of movement. The 1987 review by Solomon Islands of its constitution, for example, advocated the restoration of capital punishment, limits on the introduction of new religions, limits on the number of political parties, limits on freedom of movement between provinces, and discrimination in favor of indigenous people (Larmour 1989). Setting up a similar review committee, the prime minister of Vanuatu called upon it to overhaul Vanuatu's constitutional provisions for human rights. A review of decentralization policy in Kiribati found concern about controlling nonconformist people.

The Samoan constitution, Ghai (1986) argued, had been "deliberately intended to depart from British practice" and should be interpreted in its own terms and in the light of its own history. He was critical of the drift toward the Westminster practice of giving the head of state discretion to select the prime minister. There were substantial political implications in the head of state's discretion. It diminished the influence of Parliament. In a fluid political situation, the appointed prime minister started off with an advantage: he or she could quickly entrench support through patronage and ward off any subsequent votes of no confidence.

Ghai's criticism raises two transfer issues. The first concerns the political conditions under which a Westminster constitution operates, particularly whether it requires strong political parties. Under a Westminster constitution, the argument goes, the head of state simply chooses the leader of the largest party—neither a ballot nor discretion is necessary. But in the Pacific Islands, at least outside Fiji, parties are often weaker. They are shifting parliamentary factions rather than objects of voter choice. The remedy often considered is legislation that would require candidates to identify with political parties (thus allowing voters to choose between parties) and that would limit the ability of members of Parliament to change parties once elected on a party ticket. For these reasons, PNG introduced legislation concerning the integrity of political parties. The transfer issue is whether a particular institution (a parliamentary executive) can work in the absence of other institutions (political parties) and whether it can create the context for its operation in passing laws designed to strengthen political parties. Ghai (1986) asserted that, in the Samoan case, the constitution was "quite consistent with a party system," if a party system were to emerge. In fact it did emerge, in the rule of the Human Rights Protection Party since 1988. Ghai was also unconvinced that giving greater discretion to the head of state would resolve the problem of shifting party alliances and coalitions. Instead it might simply "transfer political intrigues from the floor and corridors of the legislature to the doors of state house" (ibid., 621).

The second issue involves informal conventions as opposed to formal rules. Douglass North (1990) argued for the importance of informal conventions underlying formal institutions in economic development. So did Joseph Stiglitz (2000), in his arguments for apprenticeships, visits, and hands-on training. In the Samoan case, we can see local traditions amplifying the written constitution. We also see the tension between the desire to keep the document simple and self-contained and the desire to spell out all the contingencies. Yet texts cannot speak for themselves. The Samoan case also shows that people bring their own, possibly self-interested interpretations to the written rules: "Reference to British conventions will produce uncertainty, and shift power unduly to officers like the Attorney-General, or expatriate lawyers" (Ghai 1986, 620). Ghai pointed to the power of professionals and their networks to promote or resist transfer: what DiMaggio and Powell (1991) called normative transfer. In chapter 8 we saw the role of professional associations in developing theories of transfer, as well as the kinds of power that professional associations deployed.

The persistence and copresence of two systems—traditional arrangements and introduced principles—are often commended as a form of adaptation or celebrated as an example of pluralism. But the situation can have pernicious effects on individuals caught between the two systems. Samoan historian and anthropologist Malama Meleisea (2000), however, made a more systematic and negative evaluation of its effects in Samoa. The much-celebrated constitution of 1962 was storing up trouble for the future, expressed, for example, in the decisions of village-level *fono* to expel or, in one case, to sanction the killing of nonconforming members. The constitution had provided "two systems of legitimacy": chiefly authority and a vaguer set of Western liberal principles. Meleisea noted that these two sets of principles could be "selectively invoked to justify almost any action" (ibid., 191). The constitution embedded contradictions rather than compromises, and its founding fathers were mistaken in thinking that "the next generation would have answers that had escaped earlier generations." Meleisea described the resulting "moral confusion," which allowed, for example, MPs and department heads named as corrupt by the controller and the chief auditor to remain in office (ibid., 193). The dual system had created what economists call moral hazard: the rules encouraged people to behave badly. When people had two routes for resolving grievances—a traditional one and an introduced legal one—they chose between them opportunistically. If they failed in one, they turned to the other. Appeals against traditional decisions were made in introduced courts. Similarly, the decisions of introduced courts were appealed to traditional authority.

Evaluations of Democracy

Not surprisingly, monarchs have often displayed a coolness toward democracy. In Hawai'i, King Kamehameha IV campaigned during the 1850s to revoke his predecessor's concession to universal suffrage in Hawai'i. His successor, King Kamehameha V, also "opposed universal suffrage very strongly and advocated a property qualification both for Representatives and for voters" (Kuykendall 1940, 31). He refused to take an oath to defend the existing constitution, called a constitutional convention, and toured the islands to press his case. When the delegates elected to represent the people refused to accept a property qualification, the king dissolved the convention and abrogated the constitution, stating, "It is clear to me that if universal suffrage is permitted, this Government will soon lose its Monarchical character" (quoted in ibid., 36). The Hawaiian monarchy was deposed by a U.S.-supported coup d'état. Its equivalent survived in Tonga, where the king was known for "citing the histories of Spain, Germany and Russia as examples of ruthless tyrannies that had democratic origins, and warning of the dangers of *coups d'état*" (Campbell 1992, 92). Similarly antidemocratic sentiments were expressed by the Taukei movement's 1987 submission to the Great Council of Chiefs in Fiji: "The two principal ideas of democracy—liberty (or freedom) and equality[—]are foreign values and indeed contrary to the Fijian way of life where liberty exists only within one's social rank and equality is strictly constrained by a fully developed social hierarchy" (quoted in Robertson and Tamanisau 1988, 81).

Fijian anthropologist Asesela Ravuvu headed a committee set up to renew the 1970 constitution after the 1987 coup d'état. He had concluded that democracy in Fiji had always been a facade: "Democracy was an illusion, a facade, a parting whim of a colonial power that had itself only practised dictatorship" (Ravuvu 1991, 87).

Fiji was the first country in which AV was used as "a deliberate instrument for 'political engineering' in an ethnically divided society" (Fraenkel 2000, 9). Joan Rydon, a political scientist, worried about the Constitution Review Commission's decision to use a paper ballot modeled on that of the Australian Senate, which allowed voters to let parties distribute their preferences, had been the commissions "greatest mistake" (2001, 47). In Fiji the results of the first election under AV were regarded by Brij Lal, an academic member of the CRC, as "hugely improbable" (1999, 4). A single party, Labour, won a majority of the seats, and the self-consciously multiracial coalition, led by the architects of the new constitution, was defeated. The result suggested that the problem with electoral engineering was not that it did not work but that it was unpredictable in its effects: "Coalitions did not respond in the way envisaged, and the new electoral laws, where these came most forcefully into play, had highly unexpected consequences" (Fraenkel 2000, 2).

Nevertheless, Ben Reilly, who had advised the Fiji Electoral Commission and was sympathetic to electoral engineering, defended the system: "It is clear that the introduction of preferential voting did play a modest role in breaking old habits of mono-ethnic politics in Fiji, facilitating cross-ethnic bargaining, and helping to build new routines of inter-ethnic negotiation and cooperation" (2001, 148). The impact of electoral engineering in Fiji then became an issue in a Court of Appeal case. The government, in its appeal against a High Court decision to uphold the validity of the 1997 constitution, had used research done by Jon Fraenkel, then a lecturer at the University of the South Pacific, on the impact of alternative voting on the subsequent election. The judgment disputed the academic's conclusion that the system was, in practice, complex and ambiguous and that "its merits as a tool for promoting ethnic cooperation were highly questionable" (Fraenkel 2000). The government asserted that such views might be "commonly held" but were "erroneous." The Court of Appeal found that even if only first preferences had been counted, the People's Coalition would still have won, that the rate of invalid voting was no higher for Fijians than for other ethnic groups, and that there was little evidence that voters were confused. The court concluded: "Even with the 'first past the post' system, government would still have been the same, and claims that indigenous Fijians in particular did not understand the system were largely unsubstantiated" (*Republic of Fiji Islands and Attorney General v. Prasad*, Civil Appeal No. ABU0078/2000S, 11–13).

Evaluations of Public Sector Reform

The international financial institutions evaluated their own work on public sector reform. The World Bank concluded that its approach to civil service reform in PNG had been "inadequate":

> It consisted mainly of wage-bill and staff reduction measures, which were not successful, leaving the budgetary burden in place, while adversely affecting efforts to build capacity in service departments. . . . At least equal attention should have been paid to improving management and the incentive framework in the civil service, which are essential for long-term service delivery improvements (2000, 9).

The bank pointed to problems of politicization and nepotism (the so-called *wantok* system) and suggested that attention to corruption prevention and accountability might have improved service delivery. However, the government itself was not blameless. As we have seen, it initiated cuts in 1981, in the mid-1990s, and again in 1999 (then advised by a renegade World Bank official). If the diagnosis was wrong, it was one shared by the

PNG Department of Finance. Dan Weise, the World Bank adviser in PNG, ended his assignment at odds with the government over its commitment to reform. In a television program, he asserted that the government had backed away from prosecuting difficult corruption cases and had slowed down on privatization. He blamed the government's fear of defeat in a forthcoming election—which it lost (Australian Broadcasting Corporation, *Four Corners*, 24 June 2002).

The ADB found that its interventions into public sector reform had "failed to take account of the need for proper pacing, sequencing and absorptive capacity" (Knapman and Saldhana 1999, 17). The urgent need to reduce public expenditure, mainly salaries, had been resolved at the expense of effectiveness—"some good staff had been lost or the wrong positions sacrificed." Institutional reform had been slow and provoked resistance. Changes in one part of the system, such as output budgeting, depended on changes in others, such as management, pay, and accounting (ibid.).

The Pacific Islands Forum commissioned consultants to perform a "stocktake," or assessment, of the process of implementing its Eight Accountability Principles. The stocktake, carried out in 2002, found "wide divergence in the extent of compliance and enforcement of the principles," particularly between the intention to implement and actual implementation (Pacific Islands Forum Secretariat 2002, 21). Countries were at various stages in economic reform, and no single solution fit every country. Some countries could not implement the accountability principles because legislation was ambiguous, inadequate, or "just too complex" (ibid., 22). The main barrier to implementation was the lack of human and financial resources. Ownership of reforms was sometimes weak, and decisions made at regional meetings were often not communicated between ministries and within countries.

Evaluations of Anticorruption

Sir Anthony Siaguru's review of the first five years of TI (PNG) operations identified several successes, particularly in curriculum development. But it also noted a lack of success regarding the National Integrity Pledge, the introduction of an ICAC, the introduction of professional codes of conduct, and efforts to persuade the Privatisation Commission to adopt integrity pacts. The first phase of the Electoral Reform Project (ERP) had clearly been a success, as the constitutional amendments and integrity of political parties legislation had been passed, and preferential voting would be introduced at the next election after 2002 (though it was not clear how much the ERPs campaign had influenced MPs in their voting).

Institutions and Development

The evaluations that most concern donors and international financial institutions relate to economic growth and development. Development is typically measured by external comparisons. Countries are ranked according to their GDP or to their human development. Transparency International devised its own ranking system, consisting of the Corruption Perceptions Index and the Bribe Payers Index.

Unfortunately, the data on economic growth in the South Pacific are weak (Chand 2003). Helen Hughes (2003) points out that the figures are highly politicized, given that they are used in arguments with donors about entitlements. Overall, the data (summarized in table 14) show a low average annual rate of growth over the last thirty years, as well as some individual cases of negative growth rates.

Institutional explanations have often been advanced for slow growth or lack of economic development. In World Bank jargon, "institutions matter." In the Pacific Islands, for example, land tenure is regularly blamed for poor performance in agriculture. Provincial government is blamed for failure to deliver services. The absence of political parties is blamed for government instability. And so on. Institutional remedies are regularly proposed: the registration of land, a new constitution, public sector reform, or a stronger anticorruption commission.

The direction of causal flow has been controversial. Fred Riggs (1964), a founding father of development administration, was critical of early World Bank recommendations for more training, expert consultants, and new institutions—the precursors of what is now called governance. He had then believed that "the administrative defects complained of are as much consequences of underdevelopment as they are its causes" (ibid., 80).

However, Daniel Kaufmann and Art Kraay (2003) more recently asserted that the flow was from institutions to development. Comparing as many as 170 countries, they found a positive correlation between per capita incomes and three measures of governance: control of corruption, the protection of property rights and the rule of law, and voice and accountability. Questions then arose: Did better governance affect per capita incomes, or did higher incomes lead to improvements in governance? Or was a third factor driving both? The authors noted that most of the differences in per capita incomes, the majority of which have emerged

TABLE 14. Average Annual Growth Rates and GNP Per Capita

	Average annual growth in real GNP per capita in 1970–2000 (%) [a]	GNP per capita in 2000 (US$ purchasing power parity)
Melanesia		
Papua New Guinea	0.3	2,180
Solomon Islands	-0.4	1,710
Vanuatu	-0.3	2,960
Fiji	2.7	4,480
New Caledonia	NA	21,820
Average	0.6	
Polynesia		
Samoa	0.8	5,050
Tonga	2.6	1,660
Cook Islands	NA	5,000
Wallis and Futuna	NA	2,000
Tuvalu	-1.4	1,100
Niue	NA	3,800
Tokelau	NA	1,500
French Polynesia	NA	23,340
Average	0.7	
Micronesia		
Federated States of Micronesia	NA	2,000
Kiribati	-1.2	950
Northern Mariana Islands	NA	12,857
Marshall Islands	NA	1,600
Palau	NA	9,000
Nauru	NA	5,000
Average	NA	
Pacific Islands average	0.6	

Source: Chand 2003.

[a] "NA" means either that data were not available or that variation greater than 25 percent between sources suggested the figures were unreliable.

only within the last two hundred years, can be traced back to older differences in institutional quality. These older differences were the result of a
Western influence, which Kaufmann, Kraay, and Zoido-Lobatón had
earlier measured in terms of the percentage of the population speaking
English or a major European language (Kaufmann, et al. 1999, 14). So
governance preceded growth. The authors used statistical tests to demonstrate that in fact a slight negative feedback from growth to governance
existed, which they explained as "state capture," or the "undue and illicit
influence of the elite in shaping the laws, policies and regulations of the
state" (ibid., 3). However, this negative causal flow was not enough to overcome the strong positive effect of particular deeply rooted, European-
influenced institutions on growth. But the absence of positive feedback
from growth to governance did suggest that there were no "virtuous
circles," in which better governance led to growth that in turn fed better
governance.

The authors' argument is clearly one for transfer. On the one hand,
European influences had a positive impact on institutional quality in some
countries, later reflected in their growth. And on the other hand, growth
would not of itself produce better institutions—it might marginally make
them worse. "Direct and sustained interventions" were needed to improve
governance in countries where it was lacking.

Consistency and Performance

New institutions are not enough in themselves. Research in the 1990s
began to suggest that the relationship between new institutions and their
context was what mattered most. Robert Putnam's work (1993) on the
performance of provincial governments in Italy was particularly influential on the World Bank.

Putnam found a general association between government performance and the level of economic development of each region. Again, the
causal flow was not clear: Did economic development encourage performance, or vice versa? Or was a third factor involved? In any case, the
considerable variation in performance was not explainable by level of economic development. Some governments in rich areas performed badly,
and some governments in poor areas performed well. Putnam's originality was in showing the significance of sociocultural factors, particularly
"norms and networks of civic engagement," when explaining differences
in government performance. He discovered that citizen membership in

sports clubs, cooperatives, mutual aid societies, cultural associations, and voluntary unions was strongly correlated with government performance. This dense network of civic associations was "path dependent," or determined by history. It could be traced back to a split in Italian government between self-governing communes in the north and feudal autocracy in the south. By disaggregating the influence of economic development and what he termed "civic-ness," Putnam also demonstrated that such civic involvement drives modernity, rather than the other way round.

Putnam did not show that good institutions were unimportant. They might be a necessary but insufficient condition for performance. Instead, he identified sociocultural factors in achieving performance from well-designed institutions. Yet his path-dependent explanation suggested that the roots of poor performance might be quite deep. Putnam's work stimulated interest in the role of civil society, NGOs, and "social capital" in development in the South Pacific, including in Papua New Guinea (De Renzio and Kavanamur 1999).

Similar research on the economic performance of North American Indian reservations has also suggested that consistency between introduced and indigenous institutions improves performance. Consistency would be particularly relevant to the formerly stateless societies of the South Pacific and their introduced Westminster constitutions. Cornell and Kalt (1995) examined how constitutions were imposed on American Indians by the U.S. Department of the Interior in the 1930s. As Putnam did in his research, Cornell and Kalt were able to hold institutions constant and then look for the impact of other factors on growth. In this case the main other factor was consistency between the introduced constitution and indigenous institutions. The authors' hypothesis was that "extra-constitutional agreement must underlie successful constitutional rule" (ibid., 403). Cornell and Kalt found big differences in levels of economic performance on Apache and Sioux reservations that could not be explained by differences in resource endowments. Instead the researchers looked to traditional political organization and its consistency with the constitutions introduced by the Department of the Interior.

Sioux traditional organization was a council of elders, who empowered a leader or leaders. Apache organization was more centered on a single chief and was thus more consistent with the directly elected, strong-chief-executive system imposed by the U.S. government. Present-day Apache leaders could draw on traditional norms and expectations about leaders in ways that the Sioux, with their more parliamentary traditions, could not.

For example, in relation to managing a tribal-owned ski resort, Cornell and Kalt noted: "[I]f Apache cultural norms locate legitimate authority in the office of the tribal chairman such that otherwise defecting support-ers are constrained by those norms to side with him when it is necessary to fire an incompetent worker at the tribal ski resort, the efficiency of labor at the site and the ski resort have better chances of being sustained" (ibid., 407).

Concerns about consistency with indigenous institutions have been introduced into the world of international institutions through work by Mamadou Dia, a World Bank official. The World Bank was driven by con-cern with Africa's dismal economic performance. Dia (1996) blamed it on the "institutional disconnect" between state and civil society, between for-mal and informal private institutions, and between corporate and societal culture. His study of institutional reconciliation in Africa turned on differ-ences between formal (and introduced) institutions and informal (indige-nous) institutions. He found that formal institutions, "not being rooted in local culture, generally fail to command society's loyalty or to trigger local ownership," and that their ineffectiveness was "compounded by the absence of the rule of law as a third-party enforcement mechanism" (ibid., 10). By contrast, informal institutions could count on "legitimacy, accountability and self-enforcement." But they also had "dysfunctional" elements—for example, discrimination on the basis of age or gender. Dia looked forward to a reconciliation between the two, resulting in institu-tions that were both "rooted" and "open." He proposed various ways of achieving this reconciliation, including having more systematic client consultation, promoting successful small businesses, and incorporating traditional values into the management practices of larger enterprises (ibid., 2–14).

The South Pacific might provide a natural laboratory for testing such arguments. Similar Westminster constitutions, for example, were imposed over a variety of traditional institutions—hierarchical in Polynesia and more egalitarian in Melanesia. However, the results are equivocal. The average annual growth rates in Melanesia (0.6 percent) and Polynesia (0.7 percent) are not substantially different (see table 14). In any case, the Westminster constitution seems consistent with both: its parliamentary aspects are sympathetic to Melanesian big-man traditions, while the power it grants the prime minister is more consistent with Polynesian hierarchic traditions (Larmour 2000a). As we have seen, some efforts were also made to adapt the Westminster constitution to local circumstances.

Evaluating Consultancy

The main concern of this book has been with the process of transfer, rather than with the institutions themselves. Missionaries and consultants played an important role in facilitating transfer, but how is their work to be evaluated?

Decolonization found Western lawyers and political scientists advising constitutional planning committees that had quite different, stateless political traditions and were looking for ways to deal with traditional leaders: chiefs, *iroij*, *matai*, and so on. Reflecting on his own advice to the Micronesian Constitutional Convention (MCC), political scientist Norman Meller (1982) questioned the consultants' "cultural competence" to advise when even apparently mundane questions about where people should meet, sit, talk, and remain silent were culturally loaded. Indeed, the familiar distinction between process and product was, Meller said, "alien to those Pacific cultures which would regard all such enterprise as comprising an integral whole" (ibid., 52). Meller was critical of Jim Davidson's account of his own approach as adviser for Western Samoa—for example, pressing for clarity when Samoans preferred silence or equivocation, and occasionally acting as an advocate for a position.

Meller distinguished two opposite methods of working. In the first, used in Samoa, a preconvention group drew up a draft for discussion and approval. The second, advised by Meller in Micronesia, involved a more incremental and reiterative method in which a series of committees, each with a broad mandate, worked in parallel and then together. Yet Meller admitted to "injecting his cultural values" of differentiation, specialization, and avoidance of delay into a situation where Micronesians might have preferred to temporize and deal with all issues together (ibid., 59).

Looking back, Meller questioned "the ethics of his interjection into the affairs of the MCC." His way of framing and deciding questions was not theirs. Nor did outsiders necessarily have much expertise in the content of the deliberations—for example, accommodating the role of chiefs. Meller wondered what role a consultant might play outside his society, concluding that a consultant should restrict himself to problems arising at the interface of the local polity with others, explaining what happened elsewhere and "assuring that knowledge on non-Island concepts is correctly—as viewed from *his* perspective—transferred across cultural boundaries" (ibid., 61).

The observations of Jim Fingleton (2002) put his own consultancies into the broader context of policy making in Melanesia. Fingleton was much more interested in reform than Meller was. As well as working on land registration, Jim Fingleton also acted as a consultant to the UN Food and Agriculture Organization (FAO) on reform of the Department of Agriculture and Livestock in PNG and on forestry legislation in Vanuatu. He later reflected on the role of consultants like himself in these processes.

In PNG he found that there was no formal approval for the policy reforms that consultants were expected to implement. No proposals had been put to ministers. The department already had its own view of its future structure as a corporation, but the consultants believed that it should remain as a government department. The consultants were never able to meet the minister of the department, who was replaced twice during their assignment as the prime minister "tried to hold his shaky coalition together" (ibid., 10). Industry opposition to reform became concerted, partly because "many years of Ministerial interference" had led to suspicion and distrust of politicians—and hence of reform—and partly because members of agricultural boards "owed their appointments to ministerial patronage and were not interested in reforms which placed the interests of growers first" (ibid., 11). The consultants' proposals were then "misrepresented" in newspaper reports as a government takeover of commodity boards and growers' funds. Growers staged a protest at a meeting in Mount Hagen and threatened to block the Highlands Highway. In August 2000 the minister of the department assured the public that the FAO's "controversial reforms" would not be implemented.

In Vanuatu there had been clear government support for a national forestry policy, and Fingleton was hired by the FAO to write new legislation to implement it. The trouble was that the government had since changed, and the new prime minister, Barak Sope, had authorized a private Australian legal firm and its local partners to draft a special law to deal with land "in which they had an interest" (ibid., 12). The prime minister's intervention was opposed by the government's legal advisers and by Forestry Department officials, and, fortunately for the consultancy, the Sope government was brought down in a vote of no confidence in May 2001.

Fingleton drew several lessons from his experience as a consultant in Melanesia. First, aid projects were no substitute for local processes of policy making. In PNG, decisions about the future status of the Department of Agriculture and Livestock had not been made before the consultants were brought in. In Vanuatu, by contrast, parliamentary approval of a new forest policy allowed officials to resist the prime minister's intervention on behalf of private interests.

Second, reform initiatives were vulnerable to turnovers of prime ministers and votes of no confidence. To survive, reform initiatives needed support from outside parliaments. Community involvement in the creation of forestry policy, though costly to achieve, gave legitimacy to the policy, enabling it to survive parliamentary instability. Fingleton proposed a revival of commissions of inquiry that could engage the public in policy making on difficult subjects like land tenure.

Fingleton's reflections demonstrated the ethical issues that pervaded the role of consultants who transferred policy. Should consultants take on board their clients' political objectives, or should they advise the opposition? What responsibility should they take for the consequences of the implementation of their advice?

Economist Dudley Seers (1962) showed how difficult it was for consultants to take refuge in the argument that their advice was purely technical. Different types of consultants faced distinctive risks. An adviser might try to play a narrowly technical role, but such a role was likely to disappoint a government client, and in any case, the exclusion of possibilities from analysis was an implicit political decision against them. Technical advisers easily became frustrated and ignored if they found the government's whole approach to be wrong. The second type of adviser, which Seers called the statesman adviser, took on board the government's goals and recommended ways of achieving them. The third type, the party adviser, took into account the government's concerns with survival and reelection: the need to assuage neglected regions or to defer to powerful interests, for example. One step further on the continuum was the personal adviser, who identified closely with particular leaders and their fortunes.

In our cases, external advice on land registration was often presented in technical terms, though it was easy to show that its assumptions had political consequences. Constitutional advice was less easy to separate from its political and partisan implications, and successful advisers like Yash Ghai, Edward Wolfers, and Anthony Regan deftly switched from the technical to the statesmanlike, the partisan, and even the personal. Principled local politicians like John Momis were often able to attract considerable personal loyalty from their expert advisers. In the 1990s, Yash Ghai became so committed to the review of the constitution in Fiji that he decided to advise a party rather than the government.

The advice on public sector reform was typically delivered in neutral and technical terms, and the IFIs' consultants could frame it in statesmanlike terms of achieving a government's goals. There was suspicion in Cook Islands and, to some extent, Vanuatu that the consultants were acting in a partisan way, sensitive to concerns of the government with its own survival. The advice on corruption was delivered in a different way, through TI national chapters. From the point of view of governments, that advice could look purely partisan.

The line between insider and outsider advice was sometimes hard to draw. In Tonga, King George adopted an Englishman as his adviser and gave him a Tongan title (Latukefu 1975, 40). Nonindigenous citizens, as well as expatriates with close personal ties to island leaders, played important roles as givers and receivers of advice from abroad. A good example would be A.V. Hughes, a former Solomon Islands finance secretary and Central Bank governor who became a citizen of Solomon Islands at independence. He later acted as a consultant to other regional governments, first through the United Nations Development Programme and later through the Asian Development Bank. And it was a nonindigenous citizen and a woman, Marie-Noelle Ferrieux-Patterson, who mobilized the Ombudsman's Office in Vanuatu, which was finally established with technical assistance from PNG in 1995 and began its functions with a scathing series of reports on government corruption and incompetence.

Conclusions

The sponsors of institutional transfer were, as we have seen, disappointed with the results. Ghai found the PNG constitution working but failing to achieve its goals. Hughes found that the expectations for customary land registration had been too optimistic. Lal was shocked at the unexpected results of the first election under the new Fiji constitution. The World Bank and the ADB were critical of their own approaches to public sector reform. The Pacific Islands Forum's stocktake of its accountability principles found that agreement at regional meetings was not being translated into changes at home. Sir Anthony Siaguru found few successes amongst TI's efforts in PNG.

Can we therefore conclude that these attempts at institutional transfer failed? The answer has to be yes if we look at particular incidents, in terms of the goals set by their proponents. But this view of institutions and their transfer may be too narrow. Reviewing the history of reform in the United States, March and Olsen (1989) asked why the government keeps announcing comprehensive reform programs, in spite of the regular lack of success: "Few efficiencies are achieved; little gain in responsiveness is recorded; control seems as elusive as before." Part of the problem, according to March and Olsen, is the attention of leaders. In the absence of that attention, "reorganisations tend to become collections of solutions looking for problems, ideologies looking for soapboxes, pet projects looking for supporters, and people looking for jobs, reputations or entertainment" (ibid., 82).

But the authors' conclusion was not cynical or defeatist. Although most reforms produced changes, those changes were minor compared with the continuing incremental changes taking place anyway. March and Olsen concluded that although any particular reorganization was likely to fail, the repetition of ideas and arguments made a difference in the long term. Ideas initially rejected became adopted when a later opportunity emerged. The climate of opinion shifted. More fundamentally, the authors argued that reform needed to be thought of not only in its own instrumental terms. Instead its symbolic importance should be noted: it reaffirmed long-standing frustrations and fears about government, and the comforting idea that leaders could bring government under control: "More generally, organisation and reorganisation, like much action, are tied to the discovery, clarification and elaboration of meaning, as well as to immediate action or decision making" (ibid., 91).

The failure of the Kenyan model in PNG was, in the longer term, only an episode in a longer-running debate about land registration in PNG, going back much earlier, to an experiment with registration by local governments in 1952, and forward to the present, when the government planned to introduce a system of registration. Meanwhile the government had been responding to demand for registration by the use of existing lease-leaseback legislation. Similarly, while systematic adjudication was actually implemented and then abandoned in Solomon Islands, it was succeeded by legislation for land records (though they could not be mortgaged). And whereas Vanuatu's leaders were preoccupied with alienated land in the 1980s, they later introduced a land tribunal that would allow for registration.

A fairly technical process of survey and registration was made to carry huge symbolic weight, by both its promoters and their opponents. On the one hand, registration was presented as the key to economic development. On the other, it was a fundamental attack on deeply held values. Its actual impact, when examined in Solomon Islands, was startlingly marginal—farmers went on doing pretty much what they had done before.

The symbolic and reiterative characters of these transfers are related. The transfers touched on important conflicts, tensions, and dilemmas that were unlikely to be resolved, one way or another, in the short term. People kept coming back to land registration. Similarly, constitutional debates about traditional leadership refused to go away. As we saw, the introduction of universal suffrage in Samoa was accompanied by an empowerment of village *fono* and a series of court cases about their rights to punish wrongdoers. To notice the symbolic and repetitive character of debates about good governance is not to belittle them. Longer-term shifts in ideas were going on through and behind them. It became generally accepted that some kind of land registration was needed in Melanesia, though the form it should take continued to be disputed. Fiji reverted to constitutionalism after coups in 1987 and 2000—there were debates about whether it was the right constitution, but there were no influential voices against constitutionalism as such. However, there was still resistance to representative democracy in principle among the elite in Tonga.

Calls for public sector reform became repeated and somewhat ritualistic. In PNG, attempts to reduce numbers were either resisted or—if accepted—later reversed. Nevertheless, a steady shift took place in the way the public sector was thought about, as well as a corresponding revaluation of the private sector. These shifts were the result of steady, repeated efforts by think tanks like the INA, multilateral banks, and tertiary education institutions that teach the new public management.

The rapid rise in international concern about corruption during the 1990s sharply demonstrated the symbolic character of debates about good governance. Laws against bribery had already been transferred and were in place. Officials had probably always taken bribes. Newspapers had always exposed scandals. There had been long-running talk about nepotism. What had changed was opinion in international agencies, in NGOs, and among the elite.

The sponsors of reform necessarily saw it in one-off and instrumental terms—a particular effort had failed to achieve the goals its sponsors set. These individual, instrumental defeats, however, should not blind us to the broader and longer-term shifts in official and professional opinion about, for example, the proper role of the state or the tolerance of corruption.

Conclusion

The metaphor of the foreign flower suggested that institutions grow out of the soil and are rooted in a local context. In this metaphor the emphasis on the soil, and the expressive character of institutions, are strongly nationalistic. But we have seen how sideways pressure supported democracy and constitutionalism. The Asian Development Bank and the Pacific Islands Forum promoted public sector reform; the Financial Action Task Force tried to press island-states to stop money laundering; and Transparency International's network franchised and supported national chapters in the Pacific Islands. In this sense small islands were not isolated. Their dependence on regional or international organizations for aid or common services made them more open to influence than larger and more autonomous nation-states were. Political scientist Goran Hyden (1983) wrote about the state floating above society in Africa. If we are going to use flowers as a metaphor, the better comparison might be with lilies on the surface of a pond: looking identical to one another, jostling up against each other, and spreading across the surface. They float above the bottom of the pond, with their roots only loosely connected to it.

Sources

Much of the borrowing of metropolitan models was indirect. Land registration was a typically colonial process, with borrowing of the Torrens title system from colonial Australia and systematic adjudication from British colonies in Africa rather than from the United Kingdom. The Westminster constitution model was borrowed through its written-up forms in India, Africa, or Australia and New Zealand. The model for independent commissions against corruption was in Hong Kong, not London. However, the new public management came fairly directly from the United Kingdom or New Zealand, as did the first principles of rational choice economics. There was continuing comparison, both positive and negative, with Africa.

Not all transfer was from place to place. There was also reference to first principles, such as the assumption that if people had their land registered, they would feel more secure and therefore more likely to invest. Some of the new public management that was promoted in the ADB reforms was based on first-principle assumptions about rent seeking by bureaucrats. It could not grasp other motivations such as nationalism. First principles and "best practice" in accountancy were also influential in the belief in the transparency and the value of external oversight in Cook Islands.

Reference to past models was selective. Proposals for customary land registration in PNG and Solomon Islands drew lessons from the failures of earlier colonial attempts. Supporters of the indigenous alternative— customary land records in Solomon Islands—drew on the early nationalist history of the anticolonial Maasina Ruru movement in arguing for registration as a way of conserving traditions. Some constitutions were adaptations of colonial predecessors, but others—like PNG's or Vanuatu's—sought to start from scratch. Public sector reformers in the 1990s virtually ignored earlier attempts to reform the civil service in each Pacific Islands nation. Rather than showing path dependency, or the weight of history, the past was often treated as something to be rejected in favor of once-and-for-all reform—an idea expressed as "We can't go on like this."

There was also "borrowing from the future"—either in generalized ideas about modernity in the West or in more utopian attempts at transformation. PNG's constitution particularly looked to the future, as did Fiji's in 1998. Public sector reform also pointed to the future, in part to justify the present pain of structural adjustment. Much of the anticorruption rhetoric was utopian, expressed in slogans like "zero tolerance" that looked forward to transformed individuals living in a world free of corruption. The rhetoric sometimes looked nostalgically to a past in which colonial officials were seen as relatively uncorrupt.

Processes

Some cases provided examples of direct, first-dimensional exercise of power to impose reform. Conditionality did work, at least for a while, in protecting PNG's forests. Indirect forms of power were used much more often, including agenda setting on the grand scale of the World Bank's *World Development Report* and on the minor scale of the content of aid negotiations with governments. Recipients resisted with weapons of the weak, such as creating delays, failing to provide information, or—in PNG —denying a visa to a bank official. The Pacific Islands Forum's *Stocktake* found that little had been done to communicate the results of regional agreements. Island governments lacked positive, enabling, infrastructural power, and so failures to transfer were often a special case of more general failures to implement policy, whether indigenous or transferred. Indigenous alternatives to the Kenyan model of registration faced similar problems of implementation, such as keeping registers up to date and servicing remote areas. Donors provided this positive, enabling form of power to island governments. The loan of funds or of police intervention allowed a government to survive, as the Cook Islands government did throughout its massive fiscal crisis and restructuring and as the Solomon Islands government did through the first year of RAMSI.

There were many examples of diversification and experiment in homegrown constitutions at independence and in Fiji in the 1990s. Yet politicians regularly complained about inappropriate institutions, while themselves imitating more prestigious—but not necessarily relevant— ones.

In times of crisis, governments looked for solutions and were forced to take what was available, even if it was not particularly relevant. When island-states ran into their first fiscal crises, in the mid-1990s, the ideas of new public management happened to be in circulation. Some NPM ideas helped justify cuts in staff. Sometimes crises were talked up in order to provide a window for transfer. The most egregious example of this tactic was the South Pacific Forum finance ministers' determination not to let economic recovery get in the way of reform. But when island governments did recognize a financial crisis, they were vulnerable to the standard, not necessarily appropriate, doctrines promoted by the international financial institutions. Looking back, both the ADB and the World Bank regretted some of the advice they had offered. The World Bank found that it should have paid more attention to improving management, incentive frameworks, and accountability and reducing corruption. The ADB found that it should have paid more attention to pacing and sequencing and to preventing the loss of good staff. In contrast to what occurred in relation to financial crises in the 1990s, civil service officials regularly had difficulty convincing Melanesian politicians in the 1970s that their nations had a crisis in customary land tenure.

Economists were often blamed for promoting one-size-fits-all solutions, but accountancy principles influenced the ADB-sponsored public sector reforms, while surveyors had a professional interest in land registration. Recently, political scientists have developed a professional interest in promoting voting systems. The most prolific form of institutional transfer was through the law, transmitted through the legal profession. The most creative and influential constitutional adviser was Yash Ghai. Yet he was strongly suspicious of the legal profession—for example, in his criticism the Samoan profession's willingness to draw on other Westminster precedents rather than on the intentions of the writers of the constitution. Academic historians—such as Jim Davidson, Brij Lal, and Alan Ward— had a surprising influence on constitutional and land reform.

Whereas professional networks promoted standardized ideas of best practice, there was an opposite risk in invention and originality. Enthusiasm for new ideas could crowd out scarce political and official attention that otherwise might be devoted to long-standing problems.

Results

The British Empire and international organizations like the World Bank have spread institutions around the world, but they have not always stuck. Table 15 summarizes the results described in earlier chapters. It shows a patchwork, with most transfers eventually succeeding but only half surviving, often with continuing external support. Customary land registration failed to transfer or (in Solomon Islands) failed to survive, though other kinds of land registration succeeded in other parts of the region. Constitutions proved more resilient, with the exceptions of those in Fiji and Solomon Islands. In Fiji, continuing attempts were made to find and entrench an alternative to the 1970 constitution, and the 1998 constitution survived the civilian coup of 2000. The constitution in Solomon Islands stayed nominally in place after the prime minister was pressured to resign in 2000. Parliament then set up a review committee to look for a more federal alternative. Yet militants and gangs outside Parliament continued to put pressure on its members, and the police were unable to maintain law and order, eventually provoking the Australian police and military "cooperative intervention" in 2003.

The institutions of representative democracy, however, seemed well

TABLE 15. Transfers and Their Survival

	Transfer	Survival of transfer
Customary land registration in PNG, Solomon Islands, and Vanuatu	No, except Solomon Islands	No; abandoned in Solomon Islands
Westminster constitutions	Yes	Yes, except for • Fiji, 1987–1990 • intimidation of MPs in Solomon Islands, 2000–2003; then RAMSI intervention
Representative democracy	Yes, except Tonga and limited suffrage in Samoa	Yes, except Tonga; universal suffrage in Samoa since 1991
Public sector reform	Yes, in staff cuts and contracts for senior staff Limited compliance with Pacific Islands Forum Accountability Principles Privatization limited	Yes, but many of the same senior staff were rehired in Cook Islands
Anticorruption	Yes; ombudsmen set up in PNG, Solomon Islands, and eventually Vanuatu	Yes, but • setbacks in Vanuatu • conciliatory role taken by Leadership Code commissioner in Solomon Islands • corruption issues in Solomon Islands 2000 coup
	Transparency International established in PNG, Solomon Islands, Vanuatu, and Fiji	TI (PNG) chapter initiatives, but little success so far
	Niue and Marshall Islands "made progress" and were removed from blacklist	Cook Islands and Nauru have legislated, but still on blacklist in 2004

established at national levels and, in Samoa, were extended through domestic decisions without external pressure. A pro-democracy movement also survived in Tonga with some external NGO support. Democracy at local levels continued to be contested by traditional leaders. Public sector reform partly succeeded—downsizing took place, but privatization programs struggled to survive. The Pacific Islands Forum's Action Plan was patchily implemented. The fate of anticorruption efforts was less clear. Transfers of ombudsman commissions, tasked with enforcing leadership codes, took place in PNG at independence and eventually in Solomon Islands and in Vanuatu, where the commission provoked strong resistance from Parliament. Chapters of Transparency International were also established in Melanesia and Fiji, but the earliest—in PNG—was having difficulty making an impression.

Effects

Many of the proponents of transfer seemed to be disappointed with the results. Research by the Lands Department in Solomon Islands found that registration had little impact. Looking back, Yash Ghai found that the PNG constitution had survived but had failed in its aspirations. The alternative voting system had not produced the ethnic moderation that its supporters in Fiji proposed, but it was going to be tried again in PNG. Public sector reform had not led to improvement in management and service delivery, though it had been accompanied by a reduction in the number of civil servants and by some sales of government assets. The ombudsman commissions produced reports, and individual officials in PNG were brought before tribunals. The real or underlying rate of corruption was hard to assess, because it took place in secret. No one argued that corruption had fallen since the introduction of leadership codes, though it might have been even worse without them. Sir Anthony Siaguru's review of the performance of Transparency International in PNG found little immediate success.

Long-term shifts in meaning and evaluation might be more significant than the results of particular episodes, which almost always disappointed their promoters. Solomon Islands and Vanuatu both introduced legislation to allow the sporadic registration of customary land, and the PNG government was ready to try again. Where constitutions had been set aside or put under pressure, the political debate was about the content of new constitutions rather than about whether to have constitutions at all. Samoa became more democratic without external pressure, and a pro-democracy movement had survived in Tonga. Officials and politicians continued to believe that the size and structure of the public service were important, even if they were hard to change. These deeply held beliefs and values were impervious to empirical evidence one way or the other, at least in the short term. Nevertheless, longer-term shifts were evident. Nongovernmental organizations and the private sector had come to be deferred to more regularly in policy making. And a consensus rapidly grew up in the 1990s that corruption was a root cause of problems in the Pacific Islands.

The Fate of the State

Great expenditures of effort have been made to maintain states, to prevent Bougainville from seceding from PNG, and now to prevent "state failure" in Solomon Islands and Nauru. Each of the policies analyzed in the previous chapters has an impact on stateness. Land registration may not have a direct influence on development, but it provides information that might allow land to be taxed in the future. Registration also makes it easier for officials to keep an eye on rural life. Constitutions set out the relationships between organs of the state, and representative democracy gives them legitimacy. Public sector reform is often a tempting option for governments when implementation of policies that affect other actors, like farmers or the private sector, becomes too difficult. States need to work through nongovernmental actors, both voluntary and profit-oriented, to get things done. Finally, the corruption that offends TI and others in the 1990s is that of ministers and officials whose private interests conflict with the public interest championed by the state.

The period of decolonization ended just as the Anglo-Saxon countries that promoted decolonization—Britain, Australia, and New Zealand —began to turn against the state, in favor of privatization and deregulation. Margaret Thatcher came to power in 1979, and Britain began to export ideas about privatization in the 1980s. The policies analyzed in earlier chapters of the present book were each components of a liberal image of the role of the state: creating and protecting private property; having a constitution that limited its power; being governed by representatives; and having a small, effective bureaucracy free from corruption. Some of these policies transferred more easily than others. Systematic land registration faltered and was reversed. The constitutions remained in place, under some pressure. Democracy was even extended in Samoa. Public sector reform had less success, and the prospects for anticorruption were uncertain. So the geometry of the transferred state in the Pacific Islands is different from that of the liberal ideal—the transferred state is constitutional and democratic, but it is not so supportive of private property and it is large and corruptible.

The compact invoked by the Fiji Constitution Review Commission and the national summits promoted by the ADB are less liberal and more corporatist in style. They see government working with and through peak organizations that represent powerful interests in society. Transparency International's ideas about coalitions are similar. New institutions like national summits were conjured up and given solidity during transfer. Civil society became treated as an autonomous and coherent actor, realized in the activities of NGOs and often funded from abroad. The Pacific Islands Forum *Stocktake* noticed that civil society was generally better organized than the private sector and therefore was better able to represent itself. The banks and donors tried to paint the private sector in a new and more favorable light. For example, the private sector, formerly characterized as the source of corruption, was now presented as one of its victims.

The Role of Culture

Consistency with local values was a determinant of transfer, but not necessarily the most important one. The individualistic values of customary land registration, for example, contrasted with the values of communal ownership. Values of political participation or chiefly hierarchy, for example, contrasted with introduced institutions of representative democracy. As Ghai (1983) argued, consultation about constitutions and local participation in their design had not resulted in constitutions that were "rooted in indigenous concepts." Nevertheless the constitutions survived better than other institutions described in table 15. Some local values, such as the Christian principles that were woven into the Vanuatu ombudsman's report, had themselves been introduced. Some proponents of transfer deliberately challenged local values. Transparency International in PNG was particularly hostile to what it saw as cultural excuses for corruption. In some cases, the argument for cultural sensitivity and appropriateness was a pragmatic one for simplicity. Land registration and constitutional requirements, for example, were often criticized as being too complicated.

Here cultural arguments slipped into what economists call transaction costs—the costs of making and keeping deals.

The thing transferred was often a relatively simple technique, like land registration, a way of counting votes, or a register of leaders' assets (in a Leadership Code Commission). This technique became surrounded, justified, and criticized by much more elaborate stories and counterstories. The relatively simple technical process of survey and registration, for example, was framed and interpreted in radically different ways—as an agricultural revolution or as a means of conserving the past. It became demonized by student radicals, but it was also a symbolic issue for economists who saw property rights as a condition for development. The indigenous alternative—customary land records in Solomon Islands—was technically quite similar, but its proponents put it in a radically different framework of meaning and valuation, harking back to the Maasina Ruru nationalist movement's grand project to write down custom. Major cultural debates took place around quite simple procedures, which were interpreted in radically different ways.

Similarly, the independence constitutions prescribed regulations, but they also made sense of them and valued them as expressions of national aspirations or protections of individual rights. For governments in fiscal crises, ideas like privatization and downsizing helped to explain an inevitable and more mundane process of budget cuts, sackings, and asset sales.

In these cases the cognitive and evaluative aspects of institutions were transferred, without necessarily much change in local behavior. Registration went from being an instrument of individualization to being reframed as an instrument of preservation. The constitution went from being an instrument of colonial rule to being an expression of popular opinion. Asset sales became privatization. And looking after one's relatives or constituents became "corruption." In this form of institutional transfer, local behavior does not change, but it is understood and valued differently—and sometimes negatively, as a deficit, or something requiring reform.

These episodes have all been of transfers into or within the region. More research is now needed on the reverse flow of Pacific Islands ideas and institutions that might have influenced the rest of the world. They have not had the force of colonialism or conditionality behind them, but we saw in chapter 8 that power is not simply one-way or zero-sum. Ideas were carried by the individuals who accompanied early explorers back to

Europe or joined metropolitan armies or came to Canberra, Wellington, or Honolulu as students sponsored by aid programs. The reverse transfer of Pacific Islands institutions is probably now being felt in church life, election campaigns, and local government in areas settled by Pacific Islander diasporic communities in the United States, Australia, and New Zealand.

References

Althusser, L. 1971. Ideology and ideological state apparatuses. In *Lenin and Philosophy and Other Essays*, ed. L. Althusser. London: New Left Books.

Anderson, B. 1983. *Imagined Communities: Reflections on the Origins and Spread of Nationalism*. London: Verso.

Appadurai, A. 1996. *Modernity at Large: Cultural Dimensions of Globalization*. Minneapolis: University of Minnesota Press.

Apter, D. A. 1955. *The Gold Coast in Transition*. Princeton, NJ: Princeton University Press.

———. 1963. *Ghana in Transition*. New York: Atheneum.

Asia Pacific Group on Money Laundering. 2003. History and background. http://www.apgml.org/content/history_and_background.jsp (accessed 30 October 2004).

'Atenisi Institute. 2000. http://kalianet.to/atenisi/institute/institute.html.

Badie, B. 2000. *The Imported State: The Westernization of the Political Order*. Stanford, CA: Stanford University Press.

Bain, W. 2003. The political theory of trusteeship and the twilight of international equality. *International Relations* 16(1): 59–77.

Bale, Malcolm, and Tony Dale. 1998. Public sector reform in New Zealand and its relevance to developing countries. *World Bank Research Observer* 13(1): 103–121.

Ballard, J. A., ed. 1981. *Policy-Making in a New State: Papua New Guinea 1972–77*. St. Lucia: University of Queensland Press.

Barcham, M. 2003. South–south policy transfer: The case of the Vanuatu Ombudsman's Office. *Pacific Economic Bulletin* 18(2): 108–117.

Barnes, J. A. 1990. *Models and Interpretations*. Cambridge: Cambridge University Press.

Beckstrom, J. 1973. Transplantation of legal systems: An early report on the reception of Western laws in Ethiopia. *American Journal of Comparative Law* 21:557–583.

Bennett, J. 2002. Roots of conflict in Solomon Islands—though much is taken, much abides: Legacies of tradition and colonialism. State, Society, and Governance in Melanesia Discussion Paper 2002/5. Canberra: Research School of Pacific and Asian Studies, Australian National University.

Bertram, I., and R. F. Watters. 1986. The MIRAB economy in South Pacific microstates. *Pacific Viewpoint* 26(3): 497–529.

Bird, N. 1945. Is there a danger of a post-war flare-up among New Guinea natives? *Pacific Islands Monthly* 16(4): 69–70. Quoted in Lindstrom 1993, 16.

Boli, J., and G. Thomas. 1999. INGOs and the organization of world culture. In *Constructing World Culture: International Non-Government Organisations since 1975*, ed. J. Boli and G. Thomas, 13–49. Stanford, CA: Stanford University Press.

Bredmeyer, T. 1975. The registration of customary land in Papua New Guinea. *Melanesian Law Journal* 3(2): 267–287.

British Solomon Islands Protectorate. 1968. Interim proposals on constitutional development. Legislative Council Paper 119 of 1968. Honiara. Quoted in Saemala 1983, 3.

Caiden, G. E. 1991. *Administrative Reform Comes of Age*. Berlin and New York: de Gruyter.

Campbell, I. 1992. *Island Kingdom: Tonga Ancient and Modern*. Christchurch, New Zealand: Canterbury University Press.

Carothers, T. 1999. *Aiding Democracy Abroad: The Learning Curve*. Washington, DC: Carnegie Endowment for World Peace.

Chand, S. 2003. Economic trends in the Pacific Island countries. *Pacific Economic Bulletin* 18(1): 1–15.

Choi, N. 2001. Land mobilisation law draft before cabinet. *PNG Land Symposium News*, 5 June. http://www.rtapng.com.pg/pngland/news (accessed 30 December 2001).

Clastres, P. 1971. *Society against the State*. Reprint, Boston: Zone Books, 1989.

Cochrane, Glynn. 1970. *Big Men and Cargo Cults*. Oxford: Clarendon Press.

Colebatch, H., and P. Larmour. 1993. *Market Bureaucracy and Community: A Student's Guide to Organisation*. London: Pluto.

Common, Richard. 2001. *Public Management and Policy Transfer in Southeast Asia*. Aldershot, UK: Ashgate.

Constitutional Planning Committee. 1974. *Report, Part 1*. Port Moresby, Papua New Guinea. Quoted in Fitzpatrick 1980, 211.

Cook Islands Commission of Political Review. 1998. *Reforming the Political Sys-*

tem of the Cook Islands: Preparing for the Challenges of the Twenty-first Century. Rarotonga.

Cooter, R. 1991. Kin groups and the common law process. In *Customary Land Tenure: Registration and Decentralisation in Papua New Guinea,* ed. P. Larmour, 33–49. Monograph 29. Port Moresby, Papua New Guinea: Institute of Applied Social and Economic Research (IASER).

Cornell, Stephen, and Joseph P. Kalt. 1995. Where does economic development really come from? Constitutional rule among the contemporary Sioux and Apache. *Economic Enquiry* 33 (July): 402–426.

Coyne, G. 1992. The impact of culture on small-scale administration: The case of Solomon Islands. In *Public Administration in Small and Island States,* ed. R. Baker, 71–83. West Hartford, CT: Kumarian Press.

Crocombe, R., ed. 1964. *Land Tenure in the Cook Islands.* Melbourne: Melbourne University Press.

Crossland, K. 2000. The ombudsman's role: Vanuatu's experiment. State, Society, and Governance Working Paper 00/5. Canberra: Research School of Pacific and Asian Studies, Australian National University.

Crouch, C., and W. Streeck, eds. 1997. *Political Economy of Modern Capitalism: Mapping Convergence and Diversity.* London: Sage.

Curtin, T. 2000. A new dawn for Papua New Guinea's economy. *Pacific Economic Bulletin* 15(2): 1–35.

Dauvergne, P., ed. 1998. *Weak and Strong States in Asia-Pacific Societies.* Sydney: Allen and Unwin.

David, R. 1963. A civil code for Ethiopia: Considerations on the codification of the civil law in African countries. *Tulane Law Review* 37:187–204.

Davidson, J. W. 1967. *Samoa mo Samoa: The Emergence of the Independent State of Western Samoa.* Oxford: Oxford University Press.

De Jong, M., K. Lalenis and V. Mamadouh, eds. 2002. *The Theory and Practice of Institutional Transplantation: Experiences with the Transfer of Policy Institutions.* Dordrecht, Netherlands: Kluwer.

Denoon, D. 1999. Black mischief: The trouble with African analogies. *Journal of Pacific History* 34(3): 281–289.

De Renzio, P., and D. Kavanamur. 1999. Tradition, society, and development: Social capital in Papua New Guinea. *Pacific Economic Bulletin* 14(2): 37–47.

de Soto, Hernando. 2000. *The Mystery of Capital: Why Capitalism Triumphs in the West and Fails Everywhere Else.* New York: Basic Books.

Dia, M. 1996. *Africa's Management in the 1990s and Beyond: Reconciling Indigenous and Transplanted Institutions.* Washington, DC: World Bank.

DiMaggio, P., and W. Powell. 1991. The iron cage revisited: Institutional isomorphism and collective rationality in organizational fields. In *The New Institutionalism in Organizational Analysis*, ed. W. Powell and P. DiMaggio, 63–82. Chicago: University of Chicago Press.

Dinnen, S. 2001. *Law and Order in a Weak State: Crime and Politics in Papua New Guinea*. Pacific Islands Monograph Series, no. 17, Center for Pacific Islands Studies, University of Hawai'i. Honolulu: University of Hawai'i Press.

———. 2002. Winners and losers: Politics and disorder in the Solomon Islands. *Journal of Pacific History* 37(3): 282–297.

Dobell, G. 2003. The South Pacific—Policy taboos, popular amnesia, and political failure. Australian Security in the Twenty-first Century Series. Delivered at Parliament House, Canberra, 12 February 2003. Menzies Research Centre, Barton, Australia.

Dolowitz, D., and D. Marsh. 2000. Learning from abroad: The role of policy transfer in contemporary policy-making. *Governance* 13(1): 5–23.

Doorn, R. J. 1979. *A Blueprint for a New Nation*. Hicksville, NY: Exposition Press.

Douglas, M. 1986. *How Institutions Think*. London: Routledge and Kegan Paul.

Ensminger, J. 1992. *Making a Market: The Institutional Transformation of an African Society*. Cambridge: Cambridge University Press.

Esman, M. 1972. The elements of institution building. In *Institution Building and Development*, ed. J. Eaton. Beverly Hills, CA: Sage.

Etounga-Manguelle, D. 2000. Does Africa need a cultural adjustment program? In *Culture Matters: How Values Shape Human Progress*, ed. L. Harrison and S. Huntington, 65–79. New York: Basic Books.

Fanegar S. 1979. Matakwalao, Malaita. In *Land Research in Solomon Islands*, ed. I. Heath, 7–18. Honiara, Solomon Islands: Land Research Project, Lands, Ministry of Agriculture and Lands.

Fiji. 1990. Constitution of the Republic. Suva: Government Printer.

Fiji Constitution Review Commission. 1996. *Towards a United Future*. Suva: Government Printer.

Filer, C. 2000. *The Thin Green Line: World Bank Leverage and Forest Policy Reform in Papua New Guinea*. Port Moresby, Papua New Guinea: National Research Institute; Canberra: Australian National University.

Financial Action Task Force. 2003. http://www1.oecd.org/fatf/.

Fingleton, J. 1981a. Customary land registration as an instrument of socio-economic change. Paper delivered at the Waigani Seminar, Port Moresby, Papua New Guinea.

———. 1981b. Policy-making on lands. In *Policy-Making in a New State: Papua New Guinea 1972–77*, ed. J. Ballard, 212–237. St. Lucia: University of Queensland Press.

————. 1985. Changing land tenure in Melanesia: The Tolai experience. PhD thesis, Australian National University, Canberra.

————. 2002. Policy-making and legislating for reform in Melanesia: Why is it so difficult? Cases from Papua New Guinea and Vanuatu. State, Society, and Governance in Melanesia Project Working Paper 02/2. Canberra: Research School of Pacific and Asian Studies, Australian National University.

Fitzpatrick, P. 1980. *Law and State in Papua New Guinea*. London: Academic Press.

Foster, R. 2002. *Materializing the Nation: Commodities Consumption and Media in Papua New Guinea*. Bloomington: Indiana University Press.

Foucault, Michel. 1980. *Power/Knowledge*. Brighton, England: Harvester Press.

Fraenkel, Jon. 2000. The alternative vote system in Fiji: Electoral engineering or ballot-rigging? *Journal of Commonwealth and Comparative Politics* 39(2): 1–31.

France, P. 1969. *The Charter of the Land*. Melbourne: Oxford University Press.

Frazer, I. 1997. The struggle for control of Solomon Islands forests. *Contemporary Pacific* 9(1): 39–72.

Fry, G. 1982. Successions of government in the post-colonial states of the South Pacific: New support for constitutionalism. In *Pacific Constitutions: Proceedings of the Canberra Law Workshop VI*, ed. P. Sack, 189–206. Canberra: Law Department, Research School of Social Sciences, Australian National University.

Geertz, C. 1963. The integrative revolution: Primordial sentiments and civil policies in the new states. In *Old Societies and New States: The quest for modernity in Asia and Africa*, ed. C. Geertz, 105–157. New York: Free Press of Glencoe; London: Collier Macmillan.

Ghai, Y. 1983. The making of the independence constitution. In *Solomon Islands Politics*, ed. P. Larmour, 9–52. Suva, Fiji: Institute of Pacific Studies, University of the South Pacific.

————. 1986. The Westminster model in the South Pacific: The case of western Samoa. *Public Law* (Winter): 597–621.

————. 1997. Establishing a liberal political order through a constitution: The Papua New Guinea experience. *Development and Change* 28(2): 303–330.

————. 2000. The implementation of the Fiji Islands constitution. In *Confronting Fiji Futures*, ed. A. Akram-Lodhi Haroon, 21–49. Canberra: Australian National University.

Gilson, R. P. 1970. *Samoa 1830 to 1900: The Politics of Multi-cultural Community*. Melbourne: Oxford University Press.

————. 1980. *The Cook Islands 1820–1950*. Wellington, New Zealand: Victoria

University Press, in association with the Institute of Pacific Studies, University of the South Pacific, Suva, Fiji.

Goldring, J. 1978. *Legalism Rampant: The Heritage of Imposed Law and the Constitution of Papua New Guinea.* Coventry, UK: Warwick School of Law.

Goodin, R. 1996. Institutions and their design. In *The Theory of Institutional Design*, ed. R. Goodin, 1–33. Cambridge: Cambridge University Press.

Hall, P. 1989. *The Political Power of Economic Ideas: Keynesianism across Nations.* Princeton, NJ: Princeton University Press.

Hampton, M., and M. Levi. 1999. Fast spinning into oblivion? Recent developments in money-laundering policies and offshore financial centres. *Third World Quarterly* 20(3): 645–656.

Haque, M. S. 1996. The contextless nature of public administration in third world countries. *International Review of Administrative Sciences* 62(3): 315–329.

Hau'ofa, E. 1988. *Tales of the Tikongs.* Auckland, New Zealand: Penguin.

———. 1993. *A New Oceania: Rediscovering Our Sea of Islands.* Suva, Fiji: School of Social and Economic Development, University of the South Pacific, in association with Beake House.

Heath, Ian, ed. 1979. *Land Research in Solomon Islands.* Honiara, Solomon Islands: Land Research Project, Lands, Ministry of Agriculture and Lands.

Held, D. 1987. *Models of Democracy.* Cambridge: Polity.

Helu, I. 1992. Democracy bug bites Tonga. In *Culture and Democracy in the South Pacific*, ed. R. Crocombe, U. Neemia, A. Ravuvu, and W. Vom Busch, 139–152. Suva, Fiji: Institute of Pacific Studies, University of the South Pacific.

Hindess, Barry. 1996. *Discourses of Power: From Hobbes to Foucault.* Oxford: Blackwell.

Hobsbawm, E., and T. Ranger, eds. 1983. *The Invention of Tradition.* Cambridge: Cambridge University Press.

Hood, C. 1998. Individualized contracts for top public servants: Copying business, path-dependent political reengineering—or Trobriand cricket? *Governance* 11(4): 443–462.

Horowitz, D. 1997. Encouraging electoral accommodation in divided societies. In *Electoral Systems in Divided Societies: The Fiji Constitution Review*, Pacific Policy Paper 21, ed. B. Lal and P. Larmour. Canberra: National Center for Development Studies with the assistance of the International Institute for Democracy and Electoral Assistance.

Huddleston, M. W. 1999. Innocents abroad: Reflections from a public administration consultant in Bosnia. *Public Administration Review* 59(2): 147–158.

Hughes, A. V. 1979. Evaluating land settlement. In *Land in Solomon Islands*, ed. P. Larmour, 232–238. Suva, Fiji: Institute of Pacific Studies, University of the South Pacific; Honiara, Solomon Islands: Ministry of Agriculture and Lands.

———. 1998a. *A Different Kind of Voyage: Development and Dependence in the Pacific Islands.* Manila: Asian Development Bank.

———. 1998b. *Solomon Islands Policy and Structural Reform Programme: An Account of the First Ten Months, November 1997–August 1998.* Port-Vila, Vanuatu: Economic and Social Commission for Asia and the Pacific (ESCAP).

Hughes, H. 2003. Aid has failed the Pacific. Issue Analysis, no. 33. Sydney: Centre for Independent Studies.

Huntington, S. 1993. *The Third Wave: Democratization in the Late Twentieth Century.* Norman: University of Oklahoma Press.

———. 2000. Foreword to *Culture Matters: How Values Shape Human Progress,* ed. L. Harrison and S. Huntington, xiv–xvi. New York: Basic Books.

Hyden, G. 1983. *No Shortcuts to Progress: African Development Management in Perspective.* London: Heinemann.

International Monetary Fund. 2001. *Conditionality in Fund-Supported Programs— Overview.* Washington, DC: Policy Development and Review Department, International Monetary Fund.

Israel, Arturo. 1987. *Institutional Development: Incentives to Performance.* Washington, DC: Johns Hopkins University Press for the World Bank.

Jackson, R. 1990. *Quasi-states: Sovereignty, International Relations, and the Third World.* Cambridge Studies in International Relations 12. Cambridge: Cambridge University Press.

———. 2000. *The Global Covenant: Human Conduct in a World of States.* Oxford: Oxford University Press.

Jeffries, R. 1993. The state, structural adjustment, and good government in Africa. *Journal of Commonwealth and Comparative Politics* 31(1): 20–35.

Johnson, J. H., and S. S. Wasty. 1993. Borrower ownership of adjustment programs and the political economy of reform. World Bank Discussion Paper 199. Washington, DC: World Bank.

Jolly, M. 1992. Spectres of inauthenticity. *Contemporary Pacific* 4(1): 49–72.

Kamikamica, J. 1987. Fiji. In *Land Tenure in the Pacific,* ed. R. Crocombe. Suva, Fiji: Institute of Pacific Studies, University of the South Pacific.

Kaufmann, D., and A. Kraay. 2003. Governance and growth: Causality which way?—Evidence for the world, in brief. WBI Governance Working Papers and Articles. Washington, DC: World Bank Institute.

Kaufmann, D., A. Kraay, and P. Zoido-Lobatón. 1999. Governance matters. World Bank Policy Research Working Paper 2196. Washington, DC:

World Bank Development Research Group, Macroeconomics and Growth; and World Bank Institute, Governance, Finance, and Regulation.

Kaufmann, Daniel. 1998. *Governance and Corruption: New Empirical Frontiers for Program Design*. Kuala Lumpur, Malaysia: Transparency International and Economic Development Institute.

Kavanamur, D. 1998. The politics of structural adjustment in Papua New Guinea. In *Governance and Reform in the South Pacific*, Pacific Policy Paper 23, ed. P. Larmour, 99–121. Canberra: National Centre for Development Studies, Australian National University.

Killick, T. 1998. *Aid and the Political Economy of Policy Change*. London and New York: Routledge.

Kirch, P. 1989. *The Evolution of Polynesian Chiefdoms*. Cambridge: Cambridge University Press.

Klitgaard, R. 1988. *Controlling Corruption.* Berkeley and Los Angeles: University of California Press.

Knapman, B., and C. Saldhana. 1999. *Reforms in the Pacific: An Assessment of the Asian Development Bank's Assistance for Reform Programs in the Pacific*. Manila: Asian Development Bank.

Knetsch, Jack, and Michael Trebilcock. 1981. *Land Policy and Economic Development in Papua New Guinea*. Port Moresby, Papua New Guinea: Institute of National Affairs.

Kuykendall, R. 1940. Constitutions of the Hawaiian Kingdom: A brief history and analysis. Papers of the Hawaiian Historical Society, no. 21. Honolulu.

Lal, B. 1988. *Power and Prejudice: The Making of the Fiji Crisis*. Auckland: New Zealand Institute of International Affairs.

———. 1999. A time to change: The Fiji general elections of 1999. Regime Change and Regime Maintenance in Asia and the Pacific Discussion Paper Series, no. 23. Canberra: Department of Political and Social Change, Research School of Pacific and Asian Studies, Australian National University.

———. 2002. Making history, becoming history: Reflections on Fijian coups and constitutions. *Contemporary Pacific* 14(1): 148–167.

Lal, Brij V., and Peter Larmour, eds. 1997. *Electoral Systems in Divided Societies: The Fiji Constitution Review*. Pacific Policy Paper 2. Canberra: National Centre for Development Studies, Research School of Pacific and Asian Studies, Australian National University, with the assistance of International Institute for Democracy and Electoral Assistance, Stockholm, Sweden.

Larmour, P. 1984. Alienated land and independence in Melanesia. *Pacific Studies* 8(1): 1–47.

————. 1989. Review of Report of the 1987 Constitutional Review Committee, by S. Mamaloni. *Contemporary Pacific* 1: 203–205.

————. 1992. States and societies in the South Pacific. *Pacific Studies* 15(1): 99–121.

————. 1994. A foreign flower? Democracy in the South Pacific. *Pacific Studies* 17(1): 45–76.

————. 1997. Corruption and governance in the South Pacific. *Pacific Studies* 20(3): 1–17.

————. 2000a. Explaining institutional failure in Melanesia. *Pacific Economic Bulletin* 15(2): 143–151.

————. 2000b. Issues and mechanisms of accountability: Examples from Solomon Islands. State, Society, and Governance in Melanesia Working Paper. Canberra: Research School of Pacific and Asian Studies, Australian National University.

————. 2003. Transparency International and policy transfer in Papua New Guinea. *Pacific Economic Bulletin* 18(1): 115–120.

Latour, B. 1996. *Aramis, or the Love of Technology.* Trans. Catherine Porter. Cambridge, MA: Harvard University Press.

Latukefu, S. 1975. *The Tongan Constitution: A Brief History to Celebrate Its Centenary.* Nuku'alofa, Tonga: Tonga Traditions Committee.

————. 1982. Constitution-making in the Pacific Islands in the nineteenth century. In *Pacific Constitutions: Proceedings of the Canberra Law Workshop VI*, ed. P. Sack, 21–36. Canberra: Law Department, Research School of Social Sciences, Australian National University.

Lawson, S. 1991. *The Failure of Democratic Politics in Fiji.* Oxford: Clarendon Press.

————. 2003. Fiji: Divided and weak. In *State Failure and State Weakness in a Time of Terror*, ed. R. Rotberg, 265–286. Washington, DC: Brookings Institution.

Leach, J., and G. Kildea. 1974. *Trobriand Cricket: An Ingenious Response to Colonialism.* Documentary film. Port Moresby: PNG Office of Information.

Lee, J. M. 1967. *Colonial Development and Good Government.* Oxford: Clarendon Press.

Leys, C. 2002. What's the problem with corruption? In *Political Corruption: Concepts and Contexts*, 3rd ed., ed. A. J. Heidenheimer and M. Johnston, 59–76. New Brunswick, NJ: Transaction Publishers.

Lindblom, Charles E. 1992. The science of "muddling through" (orig. pub. 1959). In *Classics of Public Administration*, ed. Jay M. Shafritz and Albert C. Hyde, 224–235. Pacific Grove, CA: Brooks/Cole.

Lindstrom, Lamont. 1993. *Cargo Cult: Strange Stories of Desire from Melanesia and Beyond.* Honolulu: University of Hawai'i Press.

Lipsky, M. 1976. Toward a theory of street-level bureaucracy. In W. D. Hawley et al., *Theoretical Perspectives on Urban Policy*. Englewood Cliffs, NJ: Prentice Hall.

Lukes, S. 1974. *Power: A Radical View*. London: Macmillan.

Lundberg, K. 2002. High road or low? Transparency International and the Corruption Perception Index. Kennedy School of Government Case Program C15-02-1658.0. Cambridge, MA: Harvard School of Government.

Macdonald, B. 1996. Governance and political process in Kiribati. Economics Division Working Paper. Canberra: Research School of Pacific and Asian Studies, Australian National University.

MacWilliam, S. 1986. International capital, indigenous accumulation, and the state in Papua New Guinea: The case of the Development Bank. *Capital and Class* 29:150–181.

———. 1999. Democracy and development: Fiji as exemplar for Africa. Paper presented at the African Studies Association of Australasia and the Pacific Annual Conference, University of Western Australia, Perth, 26–28 November.

———. 2002. Poverty, corruption, and governance in Fiji. *Pacific Economic Bulletin* 17(2): 138–145.

Maenu'u, L. 1979. Fiu Kelakwai scheme. In *Land in Solomon Islands*, ed. P. Larmour, 208–217. Suva, Fiji: Institute of Pacific Studies, University of the South Pacific; Honiara, Solomon Islands: Ministry of Agriculture and Lands.

Mann, M. 1986. The autonomous power of the state: Its origins, mechanisms, and results. In *States in History*, ed. P. Hall, 109–136. Oxford: Blackwell.

March, J. G., and J. P. Olsen. 1976. *Ambiguity and Choice in Organisations*. Bergen, Norway: Universitetsforlaget.

———. 1984. The new institutionalism: Organizational factors in political life. *American Political Science Review* 78(3): 734–749.

———. 1989. *Rediscovering Institutions: The Organizational Basis of Politics*. New York: The Free Press.

March, J. G., H. A. Simon, and H. S. Guetzkow. 1993. *Organizations*. Cambridge, MA: Blackwell.

May, R. 1982. Micronationalism in perspective. In *Micronationalist Movements in Papua New Guinea*, ed. R. May, 1–28. Canberra: Research School of Pacific and Asian Studies, Australian National University.

McKillop, R. 1991. Land mobilisation in the highlands. In *Customary Land Tenure: Registration and Decentralisation in Papua New Guinea*, ed. P. Larmour, 73–86. Monograph 29. Port Moresby, Papua New Guinea: Institute of Applied Social and Economic Research (IASER).

Meleisea, M. 1987. *The Making of Modern Samoa*. Suva, Fiji: University of the South Pacific.

———. 2000. Governance, development, and leadership in Polynesia: A micro study from Samoa. In *Governance in Samoa*, ed. E. Huffer and A. So'o, 189–200. Canberra: Asia Pacific Press; Suva, Fiji: Institute of Pacific Studies, University of the South Pacific.

Meller, N. 1982. Technical expertise and cultural differences: The consultant's role in the Pacific examined. In *Pacific Constitutions: Proceedings of the Canberra Law Workshop VI*, ed. P. Sack, 51–64. Canberra: Law Department, Research School of Social Sciences, Australian National University.

Meyer, J. 1981. Remarks at ASA session: The present crisis and the decline in world hegemony. Toronto. Quoted in DiMaggio and Powell 1991, 70.

Meyer, M., and L. Zucker. 1989. *Permanently Failing Organisations*. Newbury Park, CA: Sage.

Migdal, J. 1988. *Strong Societies and Weak States: State-Society Relations and State Capabilities in the Third World*. Princeton, NJ: Princeton University Press.

———. 1994. The state in society: An approach to struggles for domination. In *State Power and Social Forces: Domination and Transformation in the Third World*, ed. J. Migdal, A. Kohli, and V. Shue, 7–36. Cambridge: Cambridge University Press.

———. 1998. Why do so many states stay intact? In *Weak and Strong States in Asia-Pacific Societies*, ed. P. Dauvergne, 11–37. Sydney: Allen and Unwin.

Moore, B. 1966. *Social Origins of Dictatorship and Democracy: Lord and Peasant in the Making of the Modern World*. London: Penguin.

Moorehead, A. 1996. *The Fatal Impact: An Account of the Invasion of the South Pacific, 1767–1840*. London: H. Hamilton.

Morris, W. 1970. *News from Nowhere, or An Epoch of Rest: Being Some Chapters from a Utopian Romance*. Ed. James Redmond. Reprint, London: RKP. (Orig. pub. 1908.)

Mosley, P., J. Harrigan, and T. Toye. 1991. *Aid and Power: The World Bank and Policy-Based Lending*. London and New York: Routledge.

Munro, D. 2000. J. W. Davidson and Western Samoa. *Journal of Pacific History* 35(2): 196–211.

Neilsen, G. 1979. Ndoma, Komuvadha, and Chuva. In *Land Research in Solomon Islands*, ed. I. Heath, 19–29. Honiara, Solomon Islands: Land Research Project, Lands, Ministry of Agriculture and Lands.

Nelson, Joan M. 1984. The political economy of stabilization: Commitment, capacity, and public response. *World Development* 12(10): 983–1006.

North, D. 1990. *Institutions, Institutional Change, and Economic Performance*. Cambridge: Cambridge University Press.

Offe, C., J. Elster, and U. Preuss, eds. 1998. *Institutional Design in Post-Communist Societies: Rebuilding a Ship at Sea.* Cambridge: Cambridge University Press.

Oliver, M. 1968. *A New Constitution for a New Country.* Reno, NV: Fine Arts Press.

Olsen, J. 2003. How, then, does one get there? An institutionalist response to Herr Fischer's vision of a European federation. Jean Monnet Working Paper 7/00 Cambridge, MA: Harvard Law School. http://www.jeanmonnetprogram .org/papers/00/00f0901.rtf.

Orucu, E. 1995. A theoretical framework for transfrontier mobility of law. In *Transfrontier Mobility of Law,* ed. R. Jagtenberg, E. Orucu, and A. J. de Roo, 5–18. The Hague: Kluwer.

Ostrom, E. 1990. *Governing the Commons: The Evolution of Institutions for Collective Action.* Cambridge: Cambridge University Press.

Ostrom, V. 1987. *The Political Theory of the Compound Republic.* Lincoln: University of Nebraska.

Ottaway, M., and T. Carothers, eds. 2000. *Funding Virtue: Civil Society, Aid, and Democracy Promotion.* Washington, DC: Carnegie Endowment for World Peace.

Pacific Islands Forum Secretariat. 2002. *FEMM Stocktake.* FEMV04. http://www .forumsec.org.fj/.

Papua New Guinea. 1973. *Report of the Commission on Inquiry into Land Matters.* Port Moresby.

Parsons, W. 1995. *Public Policy: An Introduction to the Theory and Practice of Policy Analysis.* Aldershot, UK: Edward Elgar.

Platteau, J.-P. 1996. The evolutionary theory of land rights as applied to Sub-Saharan Africa: A critical assessment. *Development and Change* 27:29–86.

Pope, Jeremy. 1996. *National Integrity Systems: The TI Source Book.* Berlin: Transparency International.

———. 2000. *TI Source Book 2000: Confronting Corruption: The Elements of a National Integrity System.* http://www.transparency.org/sourcebook/index .html.

Power, A., and O. Tolopa. 2002. Land policy making in PNG. Paper presented to the Policy Making and Governance in Papua New Guinea workshop. Canberra: State, Society, and Governance in Melanesia Project, Research School of Pacific and Asian Studies, Australian National University.

Pressman, J., and A. Wildavsky. 1973. *Implementation.* Berkeley and Los Angeles: University of California Press.

Putnam, Robert. 1993. *Making Democracy Work: Civic Traditions in Modern Italy.* Princeton, NJ: Princeton University Press.

Ravuvu, A. 1991. *The Facade of Democracy: Fijian Struggles for Political Control, 1830–1987.* Suva, Fiji: Reader Publishing House; Institute of Pacific Studies, University of the South Pacific.

Reilly, B. 2000. The Africanisation of the South Pacific. *Australian Journal of International Affairs* 54(3): 261–268.

———. 2001. Examining the effect of the electoral system in post-coup Fiji. *Pacific Economic Bulletin* 16(1): 142–149.

———. 2002. Social choice in the South Seas: Electoral innovation and the Borda count in the Pacific Island countries. *International Political Science Review* 23(4): 355–372.

Rhodes, R. 1997. *Understanding Governance: Policy Networks, Governance, Reflexivity, and Accountability.* Buckingham: Open University Press.

Riggs, F. W. 1964. *Administration in Developing Countries: The Theory of Prismatic Society.* Boston: Houghton Mifflin.

Robertson, R. T., and A. Tamanisau. 1988. *Fiji: Shattered Coups.* Leichhardt, New South Wales: Pluto Press.

Rogers, E. 1995. *The Diffusion of Innovations.* New York: The Free Press.

Rose, R. 1993. *Lesson Drawing in Public Policy.* Chatham House, NJ: Chatham House Press.

Routledge, D. 1985. *Matanitu: The Struggle for Power in Early Fiji.* Suva, Fiji: Institute of Pacific Studies, in association with the Fiji Centre Extension Services, University of the South Pacific.

Rowat, D. 1973. *The Ombudsman Plan.* Carlton Library no. 67. Toronto: McLellan and Stewart.

Rueschemeyer, D., E. Stephens, and J. Stephens. 1992. *Capitalist Development and Democracy.* Cambridge: Polity.

Rydon, J. 2001. Fiji and the export of electoral systems. *Australasian Parliamentary Review* 16(1): 45–49.

Sabatier, P. A., and D. Mazmanian. 1979. The conditions of effective implementation: A guide to accomplishing policy objectives. *Policy Analysis* 5:481–504.

Saemala, F. 1983. Constitutional development. In *Solomon Island Politics*, ed. P. Larmour. Suva, Fiji: University of the South Pacific.

Saffu, Y. 1989. Survey evidence on electoral behaviour in Papua New Guinea. In *Eleksin: The 1987 Election in Papua New Guinea*, ed. M. Oliver. Port Moresby: University of Papua New Guinea Press.

Sahlins, M. 1963. Poor man, rich man, big man, chief: Political types in Melanesia and Polynesia. *Comparative Studies in Society and History* 5:283–303.

Sartori, G. 1997. *Comparative Constitutional Engineering: An Inquiry into Structures, Incentives, and Outcomes.* Reprint ed. London: Macmillan.

Scarr, D. 1988. *Fiji: The Politics of Illusion*. Sydney: New South Wales University Press.

Scharfstein, B.-A. 1989. *The Dilemma of Context*. New York: New York University Press.

Scott, J. 1990. *Domination and the Arts of Resistance: Hidden Transcripts*. New Haven, CT, and London: Yale University Press.

———. 1998. *Seeing Like a State: How Certain Schemes to Improve the Human Condition Have Failed*. New Haven, CT, and London: Yale University Press.

Scott, W. R. 1995. *Institutions and Organizations*. Thousand Oaks, CA: Sage.

Seers, Dudley. 1962. Why visiting economists fail. *Journal of Political Economy* 70(4): 325–338.

Selznick, P. 1957. *Leadership in Administration*. New York: Harper and Row. Quoted in W. R. Scott 1995, 18.

Siaguru, A. 2001. Chairman's address to the annual meeting of Transparency International (PNG) Inc. Port Moresby, Papua New Guinea.

Simpson, R. 1971. Land problems in Papua New Guinea. In *Land Tenure and Economic Development: Problems and Policies in Papua New Guinea and Kenya*, New Guinea Research Bulletin 40. Port Moresby, Papua New Guinea: New Guinea Research Unit; Canberra: Australian National University.

———. 1976. *Land Law and Registration*. Cambridge: Cambridge University Press.

Sissons, J. 1999. *Nation and Destination: Creating Cook Islands Identity*. Rarotonga: Institute of Pacific Studies and University of the South Pacific Centre in the Cook Islands.

Skocpol, T. 1985. Bringing the state back in: Strategies of analysis in current research. In *Bringing the State Back In*, ed. P. Evans, D. Rueschemeyer, and T. Skocpol, 3–43. Cambridge: Cambridge University Press.

Smith, J. 1978. Thoughts on future constitutional development in the Gilbert Islands. Public lecture delivered by His Excellency the Governor. Tarawa: USP Centre. Quoted in Van Trease 1993, 11.

Solomon Islands. 1976. *Report of the Special Select Committee on Lands and Mining*. Honiara, Solomon Islands: Ministry of Agriculture and Lands.

———. 1979. *Report of the Special Committee on Provincial Government*. Honiara, Solomon Islands: Ministry of Home Affairs.

Sope, B. N.d. *Land and Politics in the New Hebrides*. Suva, Fiji: South Pacific Social Sciences Association with UNDP and UNESCO.

Southall, A. 1968. Stateless society. In *International Encyclopedia of the Social Sciences*, ed. D. Sills, 166–167. New York: Collier Macmillan and the Free Press.

South Pacific Forum Finance Ministers. 1995. *Joint Statement*. 8 December. Port Moresby, Papua New Guinea.

Standish, W. 1978. The big-man model reconsidered: Power and stratification in Chimbu. Institute of Applied Social and Economic Research Discussion Paper 22. Port Moresby, Papua New Guinea: Institute of Applied Social and Economic Research (IASER).

Stiglitz, J. 2000. Scan globally, reinvent locally: Knowledge infrastructure and the localisation of knowledge. In *Banking on Knowledge: The Genesis of the Global Development Network*, ed. D. Stone, 24–43. London and New York: Routledge.

———. 2002. *Globalization and Its Discontents*. London: Penguin.

Stone, D., ed. 2000. *Banking on Knowledge: The Genesis of the Global Development Network*. London and New York: Routledge.

Strang, David, and John W. Meyer. 1993. Institutional conditions for diffusion. *Theory and Society* 22:487–511.

Strathern, Marilyn. 1995. The nice thing about culture is that everyone has it. In *Shifting Contexts: Transformations in Anthropological Knowledge*, ed. M. Strathern, 153–163. London and New York: Routledge.

Sugden, C. 2004. Putting the enhanced cooperation package to the test. *Pacific Economic Bulletin* 19(1): 55–75.

Sutherland, W. 1992. *Beyond the Politics of Race: An Alternative History of Fiji to 1992.* Canberra: Department of Political and Social Change, Research School of Pacific and Asian Studies, Australian National University.

Tagaloa, A. 1992. The terms of endearment in the American Pacific. In *Sovereignty and Indigenous Rights: The Treaty of Waitangi in International Context*, ed. W. Renwick. Wellington, New Zealand: Victoria University Press.

Taylor, M. 1982. *Community, Anarchy, and Liberty*. Cambridge: Cambridge University Press.

Tcherkezoff, S. 2000. Are the Matai out of time? Tradition and democracy: Contemporary ambiguities and historical transformations of the concept of chief. In *Governance in Samoa*, ed. E. Huffer and A. So'o, 113–132. Canberra: Asia Pacific Press; Suva, Fiji: Institute of Pacific Studies, University of the South Pacific.

Tendler, J. 1997. *Good Government in the Tropics*. Baltimore: Johns Hopkins Press.

Tippett, A. R. 1967. *Solomon Islands Christianity: A Study in Growth and Obstruction*. London: Lutterworth.

Transparency International PNG and the Institute of National Affairs. 2000. Proceedings from the Forum Privatisation and the National Integrity Pact, Discussion Paper 79. Port Moresby, Papua New Guinea: Institute of National Affairs.

Tully, James. 1995. *Strange Multiplicity: Constitutionalism in an Age of Diversity*. Cambridge: Cambridge University Press.

Turnbull, J. 2002. Solomon Islands: Blending traditional power and modern structures in the state. *Public Administration and Development* 22:1–11.

United Nations. 1985. Reforming civil service systems for development. TCD/SEM. 85/7-INT-85-R61. New York. Quoted in Caiden 1991, 69.

Va'a, U. 2000. Local government in Samoa and the search for balance. In *Governance in Samoa*, ed. E. Huffer and A. So'o, 151–170. Canberra: Asia Pacific Press; Suva, Fiji: Institute of Pacific Studies, University of the South Pacific.

Van Trease, H. 1993. From colony to independence. In *Atoll Politics: The Republic of Kiribati*, ed. H. Van Trease, 3–22. Suva, Fiji: Macmillan Brown Centre for Pacific Studies; Christchurch, New Zealand: University of Canterbury.

Von Savigny, Friedrich Karl. 1814. *Vom Beruf unserer Zeit für Gesetzgebung und Rechtswissenschaft*. Pamphlet.

Wade, Robert. 1996. Japan, the World Bank, and the art of paradigm maintenance: The East Asian miracle in political perspective. *New Left Review* 217:3–37.

———. 2001. Showdown at the World Bank. *New Left Review* 7:124–137.

Ward, A. 1972. Agricultural revolution: Handle with care. *New Guinea* 6(1): 25–34.

———. 1983. The Commission of Enquiry into Land Matters: Choices, constraints, and assumptions. *Melanesian Law Journal* 11:1–13.

Ward, R. G., and J. Ballard. 1976. In their own image: Australia's impact on Papua New Guinea and lessons for future aid. *Australian Outlook* 30:439–458.

Watson, A. 1974. *Legal Transplants: An Approach to Comparative Law*. Edinburgh: Scottish Academic Press.

West, D. 1986. Power and formation: New foundations for a radical concept of power. *Inquiry* 30:137–154.

Westney, D. Eleanor. 1987. *Imitation and Innovation: The Transfer of Western Organizational Patterns to Meiji Japan*. Cambridge, MA, and London: Harvard University Press.

White, G., and L. Lindstrom, eds. 1997. *Chiefs Today: Traditional Pacific Leadership and the Postcolonial State*. Stanford, CA: Stanford University Press.

Williams, H. T. 1970. *Huey Long*. New York: A. A. Knopf.

Windybank, S., and M. Manning. 2003. Papua New Guinea on the brink. Issue Analysis. Sydney: Centre for Independent Studies.

Wolfers, E. 1975. *Race Relations and Colonial Rule in Papua New Guinea*. Sydney: Law Book Company.

World Bank. 1994. *Governance: The World Bank's Experience (Development in Practice)*. Washington, DC: World Bank.

———. 2000. *Papua New Guinea—Country Assistance Evaluation.* Operations Evaluation Study, Report no. 20183. http://www-wds.worldbank.org.

World Council of Churches, DWME. 1963. Consultation statement "On church growth." Iberville, Canada. Quoted in Tippett 1967, ix.

Worsley, Peter. 1970. *The Trumpet Shall Sound.* 2nd English ed. London: Paladin.

Zucker, Lynne G. 1977. The role of institutionalization in cultural persistence. *American Sociological Review* 42 (October): 726–743.

Index

accountability, 24, 164, 175, 179; in anticorruption, 99, 112; Forum Principles
of, 89, 101, 117, 160, 174, 183; in
public sector reform, 99, 173, 188
administrative reform, 8, 52. *See also* public
sector reform; new public manage-
ment
Africa, 97, 132, 186, 187; borrowing from,
65, 89, 114, 115, 116, 186; corruption
in, 88, 97; decolonization, 14, 115;
governance in, 115; as lens, 115;
models, 46, 78, 89, 100, 115–116
agenda setting, 108, 148, 149, 188. *See also*
power
aid, 112, 118; conditions, 25, 109, 128;
corruption and, 165; critique of, 156;
dependency on, 85, 159, 186; funding
constitution review, 75, 119, 133
anticorruption: adversarial, 134; campaigns, 110, 140; commissions, 137,
175; doctrine, 153; measures, 89, 112;
new wave of, 154; rhetoric, 146, 187;
social conditions for, 125, 129, 133;
tools, 96, 133–134; transfer, 89, 110,
137, 190
antidemocracy, 72, 124, 133, 151,
171–172, 185, 191
ariki (Cook Islands), 16, 69
Asian Development Bank: corporatist, 126,
134; governance policy, 24, 47, 89;
island membership, 94; loan conditions, 11, 24, 88, 94, 103; network,
114–115; and private sector, 126, 153;
promoting corporate governance, 24;

self-evaluation, 167, 174, 183, 188;
sponsoring public sector reform, 88,
94, 102, 107, 109, 119, 153, 160, 186,
187, 189
Australia: decolonization, 14, 19, 67, 71,
73, 192; diaspora in, 128, 195; donor,
23, 24, 74, 89, 94; driving the Forum,
89, 117; funding TI, 119; interven-
tionism, 67, 72, 76, 102; models from,
24, 84, 91, 114, 116, 186; and Nauru,
67, 79, 84, 105; soft on PNG, 97
Australian National University, 44, 61, 76,
84, 126

Baker, the Reverend Shirley, 68, 74, 75
best practice, 116; in accountancy, 24, 187;
versus best fit, 88; in constitutions,
72; consultancy firms and, 51; downloading, 33; professional networks
and, 189
Bible, 4, 69, 78, 116, 117, 129; influence
on constitutions, 78, 118
borrowing: from the future, 3–4, 118, 187;
indirect, 186; from nowhere, 3–4, 52,
116; from the past, 4, 117; from private sector, 52; as reinvention, 3;
specter of inauthenticity and, 19
Bougainville: Agreement, 120; peace
process, 26; separatism, 17, 19, 76,
92, 101, 192
Britain: colonial theory, 25; decolonization,
13, 19, 67, 71–74, 192; disagreements
with Solomon Islands, 74; model, 2,
13; privatization in, 3, 13, 192

About the Author

PETER LARMOUR is a political scientist at the Australian National University. He previously taught at the University of Papua New Guinea and did research at the University of the South Pacific. Reflecting his longtime interest in the relationship between research and policy making, *Foreign Flowers: Institutional Transfer and Good Governance in the Pacific Islands* draws on the author's experience as a consultant to regional governments and aid donors. His Ph.D. dissertation was on land policy in Melanesia, and his first job was in the Lands Department in the Solomon Islands, where national leaders were rejecting introduced systems of land registration in favor of indigenous models. The editor of a number of books on government politics and land tenure in the Pacific Islands, Dr. Larmour is now doing research on Transparency International, a nongovernmental organization focused on anticorruption and based in Berlin.

Production Notes for Larmour / FOREIGN FLOWERS

Cover and interior designed by University of Hawai'i Press
production staff with text in Janson and display in Stone Sans

Composition by Josie Herr

Printing and binding by The Maple-Vail Book
Manufacturing Group

Printed on 60# Sebago Eggshell